W9-ATD-731

THE MEANING OF "FISHERS OF MEN"

THE NEW TESTAMENT LIBRARY

WILHELM H. WUELLNER

THE MEANING OF "FISHERS OF MEN"

The Westminster Press
PHILADELPHIA

To My German and American Parents

LIBRARY OF CONGRESS CATALOG CARD NO. 67-12012

Published by The Westminster Press®
Philadelphia, Pennsylvania

PRINTED IN THE UNITED STATES OF AMERICA

CONTENTS

INTRODUCTION

THE SEEMINGLY SIMPLE LITTLE PERICOPE (Mark 1:16 ff. and parallels) about Jesus' call of Galilean fishermen to discipleship poses three distinct yet related problems for which this study seeks fresh answers.

One problem concerns the literal fishing depicted or presupposed in this pericope. The question to be answered is: What was fishing in Galilee like at the time the scenes were supposed to have taken place? The answer involves a reconsideration of the traditional fisherman idyll that has dominated the tradition unchallenged since at least the time of Celsus' charge and Origen's reply in the third century A.D. This idyll has shaped just about every iconographic, exegetical, and devotional-hymnic tradition throughout the centuries, down to modern best-seller books or movies about the Fisherman, created by Lloyd Douglas and others.

And all this solely on the basis of only one or two verses in the Gospel accounts of the call of the Galilean fishermen! The idyllic tradition of "the happy, simple fisherfolk" either draws on the hypothetical oral reminiscences of the Zebedee-sons and John-sons, or rests on nothing but projections dictated, as in the case of Origen, by secondary, dogmatic premises, or simply devotional interests. Historical-critical studies of the economic and social roles that fishing played in Galilean society yield a different and, I believe, more exciting picture. The old issue of whether an allegedly illiterate fisherman from Galilee could have written First Peter, and a new issue of the social, economic context for Jesus' call to be heard and answered, will require further attention as a result of part of this study.

The second problem concerns the interpretation of the

phrase " fishers of men " which serves, in the form of a metaphor, as a job or task description for followers of Jesus. Recent studies of gospel metaphors, similes, and parables emphasize no longer the artistic creativity or originality of Jesus in coining phrases, sentences, or whole stories but, rather, the theological context, which is the very life and ministry of the historical Jesus, within which the gospel metaphors attain their full significance. This is doubly important to emphasize if, as is to be shown, fishing metaphors are widely known and used throughout the ancient Near East, in the Biblical and Rabbinical traditions no less than the Hellenistic and syncretistic literary and iconographic sources.

The task, then, is not so much to outline the variety of uses that the fishing metaphors had acquired in pre- and post-New Testament times, but to identify the transformation of meaning, which is the hermeneutical process, that went on as the metaphor passed from one culture or religion to another. Within Christianity itself, from Jesus until early patristic literature and catacomb art, the meaning attached to the fishing metaphors also changed. I can only claim to have, at best, given a brief sketch of the hermeneutical transformation in the varied interpretations of the fishing metaphors both outside and within Christianity.

The third problem is closely related to the second. I have chosen to deal with it, the hermeneutical problem proper, not in a separate section, but in critical comments interspersed throughout Part Two of the study. To deal with it fully would require a critical theological study of men-fishing, not, however, as halieutics was taken in nineteenth-century missiology, namely, a discipline apart from poimenics, cybernetics, and the like, but as an overall study of the God-man relationship. Once this is seen clearly, a number of basic questions become associated with the interpretation of the fishing metaphor. If, as the Scriptures claim, God himself, and not only his divinely commissioned fishing representatives, act as fishers of men, what is the milieu or medium in which such a catch can take place? Another way of asking the same question is, What makes man catchable or fishable in the first place? The answer to this has something to do with man's understanding of himself, that is, of his relationship to himself, to others, to history, and to nature.

In the competitive men-fishing that went on, not only between rival philosophical schools of antiquity teaching students by subjecting them to an examination of themselves and of their culture, but also between rival factions or schisms in a given religion with its orthodox center and heretical peripheries, the crucial issue remained by which norm or criterion anyone could possibly judge whether he had been fished properly or improperly. Told or imagining that he was fished by God directly, let alone by someone who claimed divine authorization for fishing his fellowmen, what would give a person the assurance that he had, indeed, been fished by God and not by some idol, demon, or, in Freudian or Marxist terms, simply been subjected to subconscious drives, or worse, to an illusion or a cultural opium?

It is not so much man's right but his duty that he examine critically, not once but unceasingly, the fishing claims made on him in order to discern whether the claim is from the true God or from false gods, from true or false prophets, from servants of God or from grand inquisitors. This examination ultimately decides whether the life of a culture and the existence of the people of God are led to full fruition and consummation or to sure destruction.

Part One

FISHING IN BIBLICAL ANTIQUITY

CHAPTER I

Fishing in Greek and Roman Times

Fishing Sacred and Profane

FISHING, FOWLING, AND HUNTING were, of course, widely known and practiced in the ancient Near East down to Roman times.[1] As sport or trade, they were also written about [2] and pictorially represented [3] in the literature and art of Near Eastern and Hellenistic cultures. As in Israel, fishing, fowling, and hunting were engaged in either professionally and commercially, or privately as a sport or as a means of supplementing the family diet. Fishing also served the purpose of providing fish for cultic meals [4] and

1. F. S. Bodenheimer, *Animal and Man in Bible Lands* (Leiden: Brill, 1960); L. Bohlen, *Die Bedeutung der Fischerei im Altertum* (Diss., Hamburg, 1936); L. Bunsmann, *De piscatorum in Graec. atque Rom. litteris usu* (Diss., Münster, 1910); Wm. Radcliffe, *Fishing from the Earliest Times* (London: Murray, 1921; 2d ed., E. P. Dutton & Company, Inc., 1926); M. I. Rostovtzeff, *The Social and Economic History of the Hellenistic World,* 3 vols. (Oxford: Clarendon Press, 1941); M. I. Rostovtzeff, *The Social and Economic History of the Roman Empire,* 2 vols. (2d ed. revised by P. M. Fraser, Oxford: Clarendon Press, 1957); Stöckle, art. "Fischereigewerbe," in Pauly and Wissowa (eds.), *Real-Encyclopädie der classischen Altertumswissenschaft,* Supplement to Vol. IV (1924), pp. 456–462.

2. On the tradition of the *halieutica,* see A. W. Mair, *Oppian: Colluthus, Tryphiodorus* (Loeb Classical Library; London and New York, 1928), Introduction, pp. xxxii–xlviii. See also Rostovtzeff, *Hellenistic World,* Vol. II, pp. 1177 f.

3. See Rostovtzeff, *ibid.,* Vol. III, pp. 1615, n. 129, on bibliography of works on graphic representations of fishing. On earliest hunting scenes, see now E. Anati, "Ancient Rock Drawings in the Central Negev," *Palestine Exploration Quarterly,* Vol. LXXXVI (1955), pp. 49–57. See also Bodenheimer, *Animal and Man,* pp. 6 f., *passim.*

4. E. Goodenough, *Jewish Symbols in the Graeco-Roman Period,* 10

for purposes of augury.[5] In certain areas certain fish, along with or instead of mammals and birds, were held sacred, e.g., the red mullet (*triglē*) at Eleusis [6] or the Oxyrhynchus fish in Egypt,[7] while other fish were held ritually unclean, e.g., the dogfish (*galeos*) at Eleusis.[8]

According to Plato's *Laws,* a person is allowed to engage in hunting, fowling, or fishing only in specified areas. The fowler, e.g., is excluded from harbors, from sacred rivers, pools, or lakes, and should not fish by using poisonous juices.[9]

Literary Accounts of Fishing Methods and Tools, and Their Metaphoric Application

One of the earliest accounts in Greek literature of the variety of methods of fishing is found in a long digression in Plato's work *The Sophist.*[10] Attempting a definition of a sophist, the dialogue takes as point of departure the well-known figure of the angler (*aspalieutēs*) as a skilled man (*technitēs*). Differentiating the acquisitive art (*technē ktētikē*) from the productive art (*technē poiētikē*), Plato

---

vols. (Bollingen Series XXXVII, Pantheon Books, Inc., Vol. I ff., 1953), Vol. V, pp. 13–22.

5. Aelian, *Peri Zōōn Idiotētos* (Book VIII:5); English translation by A. F. Scholfield (ed.), *Aelian: On the Characteristics of Animals,* 3 vols. (Loeb Classical Library; London: William Heinemann, Ltd., 1958–1959). On *Orphoi* as designation of sacred fish at the Lycian sanctuaries, and as basis of the etymology of "Orpheus," see R. Eisler, *Orpheus the Fisher* (London: Watkins, 1921), p. 14. On sacred fisheries of Artemis of Ephesus, see T. R. S. Broughton, "Roman Asia," *Economic Survey of Ancient Rome,* ed. by T. Frank, Vol. IV (The Johns Hopkins Press, 1938), p. 566. Cf. also Bodenheimer, *Animal and Man,* pp. 69 f., 125 ff.

6. Aelian, *Animals,* Book IX:51. See also Book XII:1 and 2 on sacred fish at Myra in Lycia, and at Hierapolis in Eastern Syria.

7. *Ibid.,* X:46 and XI:24. See also below, Ch. II, n. 62, on Athenaeus.

8. *Animals,* IX:65. Eisler, *Orpheus,* p. 39, holds it "most likely [that] *orphos* and *galeos* are originally only two different names, the one Lycian, the other Greek, for a peculiar kind of shark."

9. *Laws,* translated by R. G. Bury (Loeb Classical Library; London: William Heinemann, Ltd., 1959), 824 C. On a case of litigation between two parties over fishing rights in restricted areas, see Rostovtzeff, *Roman Empire,* Vol. II, p. 689.

10. Translated by H. N. Fowler (Loeb Classical Library; London: William Heinemann, Ltd., 1921).

enumerates as belonging to the former different classes, of which the class (*eidos*) of hunting (*thēreutikos*) is one besides fighting (*agōnistikos*), moneymaking (*chrēmatistikos*), and acquiring knowledge. This acquisitive art is subdivided into voluntary and coercive acquisition. The latter, whether done by words (*logoi*) or deeds (*erga*), is again subdivided into open coercion, which is the fighting (*agōnistikos*) kind, and secret coercion, which is the hunting (*thēreutikos*) kind.

With this step we are back again at the subject matter of this study. The Platonic dialogue then proceeds to distinguish between two kinds of hunting (*Sophist,* 219 E): that which goes after things lifeless (*apsychos*), e.g., diving for sea sponges, etc., and that which goes after living things (*empsychos*), or animal-hunting (*zōothērikē*).[11] After dividing the animals into land and water animals, Plato distinguishes then between water animals with wings which require the art of fowling (*ornitheutikē*) to catch, and animals in the water which require the skill of fishing (*halieutikē*) to catch.

Plato then proceeds to distinguish between two methods of fishing (*Sophist,* 220 B): the hunting by enclosures (*herkē*), in which man is more passively involved by letting several devices work for him (wicker basket or *kurtos,* net or *diktuon,* snare or *brochos,* and weel or fish trap, *porkos*), and hunting actively with strikes or blows, using the hook (*ankistron*) and spear or trident (*triodous*). This latter method is further subdivided into fishing at nighttime,[12] when hunting tools are used in connection with fire, and fishing during the daytime by using tools tipped with barbs (*ankistra*). This hunting with hooks and barbs is once more subdivided into catching fish by striking down at them with spears or tridents, and catching fish by getting them hooked in the mouth and pulling them up by

11. See Appendix I on *zōgrein,* a contraction of *zōos* and *agrein.* Eisler, *Orpheus,* p. 167, contends that the catching alive (*zōgrein*) of wild animals was part of the cultic service rendered to the "Great Hunter," Dionysus Zagreus. On the *zōgrein* of tigers and other animals with the help of mirrors, see *ibid.,* pp. 97 ff., 166 ff.

12. See Luke 5:5 and John 21:3. According to Aristotle, the night is the best time for fishing.

rod (*rhabdos*) or reed (*kalamos*).[13] When writing as advocate of the *paideia* principle of Greek culture, Plato develops, as will be seen below, still another argument about fishing.

At the point of comparing a Sophist's activities with that of an angler as a kind of hunter (*thēreus*), Plato digresses once more, this time into hunting, specifically the manhunt (*thēra anthrōpōn*).[14] What is said in this digression may have bearing on the interpretation of the Biblical and Rabbinical uses of fishing metaphors. Plato outlines four ways of catching or hunting a man by coercive means as over against the art of persuasion (*technē pithanourgikē*)[15] to which he reckons forensic oratory in court, any act of public speaking (*dēmēgoria*), or any private consultation (*prosomilia*). But the art of coercive hunting is that of piracy (*lēstikē*), of man-stealing (*andrapodistikē*),[16] of tyranny (*tyrannikē*),[17] and the whole art of war (*polemikē*).

Philological observations (Appendix I) on the tools for fishing, fowling, or hunting brought to light that some of the same tools were also used in warfare;[18] in their metaphoric meaning these terms appear interchangeably. The same is true here in Plato. In his *Laws*, Plato again deals with hunting,[19] which he calls there " a large and complex matter." After distinguishing between fishing, fowling, and hunting, he subdivides hunting into hunting of animals

13. This is the meaning of Aquila's use of *kalamos* in I Kings 14:15 where the late tenth-century B.C. prophet Ahijah says to Solomon's successor Jeroboam that "the Lord will smite Israel, as a reed is shaken in the water" (RSV).

14. *The Sophist,* 222 C.

15. On the metaphoric use of fishing and hunting in ancient Greece and Rome, see Part Two of this study, especially Lucian's work *The Fisherman,* and the metaphoric fisherman as skilled orator-counselor in Ugaritic legend.

16. See also Ezek. 19:3, 6 and Sirach 9:13.

17. In a catalog of various vices it is referred to once in the New Testament in I Tim. 1:10.

18. On the origin of the metaphoric use of warfare in Greece rather than in the Near East, see J. Leipholdt, "Das Bild vom Kriege in der griechischen Welt," *Gott und die Götter, Festgabe* for E. Fascher (1958), pp. 16–30.

19. Book VII.

and of men (*thēra anthrōpōn*).[20] This man-hunt can take place in friendship (*philia*),[21] or in war, or by robbery (*klōpeia*), robbers (*lēstai*), or pillaging army or navy squadrons (*stratopedon*).[22]

Fishing and *Paideia* Ideal

As with Plato, so with his younger contemporary Xenophon [23] the discussion of methods, of the purpose and value of the various forms of fishing, fowling, and hunting is entirely conditioned by the ideals of *paideia* as the essence of all true culture in contrast to mere technical skills.[24] What does not strengthen a person's character and render him a full human being, but makes him lazy and passive, no matter how many skills are involved, is not worthy of the *paideia* ideal. In this light we must see Plato's rejection of fishing, especially of angling (*ankistreia*), [25] and of the two forms of hunting: piracy (*lēsteia*) and man-hunt (*agra anthrōpōn*).[26] Plato also disqualifies fowling as an activity worthy of the *paideia* ideal and the "athletes" who practice it.[27]

In evaluating fishing and hunting in the light of the *paideia* ideal, "Plato goes beyond Xenophon in forbidding nets and traps, although Xenophon also ignores fishing and fowling." [28] The hunting of four-legged land animals, with the aid of horses and dogs and the hunter's own limbs (*sōmata*), most suits the *paideia* ideal by forcing a man to discipline himself in the pursuit and subduing (*kratein*)

20. *Laws,* 823 B.

21. In *The Sophist* (222 D), Plato spoke of "the lover's chase" (*thēra erōntōn*).

22. *Laws,* 823 B.

23. See the work entitled *On Hunting,* translated by E. C. Marchant, in *Xenophon: Scripta Minora* (Loeb Classical Library; London and New York, 1925).

24. Werner W. Jaeger, *Paideia: The Ideals of Greek Culture,* 3 vols., tr. by Gilbert Highet (Oxford University Press, 1945).

25. *Laws,* 823 B. But Aelian later on calls *ankistreia* "the most accomplished form [of hunting] and the most suitable for free men" (*Animals,* XII:43).

26. *Laws,* 823 E.

27. *Ibid.,* 824 A.

28. Jaeger, *Paideia,* Vol. III, p. 178.

of the animals by means of running (*dromos*), striking (*plēgē*), and shooting (*bolē*). A man engaged in this kind of hunting is truly a "sacred hunter" (*hieros thēreutēs*).

The *Halieutica* Tradition

The roots of the literary *halieutica* may go back to the fifth-century B.C. Corpus Hippocrateum, or at least to Aristotle's zoological works.[29] We have two full representative examples of the literary description of fish and fishing in the works of Oppian [30] and his contemporary Aelian (in his work *On the Characteristics of Animals*) from the second half of the second century A.D. Ovid's work from the early first century A.D. is extant only in fragments quoted by Pliny.[31] It must have been traditional with works on *halieutica* to open, as does Oppian, with a distinction between fowling (*ornitheutikē* or *ixeutikē;* Latin: *aucupium*), hunting (*kynēgesion* or *kynēgetikē;* Latin: *venatio*), and fishing (*halieutikē;* Latin: *piscatus*).

Oppian speaks of "the crafty devices of the cunning fisher's art" [32] (*haliēs polutropa dēnea technēs kerdaleēs*), but also of their hazardous and often frustrating work.[33] Unlike the hunter with his dog (s), and the fowler with his hawk (s), the fisherman has no help or guide. But both Oppian and Aelian know of a tradition that calls the dolphin the fisher's helper (*synthēros*),[34] who received wine-soaked pieces of bread as reward from the fishermen.[35] Compared

29. See, e.g., the representative work *Peri ta zōia historiōn,* or *Historia animalium,* in *Aristotelis Opera,* edited by Olof Gigon (Berlin: de Guyter, 1960), Vol. I, pp. 486–638.

30. See Mair's translation of *Halieutica, Oppian,* pp. 200–515. See also Oppian's *Cynegetica, ibid.,* pp. 2–199.

31. J. A. Richmond and O. Skutsch, "Restorations in Halieutica," *Ovidiana,* edited by N. I. Herescu, *et al.* (Leiden: Brill, 1958); J. A. Richmond (ed.), *The Halieutica Ascribed to Ovid* (London: Oxford University Press, 1962). See Pliny's *Natural History,* IX and XXXII; another zoological source is Plutarch's *De sollertia animalium.*

32. Oppian, *Halieutica,* lines 7 f.

33. Mair, *Oppian,* note on pp. 202 f., note b. Cf. The Testament of Zebulun 5:5.

34. Oppian, *Halieutica* V:425–447, esp. lines 430 f.; Aelian, *Animals,* II:18. On wolves as aids of fishermen, see *Animals,* VI:65.

35. R. Eisler, "Orphisch-dionysische Mysteriengedanken in der Christ-

with the hazards of fishing, it appears that "the feeble hairs and bent hooks of bronze (*chalkos cheilos*) and reeds (*donax*) and nets (*linon*)" [36] are out of proportion to the heavy and difficult task.

After outlining in Book I the varieties of fish [37] and amphibian animals,[38] and their various behaviors which a fisherman must know to assure the best results in fishing, Oppian goes on to give an account first of how fishes themselves hunt each other (Book II), then of how man goes about catching fish (Book III). In what appears to be conventional form, Oppian acknowledges the gift and favor of the gods [39] in the remarkable skill and knowledge man has acquired about fish and fishing. To use the tools and learn the methods of fishing, a fisherman must not only have physical stamina, but also be "cunning of wit and wise," [40] be "daring and dauntless and temperate, wakeful of heart and open-eyed." [41]

Then follows an outline of "the fourfold modes of hunting at sea" (*tetracha einaliēs thērēs nomon*).[42] One method of fishing calls for the use of a hook (*ankistron*) and line (*hormia*) made of flax or other material. The line is either

---

lichen Antike," *Vorträge der Bibliothek Warburg,* edited by F. Saxl, II. Vorträge (1922–1923), II. Teil (Leipzig: Teubner, 1925), p. 106, n. 3.

36. Oppian, *Halieutica* I:54 f.

37. *Ibid.,* I:80–408. See below, pp. 36 f., on the number of species of fish in Jewish tradition. One hundred fifty-three large fish were caught in John 21:11, see below Ch. II, n. 43. Pliny, *Natural History,* XXXII:53, mentions 144 kinds of fish; Oppian gives no specific number, contrary to Jerome's allegation in his commentary on Ezekiel (see J. P. Migne, ed., *Patrologiae Cursus Completus, Series Latina;* Paris, 1844 ff., Vol. 25, p. 474).

38. Oppian, *Halieutica* I:409–438.

39. "Poseidon or ancient Nereus or Phorcys or other gods" (*Halieutica* II:35 f.). On Sumerian goddess Nanse, "Mother of the Fishes," who provides refuge for fishes against pursuing fish and hunters, see M. Civil, "The Home of the Fish: A New Sumerian Literary Composition," in *Iraq,* Vol. XXIII (1961), pp. 154–175. For references to the Syrian god Side, also known as Agreus or Halieus, see W. Röllig, article s.v., in *Wörterbuch der Mythologie,* edited by H. W. Haussig (I. Abtlg., Syrien. Stuttgart: Klett, n. d.), p. 310. An Athenian fisherman dedicated a hook and line to a local temple, according to Lucian, *The Fisherman* (No. 47). On Babylonian sacrifices to the net, and incense-burning to the seine, see Hab. 1:16.

40. Oppian, *Halieutica* III:41.

41. *Ibid.,* III:44 ff.

42. *Ibid.,* III:72 ff. Similarly in Aelian, *Animals,* XII:43.

fixed to a rod or reed (*donax*), or held by the fisherman. The line can be leaded (*kathetos*) or have many hooks.[43] Aelian seems to be the earliest witness of the use of an artificial bait. Unlike Plato, Aelian calls fishing with a hook "the most accomplished form (*sophōtatē*) and the most suitable for free men." [44]

Another method of fishing calls for the use of nets (*diktua*). Oppian mentions ten different kinds of nets which "are not easy to identify with certainty." [45] Besides the three kinds of nets mentioned in connection with Biblical fishing (*diktuon, amphiblēstron, sagēnē*) he refers to seven other kinds of nets: *gangamon, griphos, kalumma,*[46] *panagron, peza, sphairōn,* and *hypochē*. Big nets (*diktua megala*) and other fishing gear (*paraskeuē thēratikē*) are mentioned by Aelian in connection with big-fish hunting.[47] According to Aelian, fishing with nets is comparable to capturing a camp and to the taking of prisoners. He also claims that fishing with nets is a profitable business and brings wealth (*ploutophoros*).[48] Habakkuk 1:16 also says that a fisherman "lives in luxury by them (i.e., the *amphiblēstron* and *sagēnē*)."

A third method of fishing requires the use of weels (*kurtoi*) or wicker baskets, which are tools "which bring joy to their masters while they sleep at ease, and great gain (*kerdos*) attends on little toil." [49] Aelian concedes that fishing with a weel "is a pursuit (*thēra*) that calls for much craft (*dolerōtatē*) and deep design (*epiboulotatē*)," but he also denounces it as "highly unbecoming to free men." [50] In this he is in agreement with Plato and other advocates of the *paideia* ideal.

43. Oppian, *Halieutica* III:77 f. In his Introduction to *Oppian: Colluthus, Tryphiodorus,* pp. xxxiv f., Mair comments on the use of the many-hooked line.

44. Aelian, *Animals,* XII:43.

45. Mair, *Oppian,* p. xl.

46. Used metaphorically for "deception" in Patristic Greek; see G. W. H. Lampe (ed.), *A Patristic Greek Lexicon* (Oxford: Clarendon Press, 1961), s.v.

47. *Animals,* XIII:16.

48. *Ibid.,* XII:43.

49. Oppian, *Halieutica* III:85–87. See also Mair, *Oppian,* note on p. 352.

50. *Animals,* XII:43.

The fourth mode of fishing requires the use of a long-pronged trident (*triaina*), which also serves as symbol of Poseidon,[51] the Greek divinity worshiped in all things connected with the sea, with navigation and fishing. Fishing with a trident or spear [52] can be done either from a boat or while standing in shallow water. Aelian holds that this fourth method of fishing, which he calls fishing with a pole (*kontōsis*), is "the most manly form (*andreiotatē*)," which calls for hunters of very great strength (*rhōmaleōtatos*).[53]

Besides these four most commonly used methods of fishing, there are some others. Oppian comments on them in connection with special species of fish or special local customs of fishing among certain tribes.[54] The Near East by and large was unfamiliar with ice-fishing, which Aelian describes.[55] Certain fish are best caught with bare hands, when the fisherman turns into a skilled diver.[56] At other times and other places, other fish are caught by getting them trapped in holes dug by the fishermen's feet in the sand of shallow waters.[57] The use of poison (*pharmakon*) has already been mentioned.[58] The use of music as means of decoy or chase deserves special attention.[59] The hunting

51. F. Schachermeyr, *Poseidon und die Entstehung des griechischen Göttenglaubens* (Bern: Francke, 1950).

52. On the variety of spears used in hunting, see Appendix I. On the origin of the trident as symbol, see Schachermeyr, *Poseidon,* 164 ff.

53. *Animals,* XII:43.

54. *Halieutica* IV:531 ff.

55. *Animals,* XIV:26 and 29.

56. Oppian, *Halieutica* IV:593-634. On the two divers in Jewish funerary art at Sheikh Abreiq, or Beth-shearim in western Galilee, and their yet unexplained meaning, see Goodenough, *Jewish Symbols,* Vol. I, p. 100; Vol. III, Fig. 70.

57. Aelian, *Animals,* XIV:3.

58. Oppian, *Halieutica* IV:647–693. Other sources which refer to this peculiar method of fishing are quoted by Mair, *Oppian,* pp. 452 f., note a. On the use of wine as anesthetic in fishing or hunting, and its mystical significance in Hellenistic art, see R. Eisler, "Die Jagd mit Rauschtrank und Spiegelfalle," *Vorträge der Bibliothek Warburg,* II. Vorträge, II. Teil, pp. 97 ff., esp. pp. 101 f., 176 f.

59. Eisler, "Die Jagd mit Rauschtrank und Spiegelfalle," *loc. cit.,* pp. 65 ff., 93 ff. See Aelian, *Animals,* XII:46, on the Etruscan tradition of using the music of pipes (*auloi*) besides nets and hounds to snare and catch wild boars and stags. The flute player (*technitēs aulōn*) on the walls of Etruscan tombs could then be an exact parallel to the fishermen on Christian sarcophagi.

of the sea monsters or huge fish (*ta kētea*)[60]—such as sea turtles, sharks, whales, dolphins, and the like—is in a class by itself.

These are the tools and methods used by fishermen and their "subtle wiles" (*pukinai epiphrosunai*),[61] with which they face the varying "cunning devices" (*noēmata*) of the various kinds of fish. For each has developed its own way of escaping hook, net, weel, spear, or other methods of fishing.[62] The fact that the ancient traditions about the tools and methods of fishing, fowling, and hunting hardly vary throughout the centuries of literary traditions is evidence that the tools and techniques of fishing remained the same in the different cultures of the ancient Near East. The Hellenistic age, however, seems to have brought changes to fishing and fishermen along with changes in almost every other sector of Near Eastern society.

Besides the literary sources on fishing, analyzed above, we have to take into account representations in stone or paint, dating back as far as the third millennium B.C. or earlier,[63] depicting scenes of fishing, fowling, and hunting. On the other hand, we have the book illuminations in the medieval manuscript copies of the *halieutica* works of the classical authors.[64] These illuminations may turn out to be valuable aids in the barely begun critical study of early Christian and Jewish iconographic representations of fishing scenes of mere decorative or symbolic design. In either case they provide us with another source for the interpretation of the fishing metaphors in the literary and iconographic traditions of Judaism and Christianity.

60. Oppian, *Halieutica* V:21 ff.; Aelian, *Animals,* XIII:16 f.

61. Oppian, *Halieutica* III:170.

62. *Ibid.,* III:92–168.

63. See G. Gerleman, *Contributions to the Old Testament Terminology of the Chase* (Lund: Gleerup, 1946); J. B. Pritchard, *The Ancient Near East in Pictures Relating to the Old Testament* (Princeton University Press, 1954); E. Anati, *Palestine Exploration Quarterly,* Vol. 86 (1955), pp. 49–57.

64. K. Weitzmann, *Ancient Book Illumination* (Harvard University Press, 1959), esp. pp. 26–30, on the eleventh-century Venetian manuscript copies of Oppian's *Halieutica.*

Fishing Industry in Hellenistic-Roman Times

At the time Rome took over part of the Near East, fishing seems to have been a big business, and a profitable one. Though our information about fishing and fisheries, due to the scarcity of primary sources, is defective and "does not permit us to discriminate between new and traditional methods" of fishing, historical research has shown that "new and important methods [were] introduced in the organization of the fishing industry, especially as regards the preparation of fish for the market and its preservation." [65] We can distinguish three separate but related aspects about fishing which are new in Hellenistic times. There is, first of all, the greater care that is taken in the planning and executing of fishing activities. The *halieutica* literature may be the result as well as the cause of this feature. Then there is the greater economic efficiency through the centralization of fishing activities into a regular, in some places large-scale, industry and commerce. Finally, and probably due to the centralization and industrialization, large capital investments were required to make this new fishing method possible and profitable. The tax collectors of the New Testament were such men of means, besides others, who provided the capital investment.

The change in fishing methods during this period was necessitated largely by the ever increasing food demands of the Hellenistic cities, which was due not so much to a population explosion as to the spiraling urbanization. Besides bread, processed fish (cured, pickled, salted, dried), referred to as *opson* or *opsarion* or *prosphagion,*[66] was the main food staple for the masses in town and country alike.[67] Forbes cited Cato the Elder as saying that no city could continue to exist where fish had become more expensive than meat.[68] The upper classes had delicatessen fish

65. Rostovtzeff, *Hellenistic World,* Vol. II, pp. 1178 f.

66. On ancient food preservation processes, see R. J. Forbes, *Studies in Ancient Technology,* Vol. III (Leiden: Brill, 1955), pp. 185–190; A. Alt, "Galiläische Probleme," in *Kleine Schriften zur Geschichte des Volkes Israel,* Vol. II (Munich: Beck, 1953), p. 450, n. 2.

67. Rostovtzeff, *Hellenistic World,* Vol. II, p. 1177.

68. *Ancient Technology,* Vol. III, p. 189.

imported from various renowned fishing places, which meant a lucrative business to fishermen and traders alike.

Just how profitable a business was fishing in Hellenistic-Roman times? We had already seen that the *halieutica* tradition called fishing with nets a business that brings wealth.[69] Of the fishermen of the Aegean island of Cos, Rostovtzeff says that they were "next in importance to the land owners outside the city." [70] On the other hand, there were the masses of unskilled hired hands, working for the state or privately owned systems, who lived miserably in large labor-camp-like villages under tight control.[71] An ancient Egyptian scribal "Satire on the Trades" says of them: "The fish-catcher is more miserable than any [other] profession." [72]

Besides fishing as a sport, hobby, or private avocation, if only to provide occasionally fresh fish for the family table, commercial fishing was developed along two lines. Both were widely known and practiced, especially in Egypt. Both were "conducted on capitalistic lines." [73] It is of interest here to note that "the system of state capitalism was one of the causes of the religious revolts [in Ptolemaic Egypt]." [74] The same may be said of the Zealotic movement in Galilee in the decades preceding the Jewish-Roman war of A.D. 66–70. Some of the parables of Jesus [75] presuppose the same conditions in Judea and Galilee. From the parables of Jesus, as from Rostovtzeff's studies, we conclude that the same two basic systems of commercial fishing also applied to other professions, especially farming.[76]

69. See above, p. 18, at n. 48, on Aelian, *Animals,* XII:43. On Palestinian fishing, see below, pp. 45–61.

70. Rostovtzeff, *Hellenistic World,* Vol. I, p. 243.

71. Rostovtzeff, *Roman Empire,* Vol. I, pp. 273 f.

72. J. A. Wilson, translation in *Ancient Near Eastern Texts Relating to the Old Testament,* edited by J. B. Pritchard (Princeton University Press, 1950), pp. 433 f.

73. Rostovtzeff, *Hellenistic World,* Vol. I, p. 297.

74. S. K. Eddy, *The King Is Dead* (University of Nebraska Press, 1961), p. 308.

75. The parable of the wicked tenant farmers (Mark 12:1-12 and parallels); of the laborers in the vineyard (Matt. 20:1-15); of the shrewd steward (Luke 16:1-8); and others.

76. See below, p. 43. See also Alt, *Kleine Schriften zur Geschichte des Volkes Israel,* Vol. II, p. 389, *passim.*

In one system of fishing we have the fishermen "organized by . . . either a royal concern, managed by a royal steward (*oikonomos*), or by the holder of a gift-estate (*dōrea*)." [77] If they were organized by a royal concern, they could be designated "royal fishermen" in analogy to the royal farmers (*basilikoi geōrgoi*), prevalent especially in Egypt.[78] In this system of fishing the fishermen worked under a "system of requisitions" (or "liturgies") of specified amounts of fish to be delivered at certain times. Upon delivery they received recompensations in money and/or kind, the latter largely in terms of processed fish. Papyri records reveal complaints raised by fishermen about irregular, inadequate, or outstanding payments.[79] But, as reflected in an ancient Sumerian proverb, though "change [or "breach of contract"] take place in the city, fishermen [can always] catch their own food supply." [80] Rostovtzeff concludes from the papyri records extant about this system of fishing that it brought large profits, not to the actual fisherman, who got only a small share of the profit, but to the king or the holder of the gift estate.[81] Jesus' parables of the talents (Luke 19:12-27, parallel to Matt. 25:14-30), of the unmerciful servant (Matt. 18:23-35), or of the servant entrusted with supervision (Luke 12:42-46, parallel to Matt. 24:45-51) could echo this first type of economic or industrial management.

In the other system of fishing, the fishermen lease their fish rights from *telōnai,* a word which in the New Testament has the notorious connotation of tax collector or publican.[82] Fishermen operating under this system can be called tax fishermen, in analogy to the tax farmers. They usually work with partners (*metochoi*) and sureties (*en-*

77. Rostovtzeff, *Hellenistic World,* Vol. I, p. 297.

78. V. A. Tcherikover in collaboration with Alexander Fuks (eds.), *Corpus Papyrorum Judaicarum,* Vol. I (Harvard University Press, 1957), pp. 15 f.

79. Rostovtzeff, *Roman Empire,* Vol. I, p. 424, n. 45; Vol. II, p. 721, n. 45.

80. E. I. Gordon, *Sumerian Proverbs* (University of Pennsylvania, University Museum, 1959), Collection I, No. 77, pp. 78 and 506.

81. Rostovtzeff, *Hellenistic World,* Vol. I, p. 297.

82. O. Michel, art. "*telōnēs*" in *Theologisches Wörterbuch zum Neuen Testament* (cited hereafter as *TWNT*), G. Friedrich (ed.), Vol. VIII (1965), pp. 88–106.

guoi).[83] The tax collector (*telōnēs*), or steward, "underwrote the fishing contract (*ichthyikē ōnē*), which was carried out by expert fishermen."[84] What the exact amount or percentage of taxation was that such tax fishermen had to pay is not clear in the records we have. Rostovtzeff says at one point that a fish tax of 25 percent of any catch, known as the *tetartē halieōn* or *ichthyikōn,* was levied and payable to the government besides other and minor taxes.[85] Elsewhere in his study he speaks of taxes that were as high as 30 to 40 percent of the cash value which a tax fisherman received from the sale of his catch.[86]

The following picture emerges from this brief study about the social and economic status of fishermen in Hellenistic times. On the bottom rung of the ladder are the hired hands, the fishers and sailors. In some parts of the Near East they are seasonal workers;[87] in other parts they live and work in colonies or camps the year round. Next and considerably higher on the social scale comes the one who hires laborers: the fisherman who contracts work with certain governmental or private middlemen, but who also sells and trades his catches on the local markets for his own profit. This group is made up of the professional middle-class fish catcher and fish trader. But the ones who profited most from the hired laborers and the middle-class fishermen were the "tax collectors" (*telōnai*), the holders of gift estates, the officials at sacred fisheries of the larger temples throughout the Near East, and, of course, the kings or governments.

The fishing business and industry in Hellenistic times were not so much competitive enterprises in the modern sense as means of the rich for getting richer, of the middle classes to strive to rise higher in power and prestige, and of the poor to remain poor. The Roman Government finally stepped in when the economic exploitation of the poor by the rich, of the *humiliores* or *tenuiores* by the

83. Tcherikover, *Corpus Papyrorum Judaicarum,* Vol. I, pp. 18 f.

84. Rostovtzeff, *Hellenistic World,* Vol. I, p. 297.

85. *Ibid.,* Vol. I, pp. 325, 297; and Vol. III, p. 1387, n. 101.

86. *Ibid.,* Vol. I, p. 337. On the high tax rate imposed on fisheries in Greece, see Vol. III, p. 1644; on Palestine, see below, p. 43.

87. See below, pp. 60 f.

honestiores or *potentiores,* reached perilous proportions. The "sin [that] thrusts itself in between buyer and seller," as Sirach 27:2 (cf. ch. 37:11) warns, can at best be curbed, but not eliminated, by force of law. By about the early second century A.D. legislation was enacted in Rome, designed to curtail the rising overhead prices incurred by letting fish and other staple foods pass through the hands of far too many traders and middlemen before reaching the consumer. It was decreed that a fish catch "be sold either by the fishermen themselves or by those who first buy the fish from them." [88] As a result, the distinction between fish catchers (*halieis*), fish dealers (*ichthyopōlai*), and fish producers (*ichthyopratai*) once again, as in earlier times, became less and less clear.[89]

88. Rostovtzeff, *Roman Empire,* p. 370. On the Roman Empire's controls imposed on buying and selling, see also Rev. 13:17. On trading (*ergazesthai, (dia) -pragmateuesthai*), importing (*emporeuesthai*), and making a profit or profiteering (*kerdainein*), see James 4:13 and Matt. 25:16, par. Luke 19:13.

89. See Stöckle's article "Fischereigewerbe" in *Real-Encyclopädie,* Supplement to Vol. IV, p. 456, *passim.*

CHAPTER II

Fishing in Biblical Palestine

Fishing in New Testament Times

COMPARED WITH what fishing is in Palestine today,[1] or what it was once in Biblical Israel,[2] modern critical studies of fishing in New Testament times[3] and subsequently in early patristic and Tannaitic times[4] have shown that the social, economic milieu from which the first apostolic "fishers of men" came is altogether different from the fishermen's milieu of both ancient and modern Israel. In this chapter we intend to present a picture of the social and economic aspects of fishing in Galilee during Jesus' life and the following decades prior to the Jewish-Roman War of A.D. 66–70 which, along with many other things, also changed the economic health and wealth of Palestine.

The traces we find in the New Testament of the economic role of fishing in Palestine of the mid-first century A.D. are seemingly quite marginal and insignificant, for the simple reason that the New Testament as religious wit-

1. E. W. G. Masterman, *Studies in Galilee* (The University of Chicago Press, 1909); G. Dalman, *Arbeit und Sitte in Palästina*, Vol. VI (Beiträge zur Förderung Christicher Theologie, No. 31, edited by P. Althaus; Gütersloh: Bertelsmann, 1939).

2. Gerleman, *Old Testament Terminology* (only on hunting); Bodenheimer, *Animal and Man*. R. de Vaux's study of *Ancient Israel: Its Life and Institutions*, tr. by John McHugh (McGraw-Hill Book Company, Inc., 1961) unfortunately bypasses fishing completely.

3. E. F. F. Bishop, "Jesus and the Lake," *Catholic Biblical Quarterly*, Vol. XIII (1951), pp. 398–414; F. Dunkel, "Die Fischerei am See Gennesareth und das Neue Testament," *Biblica*, Vol. V (1924), pp. 375–390.

4. M. Mainzer, *Über Jagd, Fischfang und Bienenzucht bei den Juden in der tannäischen Zeit* (Pressburg, 1910).

ness is interested in facts of political, social, economic, cultural history only as they bear out the religious witness, the *kērygma*. Therefore, the primary text for fishing in the New Testament, the pericope devoted to the call of the disciples before and after Easter (Mark 1:16-20 and its parallel in Matt. 4:18-22; also Luke 5:1-11 and John 21:3 ff.), was written for use in Christian churches and schools, and not, like Tacitus' *Annals* or Josephus' extensive writings, for general consumption. Conservative scholars keep emphasizing that the Biblical records, based on apostolic eyewitness, contain residues of factual observation of events, such as the special designation for a particular net used in Mark's and Matthew's accounts of the call of the fishermen, and many other features.

This chapter is written to expose as inadequate all three hitherto proposed, and in various camps widely accepted, interpretations about the gospel pericopes on the call of the fishermen. And the basis for this exposure is not a theological argument, but critical research of first-century literature, topography, and archaeology, and of social, economic history of the Hellenistic age in Palestine. Inadequate is (1) the conservative position that rests its case on the apostolic eyewitness and Petrine reminiscences of the Marcan tradition to assure factual reporting; (2) the form-critical position which rests its case with the verdict that this pericope on the Galilean fishermen has only kerygmatic value; and (3) the traditional view of Protestant and Catholic exegesis and devotions,[5] fostered by the apologists of the second century and perpetuated in patristic exegesis, according to which the fishing scenes in the Gospels depict the first disciples to have come from Palestine's lowest social classes.[6]

The Matthean tradition of the fish caught with a coin in his mouth (Matt. 17:27) has interest for us in this connection only insofar as it shows the disciples angling,[7] and as

5. A popular Protestant hymn by William A. Percy refers to "such happy, simple fisherfolk, before the Lord came down."

6. See below, pp. 45–61.

7. The disciples are shown with angles rather than nets only in the earliest frescoes of the Roman catacombs, and in the singular reference in the Pseudo-Clementine *Recognitions,* II. 62 f.

giving possible clues about the species of fish in question. Processed fish must have been a part of the Galilean and Judean daily diet and a staple food besides bread as everywhere else in the Roman Empire. The hungry ask for fish (Luke 11:11 and parallel in Matt. 7:10). The crowd that follows Jesus into the desert carries bread and fish with it as a matter of course (see the parallel accounts to Mark 6:35-44; 8:1-10). In the city of Jerusalem, Jesus ate broiled fish (and honeycomb) with the disciples (Luke 24:42), and fresh fish on the shore of the Sea of Galilee (John 21:9-14). All these texts bring out only one, but the important, point that the roughly half a million inhabitants of the Jewish territories of Palestine relied for their daily food not only on the Galilean farmers but also on the Galilean fishermen. What that means for the role of fishermen in the society and the economy of Palestine and for "the fishing industry which brought much prosperity" [8] to fishermen will be assessed later. First, we turn to an examination of the economic background of those place names in the New Testament which reflect some association with the fishing industry.

Bethsaida. Literally, "Fishville" or "Huntsville," Bethsaida is of primary interest to our study, for it is known in the New Testament as the native place of some of Jesus' disciples and one that Jesus visited on occasion. As the capital of Gaulanitis, the territory of the tetrarch Philip, it lay near the mouth of the Jordan at the north end of the Sea of Galilee, which there, shallower than elsewhere, was "the richest fishing-ground [where] the most valuable [fishing was found] on the whole lake." [9] Politically the center of Gaulanitis, a plateau region more than two thousand feet above sea level, Bethsaida lay at the very edge of Philip's tetrarchy at the foot of the steep slope of the plateau. Geographically and culturally, Bethsaida was part of Galilee, the adjoining tetrarchy of Herod Antipas. In placing his capital city at Bethsaida soon after he began his rule following the death of Herod the Great, Philip did early

8. L. E. Elliott-Binns, *Galilean Christianity* (Studies in Biblical Theology, No. 16; Alec R. Allenson, Inc., 1956), p. 17.

9. Masterman, *Studies in Galilee*, p. 38.

what Herod Antipas imitated decades later when he moved the capital of Galilee from Sepphoris to Tiberias.

The exact location of Bethsaida is still somewhat enigmatic even after centuries of archaeological research so well outlined by Clemens Kopp.[10] The traditional notion of two separate Bethsaidas, one in Philip's territory, the other "in Galilee" (John 12:21), has now been replaced by the conviction that there was only one Bethsaida, the capital of Gaulanitis. Nevertheless, there still remain three alternative locations for this Bethsaida: *et-Tell, khirbet el-'araj,* and *khirbet el-mes 'adiye.*[11] When Mark calls Bethsaida a village (*kōmē,* Mark 8:23), he must have "meant to designate the capital of a toparchy and its subordinate villages,"[12] of which as many as fourteen were allegedly incorporated into the "city" of Bethsaida. City and toparchic (or village) district are thus often synonymous, at least in the Palestine of New Testament times.[13] Galilean villages such as Capernaum, Chorazin, and others of the area in which much of Jesus' Galilean ministry took place, all belonged to a toparchy whose capital or city was Magdala.

In view of the lack of archaeological evidence for the city complex of ancient Bethsaida, doubt has arisen in the minds of some that Bethsaida ever became fully developed into a Hellenistic city.[14] Kopp concludes that "it would seem that the foundation of this city was not fully realized."[15] Yet he cites a Jewish source that knows of two rabbis of the second century A.D. who were natives of Bethsaida.[16] It also appears to others that a relatively small com-

10. "Christian Sites Around the Sea of Galilee: II. Bethsaida and El-Minyeh," *Dominican Studies,* Vol. III (1950), pp. 10–40. Cf. C. Kopp, *The Holy Places of the Gospels,* tr. by Ronald Walls (Herder & Herder, Inc., 1963), pp. 180–186.

11. Kopp, *Holy Places of the Gospels,* p. 185.

12. A. N. Sherwin-White, *Roman Society and Roman Law in the New Testament* (Oxford: Clarendon Press, 1963), p. 131.

13. *Ibid.,* pp. 132 f.

14. A. Alt, "Galiläische Probleme," in *Kleine Schriften zur Geschichte des Volkes Israel,* Vol. II (Munich: Beck, 1953), pp. 363–455; see p. 393, n. 2; p. 433, n. 1; pp. 447 f.; p. 451, n. 3.

15. Kopp, *Holy Places of the Gospels,* p. 185.

16. See *Dominican Studies,* Vol. III, p. 17, with reference to A. Büchler, *Der Galiläische Am ha-arez* (Vienna, 1906), p. 332.

plex of villages and a city near a small river and a relatively small inland lake belies the claim that this should have been the site of a major fishing industry and commerce, not to speak of the competition of nearby Magdala. But we have a similar case in the Near East in the fishing center on the Sangarius River in Asia Minor. Compared to its size and the reputation it had of supplying "the neighboring people with an enormous amount of fish," this place too seems to belie "its ancient and medieval reputation." [17]

Bethsaida, like Tiberias and Magdala on the shores of the Sea of Galilee, and like most Palestinian coastal towns on the Mediterranean Sea, had at best a Jewish minority population augmented by recent immigrants invited by the respective tetrarchs to help build up industry and commerce for rich tax revenues. Only a part of the Jewish populace in Bethsaida, as elsewhere, would have been professionally engaged in the fishing business either as fish catchers, or as fish traders, or sometimes as both.

That some of Jesus' disciples, the former fishermen, were from Bethsaida may mean only that it was the place of their employment, and, as Dodd insists, need not mean that they "were natives of the place." [18] Masterman observed that even nowadays, as probably also in New Testament times, "the fishermen occupied temporary huts on the shore when engaged in loading or unloading their boats." [19] Non-Jewish influence on the native Galilean Jews in Bethsaida under the reign of Herod the Great and later the tetrarch Philip is evidenced by the fact that Simon Peter's brother has the Greek name Andrew, and that another resident of Bethsaida, later on also a disciple of Jesus, had the Greek name Philip (John 12:21). It seems more than mere coincidence that these two disciples with Greek names coming from Bethsaida were approached by the Greeks in Jerusalem who sought their good offices in getting "to see Jesus" (John 12:20 ff.). It also makes one

17. T. R. S. Broughton, "Roman Asia," in *An Economic Survey of Ancient Rome,* edited by T. Frank, Vol. IV (Johns Hopkins University, 1938), p. 627.

18. C. H. Dodd, *The Historical Tradition in the Fourth Gospel* (Cambridge: Cambridge University Press, 1963), p. 309.

19. *Studies in Galilee,* p. 102. See also Mainzer, *Fischfang,* p. 41.

curious as to why, compared to Peter and the two Zebedee sons, Philip and Andrew are practically ignored in the Gospels and Acts. In any event, the Greek names reported of some residents of the Jewish community in Bethsaida may prove for this city what the hippodrome proves for Magdala, the Galilean counterpart and rival to Bethsaida, namely, "strong Gentile influence." [20]

Magdala, Tarichaea. Located only a few miles away in the adjoining Galilean tetrarchy of Herod is Magadan or Magdala, identified by the Talmud as the ancient *migdal-nunaiya,* literally, "Fish Tower," and also as the hometown of Mary Magdalene, one of the few women among the followers of Jesus mentioned by name. It is generally agreed that this is the same town which elsewhere in the New Testament goes under the name of Dalmanutha (Mark 8:10), [21] and which by the Greek-speaking residents of Galilee was referred to as Tarichaea, derived from *tarichos* which means "processed fish." Delicatessen fish was exported from here beyond the boundaries of Palestine.[22] Other places in the eastern provinces of the Roman Empire, competing with the Galilean Tarichaea in catering to the expensive tastes of the upper classes, were Amastris, Tieium, Heracleia Pontica, Chalcedon, cities on the Pontus and Propontis, besides places in the west, especially Sardinia.

Josephus' figure of forty thousand Tarichaeans [23] is probably as much exaggerated as the two hundred and thirty large fishing boats with four sailors in each, taken by him off the shore of Tarichaea at short notice for the purpose of invading rebellious Tiberias.[24] But even if

20. G. E. Wright and F. V. Filson (eds.), *The Westminster Historical Atlas to the Bible,* rev. ed. (The Westminster Press, 1956), p. 94. On Greek towns in Galilee, see V. Tcherikover, *Hellenistic Civilization and the Jews,* translated by S. Applebaum (The Jewish Publication Society of America, 1959), pp. 90 ff.

21. Kopp, *Holy Places of the Gospels,* p. 191. See also the variant readings to the Greek text of Mark 8:10.

22. S. W. Baron, *A Social and Religious History of the Jews,* Vol. I, 2d ed. (The Jewish Publication Society of America, 1952), p. 255, n. 6; Kopp, *Holy Places of the Gospels,* 192 f.; Dalman, *Arbeit und Sitte in Palästina,* pp. 105, 357.

23. *Jewish War,* II, 608.

24. *Ibid.,* p. 635.

Josephus meant by Tarichaea here the whole toparchy, we would still, even if dividing the figures by half or more, have to see in Tarichaea more than a romantic fishing village. The Tarichaean toparchy, one of eleven into which the Romans divided all Jewish territory after the death of Herod the Great, included Capernaum and Chorazin.[25] If Peter's house was in Capernaum (Mark 1:29 and parallels in Matt. 8:14; Luke 4:38), halfway between Bethsaida and Tarichaea, the former must have been the place of employment or trade.

If the men, called into discipleship by Jesus away from their employment, were in age his contemporaries or even older, it is quite likely then for them to have watched from childhood on the commercial, industrial, and cultural buildup of Bethsaida since its beginning as Philip's capital. They may have been one of the first to accept the invitation Philip must have issued to Galileans and non-Jews alike to help in the development of the rich resources of the area for the benefit of both Philip's treasury and the social, economic opportunity beckoning to the economic and cultural pioneers.

Modern historians have advanced the theory that Hellenistic cities, such as Bethsaida, and later Tiberias, were founded by decree of regional or imperial rulers to promote the economic development of the area. Alt reflects this idea in his opinion that the industrial exploitation of the fish resources of the northern part of the Sea of Galilee and the Jordan River marshes was the reason why Philip built up Bethsaida,[26] and why Herod later built up Tiberias.[27] Jones, however, contends that ancient cities were not founded primarily "to foster the economic life of the district, but to provide more comfortable travelling by the imperial post." [28] This, too, would fit Bethsaida as well as Tarichaea, for the main road north to Caesarea Philippi and Damascus passes by Bethsaida; and the main road used

25. Alt, *Kleine Schriften zur Geschichte des Volkes Israel,* Vol. II, p. 449, n. 2.

26. *Ibid.,* p. 451, n. 3.

27. Kopp, *Holy Places of the Gospels,* pp. 192 f.

28. A. H. M. Jones, *The Greek City from Alexander to Justinian* (Oxford: Clarendon Press, 1940), p. 259, *passim.*

for transporting goods from the northern part of the Sea of Galilee to the export market in Ptolemais at the Mediterranean Sea went through Bethsaida, leaving the Sea of Galilee at Tarichaea, and running through Cana.

Sidon. Literally, "Fish-catch Place," this is still another town with allusion to fishing that is mentioned in the New Testament. It is situated on the Mediterranean coast, due west of Damascus. Among the multitudes that came to Jesus during his ministry along the shores of the Sea of Galilee were reportedly also some "from about Tyre and Sidon" (Mark 3:8, with parallel in Luke 6:17, but not in Matthew). When Jesus, under pressure of political persecution at the hands of Herod Antipas, finally had to withdraw from Galilee, he first went to the district of Tyre and Sidon (Mark 7:24, with parallel in Matt. 15:21, but not in Luke; some early manuscripts omit Sidon from Jesus' itinerary). Paul later on is said to have visited friends in Sidon (Acts 27:3).

From numerous such coastal fishing places fish was either exported to the metropolitan markets of the eastern provinces, or brought to Jerusalem with its over one hundred thousand residents. There was a specially named Fish Gate (see Neh. 3:3; 12:39; II Chron. 33:14) in the walls of Jerusalem through which fish from the Galilean northwestern Mediterranean coast or from the Sea of Galilee was brought to the market regularly and sold.[29] There is evidence that fishermen sometimes acted as their own dealers in the wholesale and retail trades.[30] The rule, however, seems to have been that fishermen sold their catch to dealers. Only rarely is a deliberate distinction made in our records between fish catchers and fish traders. The author of Job 41:6 clearly refers to traders bargaining over fish, and to merchants dividing up a catch of fish. All this in connection with the contemplated catch of Leviathan! But this commercial aspect must also be kept in mind when assess-

29. On the location of the fish market in the city of Jerusalem, see J. Jeremias, *Jerusalem zur Zeit Jesu,* 2d ed. (Göttingen: Vandenhoeck, 1958), Part I, pp. 22 and 40.

30. Stöckle, art. "Fischereigewerbe," in *Real-Encyclopädie,* Supplement to Vol. IV, pp. 456–462, *passim.*

ing the social and economic milieu of the Galilean fishermen in the present Gospels.

That the tribes of Zebulun and Naphtali were those charged with fishing and the fishing trade, and that commercial fishing on the Sea of Galilee was restricted to the tribe of Naphtali,[31] was part of the old legislation of tribal territorial rights, dating back to Moses and Joshua. But in New Testament times these legal restrictions were no longer in force, in fact had not been ever since the Assyrian invasion of Israel in the eighth century B.C.[32] With or without such tribal territorial rights in force, every Israelite was, of course, free to do a limited amount of private, nonprofessional fishing. It goes without saying that "this fishing was not a lucrative business." [33] But to mention the Galilean fishermen of the Gospels in the same breath with this marginal private fishing can only augment the traditional confusion about the economic role of professional fishing in first century A.D. Galilee. Matthew's editorial remark (ch. 4:12 f.) about Jesus' ministry "in the territory of Zebulun and Naphtali" is of theological, not historical —let alone economic or sociological—significance. Matthew (ch. 4:15 f.) [34] uses the eschatological prophecy of Isaiah (ch. 9:1 f.) to characterize not only the opening but the whole of Jesus' ministry, of which the call of the Galilean fishermen to be "fishers of men" was his first act.

In conclusion of this section a brief note may be added about hunting and fowling. In the Appendix on Philologi-

31. L. Ginzberg, *The Legends of the Jews,* 7 vols. (The Jewish Publication Society of America, 1954), Vol. III, pp. 459–461; Vol. IV, p. 16. Cf. Dalman, *Arbeit und Sitte in Palästina,* pp. 357 f.; H. L. Strack and P. Billerbeck, *Kommentar zum Neuen Testament aus Talmud und Midrasch,* Vol. I (Munich: Beck, 1926), pp. 185 f.

32. For details of territorial rights of Galilean cities, royal domains and toparchies, and their changes, especially in Hasmonaean and Roman times, see Alt, *Kleine Schriften zur Geschichte des Volkes Israel,* Vol. II, pp. 363–365.

33. F. Delitzsch, *Jewish Artisan Life in the Time of Christ* (London: Hutchinson, 1906), p. 33.

34. K. Stendahl, *The School of St. Matthew, and Its Use of the Old Testament* (Uppsala, 1954), pp. 104 f., 150 f. As signifying the inclusion of the Gentiles, see J. Jeremias, *Jesus' Promise to the Nations* (Studies in Biblical Theology, No. 24; London: SCM Press, Ltd., 1958). For patristic interpretations, see E. Hilgert, *The Ship and Related Symbols in the New Testament* (Assen: Van Gorcum, 1962), p. 112, n. 24.

cal Observations it is noted that terminology as well as tools apply equally to fishing, hunting, and fowling. Acquaintance with fowling and hunting throughout the ancient Near East is clearly established by the material that Pritchard selectively collected.[35] Hunting remained during New Testament times only as a sport for the Hellenized upper classes even in Palestine, following the *paideia* ideal of the adopted culture.[36] Fowling may have remained a trade in New Testament times, if only to provide expensive fowl for the upper classes and inexpensive sparrows for the city's poor.[37] When the Septuagint occasionally changes the hunting, fowling, fishing metaphor used in the original Masoretic text into a milder expression, it does so not because either the trade or sport of hunting, fowling, or fishing was declining, though, of course, as Dalman observes, the urbanization of Palestine during the Hellenistic period and the conversion of large areas into smaller domains and toparchies restricts large-scale hunting, to be sure. Rather, the fishing, fowling, hunting metaphors of the Hebrew text are changed out of interest in safeguarding Israel's religion against anthropomorphic or theriomorphic misinterpretations or even misrepresentations, especially when the metaphors were originally applied to God.

Gerleman's study [38] seems to substantiate Dalman's evaluation of his own comprehensive account of hunting and fowling in Palestine.[39] For Dalman claimed that the widespread use of fishing and hunting metaphors in the psalms and in the wisdom and prophetic literature reveals how popular these activities had been in Biblical Israel. However, in the psalms and wisdom literature we may have only a long-established Near Eastern literary convention

35. Pritchard, *Ancient Near East in Pictures,* Fig. Nos. 109–114, 189, and the accompanying texts on pp. 33 f., 60, 262 f., 271.

36. See Josephus, *Jewish War,* I, 429, on Herod as hunter. See above, p. 15 on *paideia.*

37. On sparrows sold in the market, see Q saying, Luke 12:6, par. Matt. 10:29.

38. *Old Testament Terminology.*

39. Dalman, *Arbeit und Sitte in Palästina,* pp. 314–343. On Galilean snares and traps used today, see Fig. Nos. 60–63, 65, in Dalman's Appendix. No mention of hunting is made in R. de Vaux, *Ancient Israel.*

reflected which then says nothing about the popularity of fishing and hunting in Biblical Palestine. And about the prophet's use of the fishing metaphor Caspari argued [40] that it was prompted not by the prophet's personal or Israel's general familiarity with fishing, but by the role that fishing occupied in Assyrian, Babylonian, and Egyptian economy, cult, and mythology.

Fishing in Galilee: Its Ways and Means

Preparation for a Fish Catch. Traditionally, fishermen are said to have made their own nets from flax. This is said to have required great skill and intelligence.[41] Second-century A.D. Rabbi Jose of Galilee was a fisherman and net maker.[42] What ranked a fisherman among the social class of artisans and craftsmen was not only this ability of fashioning his own nets, suitable for the catching of the variety of fish in the various seasons of the year, but also the knowledge of what Oppian called "the crafty devices of the cunning fisher's art," that is, the variety of fishing methods and species of fish which the Hellenistic *halieutica* literature subjected to descriptive analysis. Based on Hos. 4:3, Jewish legendary tradition spoke of seven hundred species of "clean" fish, all of which, together with other "clean" animals, left the Holy Land at the time of the exile and settled in Babylon. All fish left, and except for the turbot fish, returned to Palestine by way of the abyss,[43] which ultimately connected all waterways.

Dalman gives a more realistic number of species of fish in Palestine: twenty-four kinds of fish for the Sea of Galilee (according to Josephus, "The lake contains species of fish different both in taste and appearance from those

40. W. Caspari, "Die Chaldäer bei Habakkuk," *Neue Kirchl. Zeitschrift,* Vol. 18 (1907), pp. 156–175, esp. p. 170.

41. Ginzberg, *Legends of the Jews,* Vol. IV, pp. 220 f.

42. Strack-Billerbeck, *Kommentar,* Vol. IV, p. 261, n. 1.

43. Ginzberg, *Legends of the Jews,* Vol. VI, pp. 390 f., n. 4. On the tradition of seven hundred species of clean fish, see *Midrash Rabbah,* Lamentations, poem XXXIV. On fish as exempt from the Deluge, see Eisler, *Orpheus,* pp. 182 f. See Aelian, *Animals,* IX:35, on whether or not fish have access to the lower regions, the dwelling place of the sea. See also Civil's essay cited above, Ch. I, n. 39.

found elsewhere"[44]), seventy-eight kinds of fish for the Mediterranean coast, and eleven kinds for the River Jordan.[45] Masterman lists only three families or eight species of fish in Galilee.[46] Even of this considerably smaller number of species of fish, not every one was worth fishing, either for economic reasons or because Rabbinic tradition held certain kinds of fish to be "unclean." That fish of every kind (*ek pantos genous*) had been caught in one catch according to Jesus' parable of the dragnet (Matt. 13:47-50) is, of course, a stylized theological account, as is Peter's vision in Acts 10:13 to kill and eat all kinds of animals, presumably including fish, and the figure of one hundred and fifty-three fish in John 21:11.

G. R. Wynne has argued, on the basis of the Vulgate reading of Mark 1:19, and of a Gospel scholia of A.D. 1610, that the Zebedee-sons were not sitting and mending their nets when Jesus called them to follow him (so in the translations of Knox, *The New English Bible,* Phillips, RSV, Weymouth, and others), but sitting in readiness with the net placed "in neat folds, always in view of the next haul."[47] According to Wynne, the difference between the call of Simon and Andrew and the call of James and John is this, that the latter were found by Jesus in alert readiness to cast the nets at the first sight of a school of fish near the surface, whereas Simon and Andrew were actually hauling in their catch. Before nets can be reused, they have to be washed (*plunein*) and dried. In Ezek. 26:5, 14, the place for the spreading of the nets, that is, for drying, is the bare rock. Finally, the nets are mended and folded (*katartizein*) ready for use.

Another preparation for catching fish commercially is the choice of nets suitable for the kinds of fish to be caught. The same goes for the choice of boats,[48] if any, suitable for the catch intended. The hiring of sailors for

44. *Jewish War,* III, 508.

45. Dalman, *Arbeit und Sitte in Palästina,* p. 351.

46. *Studies in Galilee,* pp. 43–48.

47. "Mending Their Nets," *Expositor,* 7th series, Vol. VIII (1909), pp. 282–285. Wynne's idea is reflected in the translations of Goodspeed and Lattey.

48. Hilgert, *The Ship and Related Symbols.*

the boats, of helping hands for the actual fishing (similar to the hiring of farm hands in the grain or grape harvest), and the coordination with one's associates or partners in joint efforts are further steps necessary before the actual catch can get under way.

Fishing Tools and Methods. The tools for fishing, hunting, or fowling are as varied as are the different kinds of game for which they were designed, and differ according to whether the fisherman, for instance, is a private amateur or a commercial businessman. Peter and Andrew in the Pseudo-Clementine *Recognitions* (II:62 f.) are said to be fishing with a line and hook, sitting on a rock, with Peter at the time falling into a religious trance. This certainly represents a different kind of fisher from the Peter who pulls a whole huge dragnet ashore singlehandedly (John 21:11) or with the help of friends (Luke 5:7). No doubt, all these accounts of Galilean fishing in the Gospels and subsequent Christian tradition have been shaped, if not indeed created, by theological interests. These accounts may therefore have little, if any, historical value. But as with the parables of Jesus, the accounts of the Galilean fishermen turned apostles may give us at least an intimation of certain economic aspects. To keep the theological and the economical aspects about the fishing accounts separate and to prevent allegorization and sentimentalization of the accounts are the purposes of this section.

Certain kinds of fishermen operate without any tools at all. They dive and use their bare hands, or with their heels dig holes in the sand of shallow waters. Others use a variety of hooks on a line or rope, either held directly or suspended from a rod. The use of bait seems to have been known. Still others would use wicker baskets or other kinds of fish traps made of nets and ropes. Still others used various kinds of spears, arrows, and harpoons. By far the most-used tool in fishing was the net. What *diktuon* is as overall designation for numerous kinds of specific nets, the word *halieus* is as common designation for various kinds of fishermen. Not even the literal meaning of *halieus,* "one who fishes in salt water," is applicable to the Galilean fishermen. Besides, fishermen could also be spoken of as hunters, partly for linguistic reasons,[49] partly because of the similarity of tools and skills used by each.[50]

One kind of net, the casting net, can be used by one person, even though the net may extend to twenty feet or more. From the fact that Mark 1:16 and Matt. 4:18 specifically mention casting nets being used by Peter and Andrew, J. G. Duncan concluded that the only place on the western, i.e., Galilean, side of the lake, where the shore does not drop off sharply into deep waters as most everywhere else on the Sea of Galilee, was the bay of the seven warm springs south of Capernaum, where "the fishes come up in shoals on account of the water from the springs." Duncan believed that "the careful selection of the correct word ['casting net'] in describing an incident has led to the identification of the spot where the incident [of the call of the apostolic fishermen] occurred." [51]

This argumentation is refuted by three considerations. For one, casting nets were used from boats as much as by fishermen wading near shore. Secondly, the Greek word for "casting net" could be used for just about any kind of net, which makes it thus synonymous with *diktuon*. Thirdly, the use of casting nets by wading near shore was restricted during the summer season when the water level of the lake fell, thus reducing even further the small rim around the lake suitable for wading.[52] Dragnets, which reach proportions of up to seven hundred feet long and fifteen feet wide, take more than one person to operate. Only when used metaphorically can a single person be said to handle a dragnet all by himself, as with Peter in John, ch. 21, or with Asherah's fisherman in the Ugaritic myth.[53] When a net is used close to shore, attending fishermen swim near it and often dive in the water to prevent the net from getting snagged and torn. Since it is reported that

49. The Mishnah *Shebiith* 7:4 speaks of "hunters of fish." In the Syriac version of Mark 1:16 f., "hunters of fish" is read instead of "fishermen," and "hunters of men" instead of "fishers of men."

50. Dalman, *Arbeit und Sitte in Palästina,* p. 359.

51. "The Sea of Tiberias and Its Environs," *The Palestine Exploration Fund Quarterly* (London, 1926), p. 20.

52. Bishop, "Jesus and the Lake," *loc. cit.,* p. 401.

53. See below, pp. 85 f.

Jesus once found Peter stripped of his clothes (John 21:7), Bishop feels justified in hypothesizing that "perhaps it was at this kind of work that St. Peter was reckoned a master hand." [54]

Unlike fishing some distance off the shore of the Mediterranean Sea, fishing on the Sea of Galilee yielded its biggest and most profitable hauls close to the shore.[55] The time for fishing in Jewish society was, of course, any day except the Sabbath. If there was not time enough, either for the game to get caught the same day the nets were set or for the hunter to check his nets or traps, the school of Shammai forbade, but the school of Hillel permitted, the setting up of the nets.[56] Anything caught on the eve of a festival day could not be emptied on the festival day itself, "unless it is known that [it was] caught during the eve of the festival day." [57]

After the Catch. This section is important insofar as it reveals the whole economic spectrum of the Galilean fishing profession, as well as the social and economic structure within which the Galilean fishing business operated. It is all the more surprising that this aspect has been traditionally least explored, if not totally ignored. I propose to treat the subject of what happens after a catch has been made and hauled in, by analyzing three distinct problem areas: (1) the sorting and counting of fish; (2) taxation of fishermen; and (3) fish trade and commerce.

1. The sorting (*syllegein*) of fish after a catch is the equivalent of the sifting (*siniazein*) [58] of wheat and weeds, of grain and chaff, in the agricultural harvest; the equivalent of the separating (*aphorizein*) of the sheep; [59] the equivalent of the selection (*apodokimazein*) of stones fit

54. Bishop, *loc. cit.*, p. 401. That fishing close to shore with casting nets means necessarily fishing for bait only (so, e.g., Foakes-Jackson, and Carrington) is too arbitrary an interpretation.

55. Masterman, *Studies in Galilee*, p. 41.

56. Mishnah, *Shabbath*, 1:6.

57. Mishnah, *Betzah*, 3:2.

58. E. Fuchs, art. "*siniazō*," in *TWNT*, G. Friedrich (ed.), Vol. VII (1964), pp. 290–291, esp. on Luke 22:31.

59. J. Jeremias, *The Parables of Jesus*, rev. ed. (Charles Scribner's Sons, 1963), p. 206, nn. 80, 81. For reasons other than those given by Jeremias for the shepherd's "sorting" of sheep, see Plato, *Laws*, 735 B.

for building,[60] the equivalent of the refining, purifying, or testing (*puroun, dokimazein, chōneuein, katharizein, peirazein*) of ores for practical uses,[61] or the equivalent of dividing (*krinein*) in legal transactions by judges or kings. The sorting of fish was required by Rabbinic law (Mishnah *Hullin* 3:7; *Uktzin* 3:8) whose roots go back to Lev. 11:9-12 and Deut. 14:9-10. Non-Jewish fishermen also sorted their fish, as reflected in Lucian's story of *The Fisherman* (No. 48) in which fish that is found to be inedible (*abrotos*), ugly (*eidechetēs*), tough (*sklēros*), and worthless (*atimos*) is thrown away right after the catch.

To be distinguished from that is the identification of fish sacred to certain gods. In Book VII of *The Deipnosophists*,[62] Athenaeus presents a list of fish considered sacred, and therefore to be eaten if at all in prescribed rituals. However, fish as staple food is infinitely more important than its cultic, sacramental function. To say that Israel did not share the common belief in certain fish as sacred to God, is not the same as Goodenough's claim that fish-eating served as "a sacramental communion with Deity" in post-Biblical Judaism.[63] Religious traditions of ancient Sumer, Syria, Phoenicia, and other Near Eastern neighbors of Israel are said to have provided the background for this practice. Other Jewish scholars have pointed out that Rabbinic injunctions against unclean fish appear to have "arisen out of opposition against the pagan cults of neighboring peoples who held such fish sacred and ate them at certain cultic meals." [64]

Besides the distinction between clean and unclean fish,

60. W. Grundmann, art. "*dokimos*," in *TWNT*, G. Kittel (ed.), Vol. II (1935), pp. 259:36 ff. and 263:31 ff. See also D. Flusser, "Qumran und die Zwölf," in *Initiation*, supplement to *Numen*, Vol. X (Leiden: Brill, 1965), pp. 134 ff.

61. F. Lang, art. "*puroō*," in *TWNT*, G. Friedrich (ed.), Vol. VI (1959), p. 949:10 ff.

62. Edited and translated by C. B. Gulick, 7 vols. (Loeb Classical Library; London: William Heinemann, Ltd., n. d.).

63. Goodenough, *Jewish Symbols*, Vol. V, p. 40; Eisler, *Orpheus*, pp. 221 f. For a more conservative interpretation, see Bodenheimer, *Animal and Man*, pp. 203 ff.

64. J. Scheftelowitz, "Das Fisch Symbol im Judentum und Christentum," *Archiv für Religionswissenschaft*, Vol. XIV (1911), pp. 1–53, 321–392, esp. pp. 339 f.

Jewish fishermen also had to face the question when fish, though clean as a species, could become susceptible to uncleanness. Mishnah *Uktzin* 3:8 records three different rulings on this question, two from pre-Christian times from the schools of Hillel and Shammai, and one from Rabbi Akiba of the early second century A.D. Jewish scholarship has called attention to the fact that Rabbinic legislation against certain food items as not kosher developed and was enforced in the interest of curbing foreign competition which was felt keenly also in the import-export trade of Galilean fish.[65] Finkelstein concurs with Ginzberg when he says of Rabbinic decisions in economic matters that they "were largely determined by local, group, or family considerations, preconceptions and even bias." [66]

In terms of Weberian sociology this means that the ethos of the Palestinian economic system, of which fishing was an important part, varied in proportion to the relationships that the fishing industry had either to the official Temple leadership, or to dealers and traders of fish in Jewish communities whose livelihood depended on fish trade. Mishnah *Betzah* 3:2 records that first-century A.D. Rabban Gamaliel, Paul's tutor, permitted Jews to buy kosher fish sold by Gentiles, though he himself apparently preferred not to patronize Gentile fishermen or fish dealers.

A fish catch was sorted into clean and unclean fish, and the haul was also often counted.[67] Bishop claims that such counting of fish was an established custom especially in partnership fishing,[68] which was characteristic of the so-called tax fishers. Not only would equity among partners, such as the Zebedee-sons and John-sons were (Luke 5:10),

65. L. Ginzberg, *On Jewish Law and Lore* (The Jewish Publication Society of America, 1955), esp. pp. 77–118.

66. L. Finkelstein, *The Pharisees: The Sociological Background of Their Faith*, 2 vols., 3d ed. (The Jewish Publication Society of America, 1962), Vol. II, p. 780.

67. J. H. Bernard, *The Gospel According to St. John*, in the *International Critical Commentary* (Charles Scribner's Sons, 1929), Vol. II, p. 699: "The simplest explanation of . . . [John 21:11] is that . . . the fish were counted [as fishermen are wont to do, because the catch has to be divided into shares], and [that the number 153 was] remembered as a notable thing."

68. Bishop, *Catholic Biblical Quarterly*, Vol. XIII (1951), pp. 403 f.

require counting, but also the apportionment of taxation due on each catch, not to speak of paying the wages to the hired hands, which was usually in kind and not in money.

2. Taxation of fishermen is an important aspect for the proper interpretation of the fishing business in Galilee which, in all probability, was patterned largely after the tax-fishing system of other eastern provinces of the Roman Empire. As independent ruler over his tetrarchy Gaulanitis, Philip could have engaged fishermen either under the liturgy or requisition system, or under the tax system. In the first instance, the "royal fishermen" would have been required to deliver at specified times specified amounts of fish for which they would be paid either in kind or cash or both. Profitable as this system was for the government which entertained it, it worked only if large capital investments had already been made to allow for maximum use or profit from the fish. It is unlikely, however, that Philip's government would have, or could have, started out this way.

The textual evidences available in the New Testament and contemporary Jewish literature for the role of tax collectors in connection with fishing seem to be less weighty than the historical argument about the need for large initial capital investments in order to launch a profitable fishing industry in Bethsaida, which favors the assumption that Galilean fishing was largely that of the tax system. Philip would have sold fishing rights to people with the means of underwriting a large industrial outlay and commercial establishment. These people would in turn lease, usually on an annual basis, fishing permits to qualified fishermen who promised the largest returns. The fisherman in turn would hire servants and sailors in living up to his economic promise and profit, both for himself and for his employer, who took a certain quota, or tax, from everything the fishermen caught. These employers were called tax collectors.

Matthew-Levi, one of Jesus' disciples called from his tax office (*telōnion*), must have been such a *telōnēs,* who had fishermen working for him on the nearby Sea of Galilee (Mark 2:14 and parallels in Matthew and Luke, but not in John). The unscrupulous profiteering of these investment brokers, loan sharks, or the like, as we would call them today, is well established by the New Testament as well (e.g., Luke 16:1 ff.; 19:1 ff.). The fact that the schools of Shammai and Hillel disputed, not the right, but the extent of the right to be dishonest to the point of perjury toward the *telōnai* (Mishnah *Nedarim* 3:4), again shows, among other things, how much religion and economics were intertwined. Rudiments of taxation and subleasing of fishing rights seem to have survived in Galilee until quite recently.[69] Delitzsch's claim, however, that fishing in Palestine was exempt from taxation[70] cannot have applied to the tax system of fishing. If he meant by it exemption from regular governmental or Temple taxes on fishing, I have been unable to find a reference to that anywhere.

3. Trade and commerce with fish, both within Palestine and beyond, is another aspect of fishing in Galilee. The reason this aspect has largely been ignored lies probably in the absence of primary sources or firsthand information. In his survey of fishing in antiquity, Stöckle observed that fishermen sometimes served as their own dealers, which may have provided them with an extra margin of profit. From the fact that Rome found it necessary finally to intervene in the fishing trade with stern legislation, we can glean that there was as much ruthless profiteering going on between retail and wholesale dealers, and between dealers and consumers, as there was between tax collectors and fishermen.

Another insight into the fishing trade is gained from a brief note in Mishnah *Shebiith* 7:4 where "hunters of wild animals, birds, and fishes" are given the permission to sell "unclean" species (of which the so-called "catfish" is one example),[71] but only if the fishermen "chanced upon" them. Mid-second-century A.D. Rabbi Judah is on record as having permitted the sale of unclean fish caught by acci-

69. Masterman, *Studies in Galilee,* pp. 37 f.

70. According to E. D. Head, *New Testament Life and Literature as Reflected in the Papyri* (Broadman Press, 1952), p. 74, n. 23.

71. Masterman, *Studies in Galilee,* pp. 45 f.

dent, provided that "this is not [the fisherman's] trade." Earlier Rabbinic tradition, however, is on record as having forbidden the sale of unclean fish under any circumstances. On the marketplace or wherever fish was handled, the scrupulous Jew, whether producer or consumer, would follow the regulation of Mishnah *Makshirin* 6:3, according to which "all fish can be presumed unclean," except certain imported and processed kinds of fish specified by name and place of origin. It is debated whether Peter's horror (Acts 10:9-16) at being invited in his vision to eat "all kinds (*panta*) of animals (*tetrapoda*) and reptiles (*herpeta*) and birds (*peteina*) which are common (*koinos*) and unclean (*akathartos*)" reveals how even early Jewish Christians still felt strongly about traditional food laws.[72]

One thing, if nothing else, should be clear by now. Prosperity, as associated with fishing in New Testament times, came to Galilean fishermen not only with the use of nets and barges, but with the bets and bargains made later in the marketplace of Bethsaida or Tarichaea, after the tax collector and hired hands had first received their due.

The Galilean Fisherman and His Social Status

Palestinian society in Roman times [73] fell into two main groups, and each again into two subdivisions. The wealthy group can be subdivided into (1) those who were estate holders of royal or imperial Roman domains and, of course, the kings and tetrarchs and their closest associates, and (2) those who provided the government and kings with the large capital investments needed for the development and maintenance of a profitable industry and commerce. Among this second group we count the *telōnai* or tax collectors, the landed gentry or aristocracy which provided the higher echelon of the priestly class, and usually

72. Affirmative, see M. Dibelius, *Aufsätze zur Apostelgeschichte* (Göttingen: Vandenhoeck, 1961), pp. 96–107. Denying that Peter's vision had anything to do with Rabbinic laws, are E. Haenchen, F. Hahn, and others.

73. Rostovtzeff, *Roman Empire,* Ch. VII; Delitzsch, *Jewish Artisan Life;* Finkelstein, *The Pharisees,* and many other studies.

also the high priests. Among them we must imagine also the owners of large fisheries, of ranches for large sheep and goat herds, and the large-scale merchants and entrepreneurs.

The other group, the villagers or common people, who by the standards of our modern society would be called the bourgeoisie, the middle or working class, can also be subdivided into (1) the small landowners, the village or town artisans and craftsmen, that is, the group which, as Finkelstein's study on *The Pharisees* has shown, provided the bulk of the manpower that went into the building of the Pharisaic movement which eventually engulfed such professional groups as priests, Levites, and scribes, as much as it did the religiopolitical movement of Zealotism. It is this group to which tentmaker Paul and landowning Levite Barnabas belonged. It is my contention that the fishermen of the Gospels also belonged to this group. (2) The other subdivision of this group included the tenant farmers or fishers, the serfs and unskilled laborers who served as hired hands in fields, vineyards, fisheries, or pastures.

It is granted that the wealth and highest social prestige was in the hands of the plutocratic oligarchy as in all other Near Eastern countries and that the commoners could, of course, not compare. But the survival of the Pharisaic movement shows where the real force of culture and social strength lay. By comparison with the capitalistic few, the artisans, craftsmen, and merchants of Galilee were relatively poor. But compared with the serfs and tenants, the small businessman was relatively well off. Moreover, the supply and demand of staple foods and other commodities led to, as Rostovtzeff saw it, a period of unprecedented prosperity in first-century Palestine. That fishermen, who traditionally had the reputation, as we saw earlier, of getting rich through their nets, shared in this prosperity is all the more likely, for they profited from the commercial value not only of regular fish as staple food for the masses of the urban population but also of delicatessen fish for export near and far to the tables of an affluent upper-class society throughout the Near Eastern provinces of the Empire.

The social reputation of fishermen in the ancient Near East fluctuated between two extremes, which, I propose, reflects the two types of people engaged in the fishing enterprise: the laborers and the managers. On the one hand, the Egyptian *Satire on the Trades* knew of no profession more miserable than the fisherman's. This tradition seems to be reflected in the literary attacks on nascent Christianity. Greco-Roman polemicists against the new religion took the poor literary style of the Gospels as evidence of the low social class background of the men who had left their fishing business to become apostles. In their reply, Christian apologists resorted to three basic arguments which became the conventional tactics against the attack that was designed to discredit the Christian movement. In the first place, it was conceded that Christianity had indeed arisen in the proletarian society of Palestine; secondly, it was emphasized that Christianity's rejection of the *sapientia mundi* was programmatic, not accidentally, but essentially; thirdly, it was taken as proof of the power of God himself at work in the new religion that "the victory over the philosophers and the grammarians [was] won by the peasants and the fishermen (*rusticanos et piscatores*)." [74]

This argument was first fully developed by Origen in his reply against Celsus who had charged that "Jesus collected round him ten or eleven infamous men, the most wicked tax collectors and sailors." [75] Origen conceded that the sons of Zebedee probably had been sailors (*nautai*), "since they left the ship and their father Zebedee." But he insisted that "Peter and his brother Andrew, who earned their necessities of life with a fishing net (*amphiblēstron*), are to be reckoned not among the sailors, but . . . among the fishermen." [76] This distinction between sailors and fish-

74. H. Hagendahl, *Latin Fathers and the Classics* (Studia Graeca et Latina Gothoburgensia, No. VI; Göteborg, 1958), p. 119, n. 3; also, p. 213, n. 5, and p. 313, n. 5. See also W. Krause, *Die Stellung der frühchristlichen Autoren zur heidnischen Literatur* (Vienna: Herder, 1958), p. 49, n. 19 and p. 271, n. 19; E. Norden, *Antike Kunstprosa* (Leipzig: Teubner, 1898), Vol. II, p. 516, n. 1.

75. Origen, *Contra Celsum,* translated by H. Chadwick (Cambridge: Cambridge University Press, 1953), Book I, 62, 63, and Book II, 46.

76. *Ibid.*

ermen is all the more remarkable, as the New Testament shows no trace of it. Josephus reports in his *Jewish War,* II, 635, that an average fishing boat on the Sea of Galilee had four *nautai.*[77] Rabbinic tradition specifies sailors, along with tax collectors and a few other professions, as people to be avoided for religious and social reasons.[78]

In Aelian's work *On the Characteristics of Animals* (XIV, 29), the terms *nautai* and *halieis* are used interchangeably. This could serve as a warning against drawing too rigid a distinction between the two terms, if not in principle, at least in certain cases. However, the later Christian iconographic tradition, for whatever it is worth, always represents Peter and Andrew with tools characteristic of their once literal, now metaphoric, fishing occupation. In the case of the Zebedee-sons James and John, nothing of the kind is ever mentioned, not even symbols related to sailing.[79] Another Christian literary tradition claims that John, the sailor-fisherman son of Zebedee, was a member of the priestly divisions serving the Jerusalem Temple before he became a disciple of Jesus.[80] Whether the idea "carries conviction" that John "the Galilean fisherman was Purveyor of Fish to his Holiness the High Priest," as has been alleged in another tradition derived from John 18:15 f., is not altogether as impossible as it is still made out to be.[81] But possibility, even probability, is one thing, proof another. And that applies to both sides in the argument over whether or not a fisherman and a priest not only can be compatible socially, but also can be one and the same person.

A totally different picture of the social milieu of Gali-

77. References to seafarers in Scripture; e.g., Ps. 107:23 f.; Rev. 18:17 f.; cf. 1 QH 3:14 f. See also G. E. Wright, "There Go the Ships," *The Biblical Archaeologist,* Vol. I:3 (1938), pp. 19–20.

78. Jeremias, *Jerusalem zur Zeit Jesu,* Vol. II, B, p. 175.

79. H. Roeder, *Saints and Their Attributes* (Henry Regnery Company, 1956), pp. 19–24.

80. E. Stauffer, *New Testament Theology,* translated by J. Marsh (London: SCM Press, Ltd., 1955), p. 40 and p. 263, n. 68. See below, p. 50. Also, J. V. Andersen, "L'apôtre Saint-Jean grand-prêtre," *Studia Theologica,* Vol. 19 (1965), fasc. 1–2, pp. 22–29.

81. Dodd, *Historical Tradition,* pp. 86–88, esp. p. 88, n. 3, and p. 246, n. 1.

lean fishermen emerges if one turns to what appears as an equally conventional assessment of a fisherman's life favored with wealth (Aelian, *Animals,* XII, 43) and with luxury (Hab. 1:16). S. W. Baron, a Jewish scholar of Jewish social history, once observed that "the numerous fishermen at Lake Tiberias or along the Mediterranean shore enjoyed a reputable, if not high, social standing." [82] From the fact that Zebedee and sons had to use hired hands to manage the volume of business, E. F. F. Bishop concluded that the "fishing industry" in Galilee was for Zebedee "a substantial business [which even implied] perhaps some other commercial partnership in a Mediterranean port." [83]

Much of what Bishop goes on to say is clearly historical fiction which nevertheless may have more truth to it than the traditional rustic idyll projected by the early Christian apologists. Bishop pictures the fishermen of the Gospels as part-time salesmen who were equally at home in the commercial and financial business centers of Bethsaida and Tarichaea, as in Jerusalem, Caesarea, Ptolemais, Tyre, and Sidon. He imagines the same men to have supplied "the high-priestly family with fresh and cured fish," carried in caravans from Galilee to Jerusalem, especially at festival times.[84]

One could go even farther in speculation. Since pilgrimages to the Temple, as well as the weekly relieving from duty of some priestly and Levitical Temple divisions by fresh ones, always took place in groups numbering scores of people from the same district and social class, it is just possible that Jesus' "triumphal entry" into Jerusalem, which now of course is thoroughly reinterpreted from the theological perspective of each Evangelist, could have been part of the Tarichaea and Bethsaida delegation of fishermen. Some of them may have served as priests or Levites in the Temple for a week at a time, some five times or so every year.

82. *A Social and Religious History of the Jews,* Vol. I, p. 254.

83. *Catholic Biblical Quarterly,* Vol. XIII (1951), p. 400. See also below, p. 52.

84. *Catholic Biblical Quarterly,* p. 402.

Records show that of the estimated eighteen thousand priests and Levites in Palestine during New Testament times most of them were engaged in full-time work during the more than ten months out of every year when they were not serving their terms in the Temple.[85] The same is true of rabbis or scribes who were engaged in regular professions besides their religious careers, and so also the members of the Pharisaic communes. Delitzsch knows of two scribes (*grammateis*) who simultaneously were professional fishermen.[86] This should be remembered in the debate over the meaning of *agrammatos* in Acts 4:13. It is intriguing to think that the two rabbis of the early second century and natives of Bethsaida were also fishermen and perhaps the same to whom Delitzsch refers.[87] The obscure early Christian tradition about John, the fisherman son of Zebedee, as also a priest before becoming a disciple of Jesus is sociologically plausible.

Baron refers to an account about Galilean fishermen who, out of Torah loyalty and religious zeal—a feature that occasionally gave at least some of them the reputation of being aligned with the Galilee-centered Zealot movement [88]—stopped all fishing for some days during Passover and again during Tabernacles.[89] Three aspects of this incident interest us in connection with the study of the social status of Galilean fishermen.

One aspect concerns the economic repercussions of this action of the fishermen. According to Baron, "widespread

85. Jeremias, *Jerusalem zur Zeit Jesu,* Part II, B, pp. 69 f. and pp. 76 f. On Egyptian priests serving as part-time *geōrgoi,* see H. Kortenbeutel, art. "*geōrgoi,*" in *Real-Encyclopädie,* Supplement to Vol. VII (1940), cols. 206 f.

86. *Jewish Artisan Life,* p. 58.

87. On Büchler's observation, see above, n. 16.

88. M. Hengel, *Die Zeloten* (Arbeiten zur Geschichte des Spätjudentums und Urchristentums, No. 1; Leiden: Brill, 1961), pp. 57–61 on "the Galileans"; see also pp. 55–57 on Simon Peter as Bar-Jona (Matt. 16:17; John 1:42; 21:15), which R. Eisler and O. Cullmann interpret as referring to Peter's association with the Zealots. Finkelstein, *The Pharisees,* Vol. I, p. 5, speaks of the Galilean middle class as "usually zealot, sometimes sectarian." Cf. also B. Reicke, *Diakonie, Festfreude und Zelos* (Uppsala: Univ. Arsskrift, 1951–1955), pp. 236 f., on Palestinian early Christian Zealotism.

89. *A Social and Religious History of the Jews,* Vol. I, pp. 254 f.

complaints" came from consumers, especially the festival crowds who "found themselves deprived of [fish]," which he claims was an "integral part of [the Jewish] holiday meal during the latter days of these important festivals."[90] Even if only the crowds gathered for the festival are implied, it would still mean that tens of thousands were clamoring for their fish. And for the fishermen a sizable business opportunity was deliberately bypassed! Whether the event that Baron reports would or would not strengthen Goodenough's thesis that fish was eaten in Jewish society of New Testament times with sacramental significance need not concern us here.

What furthermore interests us in Baron's account is the implied Torah loyalty of the Galilean fishermen. Delitzsch must have had something similar in mind when he, after first lumping "sailors" and "fishermen" together, recalls Rabbinic tradition about sailors as by nature very devout "because of their having to do with the uncertain and dangerous elements."[91] This alleged piety of the Galilean fishermen would well fit in with the tradition preserved in John 1:35 ff., according to which the fishermen had been followers or students of John the Baptist.[92] Max Weber has shown how throughout history a person's or group's religious zeal and loyalty often went hand in hand with an enterprising spirit of economic, capitalistic adventure.[93]

Finally, the incident about the Galilean fishermen at Jerusalem during festival time led Baron to stipulate that part of the time they had taken out from fishing was spent "forming a professional association."[94] Like most other trades in Greco-Roman times, fishermen and fish salesmen had their craft guilds (*collegia fabrorum*)[95] which could be considered a kind of primitive ancestor to modern labor unions and service clubs. These guilds had acquired over

90. *Ibid.*

91. *Jewish Artisan Life,* p. 33.

92. Dodd, *Historical Tradition,* pp. 302 ff.

93. *The Protestant Ethic and the Spirit of Capitalism,* translated by T. Parsons (Charles Scribner's Sons, 1930), p. 58.

94. Baron, *A Social and Religious History of the Jews,* p. 254.

95. Head, *New Testament Life and Literature,* Ch. VIII; Jeremias, *Jerusalem zur Zeit Jesu,* Part I, pp. 22–23.

some centuries of their existence throughout the Eastern provinces of the Empire a well-deserved reputation of being seedbeds and nurseries of political rebellion. Emperor Augustus finally decreed in the *lex Julia de collegiis*[96] of the year 22 B.C. that the most dangerous of the clubs be closed, and that special imperial or provincial permits would henceforth be required for continuing old or founding new guilds. That things did not change overnight is evident from Josephus' account (*Vita* 62) about sailors (*nautai*) from Tiberias making common cause with the local proletariat (*aporoi*) in demolishing Herod's palace. Among the causes of "the social unrest in the fishing community of Tiberias" F. M. Heichelheim[97] lists "excessive obligations to the government" besides religious and nationalistic causes.

We must guard against the temptation, heightened by the contrast of the traditional image of the Galilean fishermen as poor and illiterate, to make them out as wealthy middle class in the modern American sense. It is good to remind oneself that the total volume of the Galilean fishing industry "was relatively small" in comparison to what fishing was in other ancient cities.[98] Mindful of his own warning, Jones has to concede that there was "extensive trade in staple foodstuffs, such as dried or salted fish," and that industry and commerce of these staple foods "were sufficiently important to make the fortunes of a few cities and to contribute substantially to the prosperity of a number of others."[99]

To be sure, the bourgeois class of Palestine society, the class to which most priests, Levites, scribes, and Pharisees belonged, was clearly distinct from the wealthy upper class that provided a city like Bethsaida with the fiscal securities for economic growth. It is equally clear that the social status of a Galilean fisherman was not identical automatically with poverty and illiteracy. My contention that fishing in Galilee was "big business" and was synonymous

96. H. Last, "The Social Policy of Augustus," in *The Cambridge Ancient History*, Vol. X (Cambridge: Cambridge University Press, 1952), Ch. XIV, p. 459, nn. 6 and 7.

97. "Roman Syria," in *An Economic Survey of Ancient Rome*, p. 230.

98. Jones, *The Greek City*, p. 260.

99. *Ibid.*, pp. 261, 262.

with prosperity does not invalidate the observation of A. N. Sherwin-White and others that Galilee, compared with other areas inside and outside of Palestine, was "less dominated by a landowning class or a middle class of moderately wealthy *bourgeoisie*." [100]

When we look to the New Testament for information about the life of the Galilean fishermen before their call to discipleship, we learn very little. And the little it seemingly does contain has all too often been inadequately or misleadingly interpreted.

The Gospel References. Before turning to the Synoptic tradition, let me briefly present the Johannine material. In a tradition independent of the Synoptics, the Fourth Gospel reports in John 1:35 ff. that Andrew and Simon Peter (the Synoptics prefer the reverse order of listing the names) at the time of their response to the call of Jesus were not in Galilee, and that they were followers of John the Baptist. Both observations apparently belong together. That they follow Jesus from the beginning of his recorded public ministry, which in varying form the Synoptics also report, may be based on the dogmatic tradition that these men were eyewitnesses "from the beginning" (John 15:27; I John 1:1 f.; Acts 1:21). Of course, the reverse may be true that the dogmatic tradition arose because these men really had been with Jesus from the beginning. Besides the sons of Zebedee (John 21:2), Andrew and Simon are the only ones mentioned by name and their patronymic as "son of John" [101] or Johnson. Only by a passing reference are they associated with Bethsaida (John 1:44). According to Dodd, the author of the Fourth Gospel found this information in the Johannine tradition which Dodd believes to be Jerusalem-centered, while the Galilee-centered Synoptic traditions do not associate Peter and Andrew with Bethsaida, but only with Capernaum which politically belonged to the toparchy of Tarichaea.

In John 21:1-14, in the time after Easter, the disciples of Jesus (five by name, two anonymous, with Andrew conspicuously absent) are depicted as fishermen in Galilee.

100. *Roman Society and Roman Law*, p. 141.
101. Dodd, *Historical Tradition*, p. 307.

Dodd identified this report form-critically as belonging to the "circumstantial type (analogous to the *Novellen,* or tales)."[102] The narrative pattern or scheme of this type consists of five elements (the desolate disciples without Jesus; his appearance; his approach and greeting; their recognition of him; his commission to them). Each of the five elements is modified in a variety of ways in each of the three basically independent gospel traditions, the Lucan, the Johannine, and the one in Matthew-Mark. But even if one were to attribute the remarkable details in the fishing scene of John 21:3 ff. to an eyewitness, and even if the men depicted engaged in fishing presumably were professional fishermen, neither the Johannine tradition nor the Fourth Gospel provides any clue about the social status of the men mentioned in John, ch. 21, or in ch. 1:35 ff., or, for that matter, in ch. 6:16 f. There all the disciples pile into a large fishing boat to cross over to Capernaum. Even if that were, as alleged, to prove that all or at least the fishermen among them were expert sailors, this portion of the tradition also neither proves nor disproves anything anybody might claim about the social status of these men. The Johannine tradition and the fourth Evangelist preserve only the association of some of the disciples with fishing in Galilee; about their social and economic status the records simply are either uninformed or disinterested.

In the Synoptic tradition we are only seemingly better off. The pericope of the call of the first disciples (Mark 1:16-20 and parallels) leaves no doubt that these men were fishers. But questions as to the relative poverty or prosperity of these Galilean fishermen lie clearly outside the scope of the pericope. Jesus visits in the house (*oikia*) of Peter, in Mark and Matthew after the call to discipleship, in Luke even before then. More general is the only other statement about the social, economic status of the Galilean men who answered Jesus' call to discipleship. The statement appears now in each of the three Synoptists as part of, or appended to, the pericope of the rich man who approached Jesus on his journey to Jerusalem (Mark 10:17-

102. *Ibid.,* p. 143. See below, p. 193.

31; Matt. 19:16-30; Luke 18:18-30). Peter as spokesman of all disciples, and not just the Twelve, or even the Galilean fishermen, confesses that they had left "everything" (*panta,* Mark 10:28; Matt. 19:27). Luke 18:28 has them give up *ta idia,* which Goodspeed, Moffatt, RSV, and other translations render as "home (s)"; other translations prefer "belongings," "possessions," and the like.

It may be too much to expect at this point recollections about nets and boats and servants that were left behind. But one may be tempted or intrigued by the implication here that the disciples did not exchange one economic hardship for another when they responded to Jesus' call. Precarious as this inference is, made from Mark 10:28 and its parallels, the decisive thing, however, is that all traces of the economic background of the Galilean disciples of Jesus were absorbed or obliterated by the theological interests at work in the gospel traditions and later compositions. The catechetical purpose of this whole pericope should be seen in the context of the tradition on property asceticism peculiar to sectarian Judaism and early Jewish Christianity.[103] One cannot press the independent logion (Mark 10:29-30; Matt. 19:28-29; Luke 18:29-30) that speaks of the Galilean disciples as having left "house[104] and home"[105] into yielding information about the former social and economic status of the Galilean fishermen.

The References in Acts. For Peter to say that he has "no silver and gold" (Acts 3:6) does not prove his poverty as fisherman, but proves him as practitioner of the property asceticism as announced in Acts 2:44 f. (cf. ch. 4:32, 34 f.). The only other text left is Acts 4:13 where a group of professional religious leaders (vs. 5 f.) in Jerusalem speaks of Peter and John as *agrammatoi* and *idiōtai.* The translation

103. H. Braun, *Spätjüdisch-häretischer und frühchristlicher Radikalismus* (Tübingen: Mohr, 1957), Vol. II, pp. 73–80.

104. *Oikia* and *agroi* specify the real estate, as does *ktēmata* in Mark 10:22; Matt. 19:22; the variant reading *chrēmata* generalizes. So does Luke 18:23 and the tradition behind Mark 4:19. On Jesus without *oikia,* see Luke 9:58; Matt. 8:20; Gospel of Thomas, logion 86.

105. Luke 2:41-51 is a good illustration of how homelessness and breaking with family ties belong together. Notable exception: marriage. See I Cor. 9:5 in the context of Luke 12:51-53; Matt. 10:34-37; Thomas, logion 16.55.101.

of these terms as referring to illiterate and uncultured men has contributed more than any other single factor, except perhaps the interpretation of the patristic apologists, to the understanding that the Galilean fishermen were economically poor, culturally inferior, and socially of the lowest status.

A purely philological argumentation will be indecisive. In the context of the Corpus Hellenisticum, *agrammatos* indeed does mean "illiterate" as we know since at least Wettstein.[106] To argue on the grounds of the Hellenization of Palestine and the influence of Greek culture over Galilee's native population that Palestine's uncultured people could have been bilingual, and, after all, "have had some Greek culture," [107] is only to provoke warnings like that by V. Tcherikover against overemphasizing the Hellenistic cultural element,[108] or to provoke skepticism, best expressed in discussions of the authorship of The First Letter of Peter.[109]

We can free ourselves from the present stalemate in the discussion by integrating the technical philological and the general argument about the Hellenization of Palestinian Judaism with the historical-critical study of the social and economic aspects of Galilean society of the Greco-Roman period. This has not been done. Moulton's often-quoted contention "that Peter's Greek may well have been better than his Aramaic," and that the noticeable Galilean accent at the occasion of his Jerusalem denial of Jesus (Matt. 26:73) "does not necessarily imply defective cul-

106. Origen, *Contra Celsum* I, 62, agreed with Celsus that the fishermen lacked learning, i.e., "a primary education." But Origen comes to this conclusion by contrasting the word of God with "the power of speaking [according to] the standards of Greek dialectic or rhetoric arts" (Chadwick, tr., *Contra Celsum,* p. 57). On the same premise operate G. Schrenk, in *TWNT,* G. Kittel (ed.), Vol. I (1933), p. 762:60; Bauer's *Wörterbuch;* Arndt and Gingrich's translation, and most modern Bible translations (Knox, Phillips, Goodspeed, *et al.*).

107. G. Dalman, *Sacred Sites and Ways,* translated by P. P. Levertoff (The Macmillan Company, 1935), p. 165.

108. *Hellenistic Civilization,* pp. 114–116.

109. E. G. Selwyn (ed.), *The First Epistle of St. Peter,* 2d ed. (London: Macmillan & Co., Ltd., 1947), p. 7, n. 1; F. W. Beare (ed.), *The First Epistle of Peter,* 2d ed. rev. (Oxford: Basil Blackwell & Mott, Ltd., 1958), p. 28.

ture," [110] lacks the supporting evidence compatible with the *agrammatos* of Acts 4:13.

The task is to provide the evidence that can sustain the claim that the social milieu and economic class, and with both the cultural potential, of Galilean fishermen is identical with that of Paul, the tentmaker or leather tanner.[111] It has been argued on linguistic grounds that the style of First Peter, long recognized as resembling that of Paul's, is not that of the colloquial spoken koine Greek, but that of the Hellenistic synagogue.[112] One does not therefore have to resort to the fiction of a classical education in the Hellenistic sense for the Galilean fisherman any more than for Paul and his Jerusalem education.[113] The social class of Galilean villagers or small landowners—the middle class that furnished most of Israel's priests, Levites, and scribes—is compatible with the literary style of the koine Greek of the Hellenisitc synagogue not only of the Dispersion but also of the homeland. The question is, Is it also compatible with the *agrammatos* of Acts 4:13?

The answer is yes, provided one has fully dissociated oneself from the still prevailing tradition of the Greco-Roman understanding of the learning of *grammata* as synonymous with "learning to read and write." G. Schrenk, though advocating "illiterate" (*analphabētos*) as the meaning of *agrammatos* in Acts 4:13, is fully aware that in Jewish tradition "the learning of *grammata* is especially related to knowledge of the law (cf. Test. Ruben 4:1)." [114] When Sirach 38:24 ff. flatly announces that people too busy with making money or a living and lacking leisure

110. J. H. Moulton and W. F. Howard, *A Grammar of New Testament Greek* (Edinburgh: T. & T. Clark, 1929), Vol. II, p. 26.

111. E. Haenchen, *Die Apostelgeschichte,* Kritisch-exegetischer Kommentar, edited by H. A. W. Meyer, 11th ed. (Göttingen: Vandenhoeck, 1957), p. 476.

112. A. Wifstrand, "Stylistic Problems in the Epistles of James and Peter," *Studia Theologica,* Vol. I (1947), I–II, pp. 170–182.

113. W. C. Van Unnik, *Tarsus or Jerusalem,* translated by G. Ogg (London: The Epworth Press, Publishers, 1962).

114. Art. "*gramma,*" in *TWNT,* Vol. I (1933), p. 762. On Jewish vs. Hellenic education, see S. Zeitlin, *The Rise and Fall of the Judaean State* (The Jewish Publication Society of America, 1962), pp. 420–426; Van Unnik, *Tarsus or Jerusalem,* pp. 59–72, on *anatrophē* and *paideia.*

cannot become wise and learned, it is not claimed that such people cannot attain a decent education. What the passage does say, contrary to Rabbinic practice, is that religious knowledge and preoccupation with technical skills or economics are incompatible. Delitzsch, who devotes a whole chapter to "the connection between letters and handicraft" in his small study on *Jewish Artisan Life in the Time of Christ* can show that some of the very artisans that Sirach excludes from wisdom and learning were distinguished scribes. It is in this connection also that Delitzsch refers to two scholars, Rabbi Ada and Rabbi Jose, who were professional fishermen.

For the Galilean fishermen to be called *agrammatoi,* without denying them full education, respectable social status, and some degree of cultural potential, is altogether reasonable if we interpret *agrammatos* and its close parallels as *anomos, adikos,* and the like,[115] in the context of Israel's *am ha-arez* tradition. It has long been observed that "the *am ha-ares* was not necessarily of the lowest social class; priests, even the High Priest, might be without rabbinical education" [116] or an antagonist to the Pharisaic movement. Even though a man might have had a proper rabbinic education, i.e., had become a *nomikos,* or a *talmid chakam,* or even a *grammateus,* he could still be called *agrammatos* if, as Moore points out, he did not keep up with his studies, or even worse, like Paul, embraced a rival interpretation which created a conflict similar to that between the mutually exclusive standards of learning of the Teacher of Righteousness at Qumran and Jerusalem orthodoxy. Another way of getting oneself denounced as *agrammatos* was to choose an occupation (e.g., tax collector) which by some standard or another (Pharisaic, Sadducean, Zealotic, or Essene) was held incompatible with religious, not cultural, values. In the eyes of the irate Tem-

115. In John 7:49 Pharisees characterize the very crowd assembled for the Feast of Tabernacles in Jerusalem as ignorant of the law. I Cor. 15:34 refers to fellow Christians as "having no knowledge of God." Cf. also *amathēs* in II Peter 3:16, or *amathēteutos* in Patristic Greek.

116. G. F. Moore, "The Am Ha-ares," in *The Beginnings of Christianity,* 5 vols., edited by F. J. Foakes-Jackson and K. Lake (London: Macmillan & Co., Ltd., 1920–1933), Vol. I, pp. 441 f.

ple crowd (Acts 21:28) Paul and his associates were *agrammatoi* even though they followed the letter of the Law about purification.

Rabbinic tradition knows of some among its illustrious teachers who, up to a certain age (in the case of Johanan ben Zakkai, for instance, till age 22; in Akiba's case till age 40), had been *agrammatoi*. B. Gerhardsson [117] takes this to prove that uneducated men succeeded later on in life in becoming highly articulate scholars, proficient in one or more literary style. I take the same sources to mean that the men in question did not begin their rabbinic training until later in life, and that therefore *agrammatos* does not necessarily imply lack of primary education, low social, economic, cultural background, or the like. This, of course, does not deny the fact that some scribes did rise from the humblest of social circumstances. Even to a modern Jew,[118] *agrammatos* as "lack of learning" carries a connotation different from that which a non-Jew would associate with it.

When Jesus contrasts a Pharisee and a tax collector, with the latter as a perfect example of what a Pharisee would call an "illiterate and common man," he does not contrast two social or economic classes of people. Socially, economically, and culturally the tax collector was most likely in every way superior to the Pharisee who by Hellenic standards may have been illiterate or barbarian. Finkelstein's contrast between "the urbanity of the Pharisees" and the boorishness, crudity, and ill-breeding of the *am ha-arez* is utterly misleading if, as often is done, this is taken as also a social, economic classification.[119] One gets a more adequate picture of the Galilean *am ha-arez,* to which the fishermen belong, from Finkelstein's chart of "the sociological strata of Jewish Palestine during the last decade of the Second Commonwealth." [120] The chart makes clear that the fishermen belonged to what Finkelstein calls "Middle

117. *Tradition and Transmission in Early Christianity* (Coniectanea Neotestamentica, No. XX; Lund: Gleerup, 1964), pp. 25 f., n. 50.

118. See, e.g., J. Neusner, *History and Torah* (Schocken Books, Inc., 1965).

119. Finkelstein, *The Pharisees,* pp. 82 ff.

120. *Ibid.,* pp. 4 f.

Classes"—"usually zealot, sometimes sectarian"—who are anything but cultural barbarians or illiterate hillbillies.

Before we draw the final facet of this portion of the study, a few words must be added about seasonal and dual employment of fishermen, and about the employment of hired hands in coping with the volume and various aspects of the fishing industry and trade.

Besides the division of labor that a professional scribe, for instance, would have to allow if he were also a full-time fisherman, we have a tradition in post-Biblical Judaism that knows of dual and seasonal employment for fishermen. The Testament of Zebulun 6:8 says that Zebulun "caught fish in the summer," while "in the winter [he] kept sheep with [his] brethren." From this reference it would appear that fishing was carried on largely during the dry season from June to September, the climax of the agricultural year, and that, instead of idling during the rainy seasons, the same men would turn to shepherding from October through May. But Masterman observed that fishing in the Tarichaea-Bethsaida area reached such a pitch in the period from mid-January to mid-April that fishermen built temporary tents or reed huts on the shore close to the mills [121] for maximum efficiency.

The seasonal employment of fishermen is likely to apply mostly, if not exclusively, to the hired laborers.[122] In his book *On the Characteristics of Animals* (XIV, 29), Aelian speaks of certain fishermen earning double wages (*misthos*) by serving alternately as sailors (*nautai*) and farmers (*geōrgoi*). Esau, of course, was both "a skillful hunter" and "a man of the field" (Gen. 25:27).[123] In Ptolemaic Egypt "royal farmers" worked seasonally as fishers also, or as shepherds and the like, even as priests.[124] It is pure fancy, but nevertheless intriguing, to speculate that the

121. *Studies in Galilee,* p. 38.

122. See *ergatai,* Matt. 20:2; *misthōtoi,* Mark 1:20; other terms are *misthios, ekdidonai;* cf. also *doulos, oiketēs.* Not used in Biblical tradition are *thēs, ōnētos,* and others.

123. On the allegorical significance attributed to Esau's dual occupation, see Philo, *Questions and Answers on Genesis,* Book IV, 165, translated by R. Marcus (Loeb Classical Library, Supplement to Vol. I; London: William Heinemann, Ltd., 1953).

124. Kortenbeutel, in *Real-Encyclopädie,* Supplement to Vol. VII, cols. 206 f.

shepherds of Bethlehem, "hirelings" as John 10:12 calls them, later witnessed as hired servants on Galilean fishing boats how "the Good Shepherd" revealed himself as "Fisher of Men."

The term "fishermen" is used also for referring to these hired servants. It is therefore quite important to keep at all times clearly separated in one's mind one type of fisherman who is owner of boats, nets, marketing equipment and the like, who also signs the fishing contract with the "tax collector," who pays the taxes and wages, and, like the owner of a farm or vineyard in Jesus' parables, may occasionally go on business or pleasure tours. This type is to be distinguished from the hired servant and sailor. Of this second type it has been said that they enjoyed little social prestige or economic wealth.[125] That this second group has not been distinguished from the first is another factor that has been, and still is, contributing to the distorted view of the Galilean fishermen whom Jesus called to discipleship. The New Testament evidence that prevents us from identifying Peter, Andrew, and the Zebedee-sons with the second type of fishermen is found in Luke's reference to the partnership existing between them,[126] and Mark's reference to Zebedee's hired servant-fishermen.

Conclusion of Part One

In the light of territorial studies of the area around the Sea of Galilee and of the last decades of the Second Commonwealth, the study of fishing in these territories has brought to light, first, that fishing was a vital industry to the tetrarchy of Herod Antipas, king of Galilee, and to the tetrarchy of Gaulanitis ruled by Philip. It appeared that Philip founded the city and toparchy of Bethsaida at least in part as a fishing establishment to rival the already established Galilean fishing center in Tarichaea, which was both a city and the center of a toparchy that included Capernaum, the home of the gospel fishers, accord-

125. Stöckle, in *Real-Encyclopädie*, Supplement to Vol. IV, col. 458:45 ff.

126. See *metochos* in Luke 5:7; on *koinōnoi* in Luke 5:10, see F. Hauck, art. "*koinos*," in *TWNT*, G. Kittel (ed.), Vol. III (1938), p. 804, n. 49.

ing to the Synoptics. The rich revenues derived from the fish resources of the Sea of Galilee, especially in its northern part, could not only sustain a profitable industry for commercial and industrial entrepreneurs, but also provide tax revenues for the tetrarchs' ambitious cultural and political programs.

Secondly, it can be argued now that the information of the four Gospels about the hometown of the gospel fishermen (Capernaum, according to the Marcan tradition; Bethsaida, in the Johannine tradition) need not be taken as evidence of mutually exclusive traditions. For in the wake of the policy of the tetrarchs, the successors of Herod the Great, Hellenistic cities were founded, and toparchies organized, for which the governments invited or recruited people, both resident Jews and immigrant non-Jews to provide the manpower for the envisioned commercial and industrial development. The people who responded to the call of this new frontier were given every economic advantage and financial assistance by the tetrarchs who were cooking their own goose. People often maintained their homes in the nearby villages or hamlets that they had left for the new cities and the prosperity they promised. Peter could well have kept his parental home in his native Galilean village of Capernaum while later on moving only a few miles east to Bethsaida to establish himself as prosperous fisherman with the aid and encouragement of Philip's government.

Thirdly, we came to realize that fishing in Galilee was a "big business" whose capital investment and security was provided by either the government of Herod and Philip or private men of means who in turn subleased fishing rights to promising, capable fishermen for maximum return on their investments. The supply in fish was exploited to the limit of the maximum demand made by (1) the population masses, especially in the cities which depended on fish next to bread as staple food; (2) the profitable business in delicatessen fish for the upper classes of society at home and abroad; and (3) the governments' need for ever greater revenues to maintain the political and cultural programs.

Fourthly, we were led to distinguish between two social and economic classes of fishermen, besides the government's own hand and the tax collector's interest, in the capital investment and profit from fishing. One class was made up of the men who actually went out to do the sailing and fishing, who cared for the nets and boats, who sifted, counted, and processed the fish, and who, like the laborers in Matt. 20:1 ff., in off seasons might wait in the marketplaces to be hired for farming, shepherding, or other menial tasks. The other class was made up of those who hired and paid wages to those of the first class, who saw to it that the quota was paid to the tax collector or the government as the case might be, who besides furnishing the equipment for the actual fishing might also maintain some or all aspects of the varied kinds of fish to be processed for sale and shipment, and who would do their own bargaining and trading in fish or even fishing equipment. It was in this second class that fishermen operated in legal partnership with others and acted in solidarity as members of trade-union-like professional associations. It is to this class that we must look when reading, for instance, of scribes as professional fishermen.

Fifthly, it was learned that Galilean fishermen were devoted to the Temple and its festivals, and loyal to Torah and covenant, sometimes as Zealots, occasionally as sectarians. The latter lends credence to the report in John 1:35 ff. that the gospel fishermen had once been associated with the Baptist movement whose center of activity lay outside of Galilee. As such sectarian followers, like the earlier Qumran Teacher of Righteousness, these devout men were denounced by the ruling Pharisaic orthodoxy in Jerusalem as "uneducated and common men," which, we concluded, does not reflect on their education or social, economic status.

It will be our task in Part Two of this study to determine the various meanings attributed both to the call to discipleship that Jesus issued to such fishermen now properly understood in their social, economic, and religious Galilean milieu, and to the task of "fishing men" to which Jesus commissioned and committed them.

Part Two

FISHERS OF MEN

CHAPTER III

Fishers of Men in Non-Christian Traditions

PLATO'S *The Sophist,* briefly reviewed earlier in Chapter I, gave us a first example from pre-Christian times of the metaphoric use of fishing activities in the description of teacher-student relationships. It is the contention of this and the following chapter that the advocates of Jesus' originality in using the fishing metaphor are laboring at best with a half-truth. For the originality or creativity of Jesus in this case, as with other metaphors, similes, and parables that he used, is to be seen in the specific manner and context in which he used and interpreted them rather than in the claim that he newly coined a phrase out of the depth of his poetic genius.

Our intention is not to prove that the fishing metaphor was known and used in non-Christian traditions, or how widely, but to trace the creative transformations of the metaphoric uses of fishing as they reflect man's relationship to others and to events and values in life. In covering Greco-Roman and Near Eastern syncretistic traditions, then Israel's Biblical and post-Biblical Rabbinic and sectarian traditions, it is the intention of this condensed review to avoid the trap of "parallelomania." [1] Instead, an attempt is made to expose the hermeneutical process at work in different cultures and religions, all employing the same set of symbols—the fishing or hunting metaphors depicting man's varied experiences of retributive supreme

1. S. Sandmel, *Journal of Biblical Literature,* Vol. 81 (1962), pp. 1–13.

justice, of ultimately transforming renewal, and of irresistible commitments to saying or doing something that transcends everything else.

As representative member of the "history of religions" school, R. Eisler, in his *Orpheus the Fisher* of 1921, drew attention to a wider range of evidence for the background of the Christian use of the fishing metaphor than earlier classical philological studies in the tradition of Wettstein [2] had presented, not to speak of the narrow focus on Old Testament sources since early patristic times. Eisler freed the critical study of the meaning of the fishing metaphor from the barren alternative of tracing the background to either classical Hebrew or classical Greek traditions. Like other members of the "history of religions" school, Eisler saw even earliest Christianity as a syncretistic phenomenon arising yet different from the syncretistic milieu of sectarian Jewish apocalypticism, esoteric Rabbinic "gnosticism," the Baptist movement, and the since discovered Qumran sources. Eisler's legacy, though rarely explicitly acknowledged, continues to be felt in the recently renewed discussion of the meaning of the fishing metaphor.[3] This legacy, however, operates mostly in the negative sense of a continued preoccupation with what Sandmel called parallelomania.

What is long overdue in the old and now renewed discussion about the meaning of the fishing metaphor is a concerted effort of spelling out the changing norms or criteria by which it came to be interpreted. C. W. F. Smith, for instance, observed that Jesus' use of the fishing meta-

2. Jacobus Wettstein, *Novum Testamentum Graecum*, 2 vols. (Amsterdam, 1751–1752; reprint Graz: Akademische Druck- und Verlagsanstalt, 1962), ad Matt. 4:19.

3. J. Manék, "Fishers of Men," *Novum Testamentum*, Vol. II (1958), pp. 138–141; C. W. F. Smith, "Fishers of Men," *Harvard Theological Review*, Vol. LII (1959), pp. 187–203; O. Betz, "Donnersöhne, Menschenfischer und der Davidische Messias," *Revue de Qumran*, Vol. III (1961), pp. 41–70; W. Wuellner, "Early Christian Traditions About the Fishers of Men," *The Hartford Quarterly*, Vol. V (1965), pp. 50–62. On fish, fishing, and fisher as archetypal symbols in modern research in the phenomenology of the self, see the five essays in *The Collected Works of C. G. Jung*, Vol. 9, Part II, edited by Herbert Read, *et al.*, translated by R. F. C. Hull (Bollingen Series XX; Pantheon Books, Inc., 1959), pp. 72–94 and 103–172.

phor did not depart from the original Old Testament sense ("organs of the pending final judgment"), while the subsequent gospel traditions and Evangelists gave the metaphor a more positive soteriological meaning. Betz in his critique rightly insists that the decisive transformation in the meaning of the metaphor originated with Jesus and not later. But Betz in turn fails to recognize what, one-sidedly to be sure, Smith rightly insists on, namely, that the hermeneutical process of reinterpretation continues for better or worse. Recent studies of the parables of Jesus [4] and of the Evangelists' use of the gospel traditions [5] in general have shown how crucial this continuing theological process and critical interpretation was.

The non-Christian uses of the fishing metaphor, especially in the Jewish traditions, are also charged with theological content, with the questions of authority and power of divine origin, and supercharged when controversy smolders or flares up over the critical choice between true and false men-fishing at the sight of rival fishers of men. As also in the orthodoxy-heresy problem even in nascent apostolic Christianity,[6] the fierce competition over who or what constitutes true fishing and fishers of men was not an accidental historical problem, but evidence of the sometimes ignored fact that the hermeneutical, critical examination of the truth claims implicit or explicit in religious and some cultural activities was recognized as a crucial concern. The history of the interpretation of the fishing metaphor can be understood as part of the general history of man's search for criteria that test and assure the health of a culture presumed to be subject to the same force that is claimed to have authorized the fishing of men. Whether that power is divine or demonic, whether it is derived from ultimate reality or mere penultimate idols, is the crucial test to be made, hopefully by ourselves freely and radically.

4. Jeremias, *The Parables of Jesus,* pp. 23–114.

5. G. Bornkamm, G. Barth, and H. J. Held, *Tradition and Interpretation in Matthew* (The Westminster Press, 1963); H. Conzelmann, *The Theology of St. Luke* (London: Faber & Faber, Ltd., 1960): C. H. Dodd, *The Historical Tradition in the Fourth Gospel.*

6. H. Koester, "*Gnōmai Diaphoroi,*" *Harvard Theological Review,* Vol. 58 (1965), pp. 279–318.

For if not, inevitably history itself will bring the conviction.

Greco-Roman Fishing Metaphors

Men-Fishing as Cultic Act. In the cultic context of Dionysian religious traditions the fishing metaphor is applied to Dionysus himself and to his devotees. In the sacrificial death of Dionysus as *"der gefischte Gott,"* [7] which means that the hunter- or fisher-God himself gets caught or bagged, participants in the Dionysian rite are caught, and thus experience "the joyful release of vitality." [8] The ecstatic nature of Dionysian cultic men-fishing is evidenced by scenes depicting bacchic fishermen surrounded by satyrs,[9] or later on by cupids.[10] The divine fisherman uses wine as *pharmakon* to catch the fish and thereby bring them to the experience of salvation.[11] One of the best examples of this men-fishing is the mosaic pavement of the bacchic mystery hall at Tramithia on the isle of Melos.[12] Dionysus is depicted fishing from a ship in the midst of a circular *piscina,* using a bottle full of wine as bait at the end of a rope. The initiates in the ritual may have been dressed in fish masks, Eisler speculates; he also sees traces of "the wine-bibbing fish of the Dionysian mysteries" in Oppian's *Halieutica* (I, 649), and in Lucian's *The Fish-*

7. Eisler, *Bayrische Hefte für Volkskunde* (1915), pp. 116 ff. Cf. also the gnostic term "saved savior" and Goodenough's phrase "God born and torn for us" applied to Dionysus as Eros-Horus, in *Jewish Symbols,* Vol. VIII (1958), p. 10.

8. E. R. Dodds (ed.), *Euripides: Bacchae* (Oxford: Clarendon Press, 1944), p. xliii. See Goodenough's critique of Dodds's interpretation in *Jewish Symbols,* Vol. VI (1956), pp. 17 ff. On the "Semitic Elements in the Cult of Dionysos," see M. C. Astour, *Hellenosemitica* (Leiden: Brill, 1965), pp. 176–194, 203 f.

9. Eisler, "Orphisch-dionysische Mysteriengedanken in der Christlichen Antike," *Vorträge der Bibliothek Warburg,* II. Vorträge, II. Teil, pp. 102 f.

10. See Goodenough, *Jewish Symbols,* Vol. VIII, pp. 6 f.

11. Eisler, *Vorträge der Bibliothek Warburg,* II. Vorträge, pp. 119 f., 176 f. On *pharmakon* as means of fishing, see above, Ch. I, n. 58. Oppian, *Cynegetica,* IV, in Mair, *Oppian,* pp. 320–353, knows of leopards being caught with wine.

12. Eisler, *Orpheus,* Plate LXVI. Goodenough, *Jewish Symbols,* Vol. VI, pp. 55 f., Fig. 235.

erman.[13] The channels through which these Dionysian symbols entered into Jewish and Christian art are not always clear, but intimations of the symbols are certainly there in the juxtaposition of angling fisher and vine branch,[14] or in the use of the mystic winnowing sieve beside the sacred net.[15]

It is debatable whether, like the netted or hooked fish, the butterfly, symbol of Psyche, represents "fascinated victims of the great fisher and hunter of all living beings," [16] or whether it is an eschatological symbol of assured eternal life beyond death. As Goodenough pointed out in a critique of Dodds's interpretation of Euripides' *Bacchae,* this would be an altogether alien alternative for most Greek religious traditions as it would be for certain strata of the Priestly and Wisdom traditions of Israel in a contrast not to be drawn too sharply with prophetic and apocalyptic traditions. Orphism and its eschatology attempted to reform and rescue Dionysian traditions from their Bacchanalian distortions, but with dubious success. The metaphoric use of fishing in Orphism carried the same meaning of eschatological salvation in the sense of participation in the eternal life of God as Dionysian-Orphic symbols of fishing had in synagogal art by employing the symbolic figures of Dionysus-Orpheus and Eros.[17]

Men-Fishing as Social, Cultural Activity. The patron gods of hunting, Apollo and Artemis,[18] teach the literal art of hunting and fishing to the centaur Chiron, who in turn teaches the art to many of the early heroes. The hunting and fishing arts seem to acquire a metaphoric sense when Chiron's teaching is said to have contained

13. *Orpheus,* pp. 278 f.
14. *Ibid.,* p. 186, n. 4.
15. *Ibid.,* p. 293.
16. *Ibid.,* p. 29.
17. See below, pp. 123 ff.
18. On Diktynna or Britomartis, the Minoan counterpart to Artemis, see A. Evans, *The Palace of Minos* (London: Macmillan & Co., Ltd.), Vol. I (1921), pp. 511, 548; IV:2 (1935), pp. 577 f., Figs. 560, 561. On fishing with a net, see Vol. III (1930), pp. 40 f., Fig. 26. On an Assyrian deity hunting with bow and arrow, see H. Gressmann, *Altorientalische Texte und Bilder zum Alten Testament* (Tübingen: Mohr, 1909), Vol. II, Fig. 103.

also instruction in healing,[19] with which Asclepius is associated as one among over forty healing deities, heroes, and heroines of Greek mythology.[20] Eisler devotes a whole chapter to "the Fisher-god as Culture-Hero and Teacher of Humanity." [21] The same tradition appears earlier in Near Eastern mythology associated with the fishing practices of Ea priests as exorcist healers and wisdom teachers,[22] and also in Jewish legendary tradition about angels (or "the watchers," or "the holy ones") chasing the daughters of men in Gen., ch. 6,[23] and possibly also in the centaur symbol in the ceiling of the Dura synagogue.[24]

Not to be confused with the Dionysian religious tradition is the men-fishing associated with the frenzies revealing that a person has been hooked by Eros-Adonis and his female companion Aphrodite-Ishtar-Venus. A Pompeian fresco [25] shows Eros and a female figure (which could be either a ceremonially dressed bride or Aphrodite) both in the act of angling for fish. But only the social, cultural context within which the symbol is used could reveal whether the symbolized passion or consuming obsession is that of sexual eros, or that of some nobler or even baser form of eros. According to Oppian (*Halieutica* IV, 1 f.), fishermen often make their most successful catch at the time fish are consumed by "fatal mating," when the "assault" of passion makes them an easy prey. The important thing to keep in mind when interpreting the mythological figures engaged in men-hunting or men-fishing is that man's state of being caught does not so much represent the frenzied abandon experienced in love, passion, or noble aspiration of one kind or another, but rather the change and transformation that takes place as a result.

A teacher's or Sophist's hunting or fishing of students differs, so Plato criticized, from "the lover's hunt" in that

19. Jaeger, *Paideia,* Vol. I, pp. 25 f. Cf. Astour, *Hellenosemitica,* pp. 299 ff., on Chiron and Asclepius.

20. W. A. Jayne, *The Healing Gods of Ancient Civilizations* (University Books, The Exposition Press, Inc., 1962), p. 240.

21. *Orpheus,* pp. 42–50.

22. See below, pp. 78 f.

23. See below, pp, 119 f.

24. See below, p. 125.

25. Eisler, *Orpheus,* Plate LXIII.

the teacher expects or demands gifts or payments for his fishing. Artemidorus[26] (*Onirocriticon* II, 14) gives an account of a Sophist's dream about catching many and large fish, i.e., wealthy students, by his teaching. The idea of fishers of men being or becoming falsely motivated in their fishing by letting themselves be baited by bribes of food, money, or other pleasures is quite prevalent in antiquity. The prophetic criticism leveled against Israel's fishers of men as having become baited themselves by bribes (Jer. 5:26-28a; Ezek. 13:18 f.) or the ubiquitous warnings in the New Testament against the snares of riches (I Tim. 6:5 ff.; I Peter 5:2 f.) are but versions of the continuous note of criticism in Greek tradition from Plato's *The Sophist* (222 A) to Lucian's satirical critical essay on *The Fisherman.*

But the central idea is that of the teacher or educator as a fisher of men. That he appears as "paid hunter" is as legitimate as Paul's apology for the *exousia* which apostolic fishers of men have for food and drink (I Cor., ch. 9). Incidentally, Plato (*Sophist,* 231 D) employs the image of merchant, athlete, and purger, besides that of fisher or hunter, for characterizing the Sophist's activity. We had occasion earlier to observe the close relationship not only between fish-catching and fish trade, but also between the sorting of fish and refining metals.

A. D. Nock explored the uses of the fishing or hunting metaphors in connection with learning and teaching practices in the schools and academies of Greco-Roman antiquity.[27] Nock distinguishes between two main periods in a student's life when he is reputed to be most receptive to the pedagogical fishing: the time before and the time after his adolescence. This may reflect the same distinction Van Unnik pointed out about *anatrophē* as always prior to *paideia.*[28] The meaning of the pedagogical men-fishing is twofold. First, the student, "caught" by the teacher, or

26. R. A. Pack (ed.), in *Bibliotheca Scriptorum Graecorum et Romanorum Teubneriana* (Leipzig: Teubner, 1963), Vol. I, pp. 128 f.

27. "Conversion and Adolescence," *Pisculi. Studien zur Religion und Kultur des Altertums,* F. J. Dölger, *Festschrift. Antike und Christentum,* Supplement to Vol. I (Munich, 1939), pp. 165–177.

28. *Tarsus or Jerusalem,* pp. 59–72.

rather the ideas the teacher holds out as bait, is thus rescued from the snares and lures of a life of pleasure, and, secondly, thereby rescued for full civic responsibility and cultural values, the ultimate objective of the *paideia* ideal. "Being caught" comes thus close to "being brought, or made, fully alive," which appears as the meaning of *zōgrein,* as set forth in Appendix I. Inspired by the classical Greek *paideia* ideal, "man-fishing" and "disciple-making" (*mathēteuein*) become interchangeable. The same is true for the Rabbinic tradition, regardless of whether one considers the metaphoric use of fishing as Hellenistic influence or as part of traditional Near Eastern educational ideas.[29]

The fisher of men as educator may be a philosopher or wise man (*sophos* or *sophistēs*). He may have additional bait to offer besides his wisdom, if he can accompany his teaching with "signs" as experimental proof of the power or skill to be conveyed, as specially characteristic of the *theios anēr.*[30] He may, like Israel's classical prophets, write and recite as poet rather than, or along aside of, his teaching and possibly other duties.[31] This is best illustrated by Cercidas of the second half of the third century B.C. In his *Meliam* (IV, 9 f.) he characterizes his mission as poet in terms of a "fisher" (*halieutas*) and "keenest tracker" (*ichneutas aristos*) of all the Pierian maids, that is, the Muses of the community of Pieria in Macedonia.[32] Society critic and essayist Lucian can speak of himself metaphorically as fisher of men in his attempt to bring the teachers of his days—the target of his satire—to justice and, by chance, back to full life (*anabioun*) as the subtitle of his work on *The Fisherman* says so suggestively.[33]

29. L. Dürr, "Das Erziehungswesen im Alten Testament und im Antiken Orient," *Mitteilungen der Vorderasiatischen Gesellschaft,* Vol. 36 (1932), pp. 1 ff.; W. McKane, *Prophets and Wise Men* (Studies in Biblical Theology, No. 44; London: SCM Press, Ltd., 1965), Part I.

30. L. Bieler, *Theios Anēr* (Vienna, 1935), pp. 122–129.

31. On an ancient poet's combined roles as wise man, priest, and educator, see G. Rohde, "Die Aufgabe des Dichters in der Antike," *Studien und Interpretationen* (Berlin: de Gruyter, 1963), pp. 273–289.

32. A. D. Knox (ed. and tr.), *Herodes, Cercidas and the Greek Choliambic Poets* (Loeb Classical Library; London: William Heinemann, Ltd., 1953), pp. 206 f.

33. A. M. Harmon (ed.), *Lucian* (Loeb Classical Library; London: William Heinemann, Ltd., 1921), Vol. III, pp. 1–81.

Diogenes Laërtius reports that Solon, the great Athenian statesman and reformer, once used either an already familiar, or since his use, familiar proverb which freely translated says: "Fishermen endure being sprayed by the Sea when catching fish; why shouldn't I when catching (*halieuein*) a man?" [34] Solon reportedly said this when someone whom he tried to win over by what Plato called the persuasive hunting of rhetorical skill spat on him. Again, the important point is that the man-fishing here, though employing the skilled means of rhetorics, is identical with coming under the captivating spell of some idea, in this case here the very practical, political, civic reform program.

Men-Fishing as Retribution and Vindication. In the mythological tradition this aspect of men-fishing is preserved in the reports about the hunting activities of Nemesis, the mythical hunter or punisher of people guilty of speaking careless words (Plato, *Laws,* 717 D), or of the Erinyes which justly avenge the spirits of the slain. Once again the *halieutica* tradition provides a later contact with earlier mythological tradition when Aelian, *On the Characteristics of Animals* (I, 24; cf. XV, 16), compares the devouring "brood of vipers" with the avenging Erinyes. Related but independent of the Erinyes tradition is the menfishing that Hades, "the Unseen," the god of retributive justice, "the punisher of wrongdoers" (as Plato called him in *Laws,* 870 D–E; 881 A–B), carries on with his net (*diktuon Hadou*). The term "gates of Hades," known from the New Testament in only its negative connotation, is actually synonymous with "net of Hades." [35] Whether Hades was ever represented pictorially with a net as the symbol of his critical power, analogous to the scales of Dikē-Justitia, is so far undocumented for Greece, as it is for the Near Eastern parallel to Hades which is Shamash, the celestial judge. To get caught in the net of Hades, as in that of

34. On the tradition of this proverb, see J. Freudenthal, in *Rheinisches Museum,* Vol. 35 (1880), p. 413, n. 12.

35. See J. Jeremias, art. *"pulē,"* in *TWNT,* G. Friedrich (ed.), Vol. VI (1959), pp. 923 ff. Cf. I QH 3:17 f.; 6:24, 31. On the relation between Hades and Sheol-Gehenna, see T. F. Gleason, *Greek Influence in Jewish Eschatology* (Biblical Monographs, No. 1; London: S.P.C.K., 1961).

Shamash, Nergal, or other related Near Eastern deities, is to be brought to justice by trial, whose outcome, as often in Yahweh's trials with Israel, is either vindication or condemnation of the accused.

A trial also provides the framework for Lucian's essay on *The Fisherman,* whose task it is, like that of Israel's prophets, to bring the cultural, religious leaders of the people to justice, that is, to fish them with the result that the caught are brought to their senses, i.e., back to their original tasks and thus back to full life, or they are brought to ruin. Lucian's Fisherman is technically a *rhetōr* (par. 23), who is surnamed Frankness (*parrēsiadēs*). Charged with having falsely accused the philosophers and educators, i.e., the fishers of men, of his days as not doing what they are commissioned to do, Frankness appears in court, presided over by Lady Philosophy. The jury consists of Virtue (*aretē*), Temperance (*sōphrosunē*), Justice (*dikaiosunē*), Culture (*paideia*), and Truth (*alētheia*), with the latter insisting that Liberty (*eleutheria*) and Free-Speech (*parrēsia*) be added to the jury. The accused Fisherman is granted the request to use as his legal aids Investigation (*elenchos*), who consents to serve provided he can bring along his assistant, Proof (*apodeixis*).

With their help, Fisherman-Frankness vindicates himself before the court and the accusing fishers of men by empirical proof, with a hook and line taken from a nearby temple, where they had been placed as votive offering of an Athenian fisherman, and with bait appropriate for the catch, figs [36] and gold.[37] Not only is he vindicated; he is also commissioned by the court to resume his role of fisherman, now no longer on his own authority but by order (*parēngelmena*) of the supreme court, and with the continuous assistance of Investigation. Lucian's fisher of men is "not of man, but of God," as the New Testament would put it. And like the Counselor of the Fourth Gospel (John

36. In par. 46 a triple bait is mentioned: gold (*chrusion*), fame (*doxa*), pleasure (*hēdonē*). On figs as sexual symbol, see Eisler, *Orpheus,* p. 108, n. 5. Cf. the triple bait with the three nets of Belial in post-Biblical Judaism.

37. Lucian, *The Fisherman,* par. 47.

16:7 f.), Lucian's Fisherman makes men come under the conviction of truth itself, which leads them either to regeneration and new life or to judgment. What distinguishes this Hellenistic interpretation of divinely commissioned men-fishing from that in the Old and New Testaments are the respective interpretations of divine justice in terms of covenant steadfastness of Yahweh, or the love of God in Christ Jesus.

Men-Fishing as Prophesying. The Greek prophetess Cassandra in Aeschylus' play *Agamemnon* (lines 1115 f.) pronounces a "net of Hades" to fall over Clytemnestra, Agamemnon's wife, who was plotting the murder of her husband at his return from Troy. The prophetess speaks the fatal word, as the Babylonian prophet or priest was compelled to speak the word or command (*amatu*) of Nergal, which brought a widespread plague as "a snare prepared on the shore of the sea, out of the meshes of which the fish cannot escape and a net in which man is taken." [38] More important than the retributive justice implied in Cassandra's fishing with the net of Hades is the idea that the prophet brings to language, and thus to decision-making, what otherwise would loom as brute fate in history and over life itself. But equally important is it to realize that it is not Cassandra or, for that matter, any other prophet speaking "the word" who does the actual fishing of men. Neither the prophet nor the poetically or otherwise technically competent word of the prophet has the power to catch men. Only that which or he who is mediated by the prophet's life and word can do so. In the contest between rival prophets, however, the hermeneutical issue breaks wide open in the critical challenge and test of every authority and value exerting such claim.

Other Metaphoric Uses. There are a number of uses of the fishing metaphor less relevant to our discussion than those mentioned above. Nevertheless, they all show, in varying ways, how man motivates his demands over other men, or how events captivate people. When Artemis, for instance, is said to be the Zeus-appointed "lion against

38. M. Jastrow, *Die Religion Babyloniens und Assyriens,* 3 vols. (Giessen: Ricker, 1905–1912), Vol. I, pp. 475 f.

women" to hunt and kill of them whomever she will (Homer, *Iliad,* XXI, 483 f.), the man-hunt here refers, of course, to the until recently quite frequently fatal childbed fever that befell women after childbirth.[39] Another example is Lucian who in his *Timon*[40] has people use the dragnet of bribing someone for favors, but failing because the big fish, though swallowing a quantity of bait, escapes by showing favors to others. Greek, as well as Jewish and Christian, and ancient Near Eastern literary and iconographic traditions show themselves familiar with the metaphor of catching man in a net as the expression of complete enslavement, loss of identity, and therefore ultimate doom and ruin.[41] That folly (*anoia*) can get a man entangled in "the inextricable net of calamity" (Aeschylus, *Prometheus Bound,* line 1078), or that superstition (*deisidaimonia*) can catch one as in a great dragnet, as Plutarch says of the Jews who let themselves be conquered rather than break the Sabbath (cf. I Macc. 2:32 f.), are but the negative side of something that the Greek tradition can spell out in positive terms. For in the *paideia* tradition it is taught that man, in search of true identity and the full realization of himself, should at all times pursue or hunt after or let himself be caught by the ultimate values of "the good and the beautiful" attested to by classical Greek civilization.

Fishing Metaphors in Ancient Near Eastern and Syncretistic Traditions

Mythological Fishing Among the Gods. The tradition of the use of nets in ancient Near Eastern mythology is closely related to that of warfare between the gods.[42] On

39. On other childbirth deities, see Jayne, *Healing Gods,* pp. 53, 85 f., 415, 442, 456.

40. Harmon (ed.), *Lucian,* Vol. II, pp. 350 f.

41. See Appendix I on *sagēneuein.* On the metaphoric use of *sylagōgein,* see Col. 2:8. On "fishing" in the sense of enslaving (*katadouloun, lambanein, halosis*), see Epictetus, *Discourses,* IV, 30 f., and W. Grundmann, art. "*tapeinos,*" in *TWNT,* Vol. VIII (1965), pp. 11 f., on *aichmalōsia* as synonym of *tapeinōsis.*

42. Cf. E. D. van Buren, "How Representations of the Battles of the Gods Developed," *Orientalia,* Vol. XXIV (Rome, 1955), pp. 24–41.

the stela of Eannatum, the king of Lagash in mid-third-millennium Sumer, the king is shown with the royal rod smiting men caught in a net while with his other hand he is holding the symbols of the god Ningirsu over the net called "the great dragnet of En-Lil." [43] In the Greek *halieutica* tradition the taking of prisoners is still compared to fishing with nets (Aelian, *On the Characteristics of Animals,* XII). Akkadian mythology pictures Marduk, Ea's avenger, using a net, "the gift of his father Anu," [44] in catching Tiamat and her consorts of gods and demons. The note of avenging in this story brings this netting activity into close parallel with the execution of retributive justice also symbolized by Marduk. People rejoice in Marduk because "sinner and transgressor will be confounded before him." [45]

Marduk uses other tools besides the net, such as bow and arrow, mace or club, and four winds, with seven more added to match Tiamat's eleven demon monsters. The relationship between Marduk's net and the holy spells will be explored later in the section on the cultic context of men-fishing. In later Babylonian tradition Marduk became associated with the zodiacal *sagittarius* or centaur, familiar also in Greek mythology. Other gods besides Marduk can be associated with the zodiacal centaur, such as Nergal, the god of war whose function is related to Adar, the god of hunting and the god of judgment.[46] With the sun as their common symbol, we recognize here again the close relationship between hunting, warfare, and retributive justice.

Vindication of Justice as Fishing. This aspect of the fishing or hunting metaphor is very pronounced throughout the ancient Near East. The agents to wield the unfailing, inescapable net of justice and retribution are first of all

43. S. N. Kramer, *History Begins at Sumer* (Anchor Books, Doubleday & Company, Inc., 1959), Fig. 6, and pp. 243 f.; Eisler, *Orpheus,* Plate VIII; G. A. Barton, *The Royal Inscriptions of Sumer and Akkad* (Yale University Press, 1929), p. 65.

44. E. A. Speiser, "Akkadian Myths and Epics," in Pritchard (ed.), *Ancient Near Eastern Texts* (rev. ed., 1955), p. 66.

45. *Ibid.,* p. 72, Epilogue.

46. W. Muss-Arnolt, "The Names of the Assyro-Babylonian Months and Their Regents," *Journal of Biblical Literature,* Vol. 11 (1892), pp. 72–94 and 133–176.

certain gods. Supreme among them is Shamash, a deity common to all Near Eastern religions, and under various names and symbols venerated also in other religious traditions.[47] Besides the sun as symbol, Babylonian and Egyptian traditions often employ the symbol of a charging eagle or lion.[48] All these symbols left traces on Israel's conception of Yahweh as hunter of men.[49] Among the many functions of Shamash, "the shepherd of men," [50] is that of the celestial judge who casts his net over evildoers to "bring them to light." [51] An Akkadian proverb explicitly states that Shamash hunts men for the sake of retribution.[52] Ginzberg cites a tradition preserved in post-Biblical Judaism which mentions the sun as witness against Adam's trespass.[53] The angel Ariel, the lion of God,[54] may be a late Jewish adaptation of the Near Eastern principle of inescapable retribution embodied in Shamash. Transgressors against the ordinances of an anonymous Egyptian goddess are warned that they will be pursued by her "with the smiting of a savage lion." [55] The net of Shamash is for the Semites what the net of Hades is for the Greeks. C. H. Gordon believes that the two traditions may both have been derived from a common Mesopotamian stock.[56] The god

47. F. J. Boll, *Die Sonne im Glauben und in der Weltanschauung der alten Völker* (Stuttgart: Franch., 1922) ; H. R. Engler, *Die Sonne als Symbol. Der Schlüssel zu den Mysterien* (Zurich: Helianthus, 1962) .

48. Aelian, *Animals,* XII:7; Goodenough, *Jewish Symbols,* Vol. VII, pp. 29–86; Vol. VIII, p. 254; Index, "lion." On the fusion of eagle and lion, see *Jewish Symbols,* Vol. VIII, pp. 126 f.

49. See J. Hempel, "Jahwegleichnisse der Israelitischen Propheten," in *Apoxysmata,* J. Hempel, *Festschrift,* edited by G. Fohrer (Beihefte zur Zeitschr. f. d. Alttest. Wissenschaft, No. 81; Berlin: Töpelmann, 1961), pp. 1–29, esp. pp. 14 f. See below, pp. 88–92 and 109 f.

50. Eisler, *Vorträge der Bibliothek Warburg,* II, p. 57, n. 4.

51. Speiser, "Akkadian Myths and Epics," in Pritchard (ed.), *Ancient Near Eastern Texts,* p. 115 (A-2, lines 20 f.) ; p. 116 (C-2, lines 38 f.) .

52. R. H. Pfeiffer, "Akkadian Proverbs and Counsels," in Pritchard (ed.), *Ancient Near Eastern Texts,* p. 427. See Aramaic parallel on p. 430, and Hittite parallel on p. 398:13 f.

53. *Legends of the Jews,* Vol. I, p. 79; Vol. V, p. 38, n. 105; p. 102, n. 89.

54. G. G. Scholem, *Jewish Gnosticism, Merkabah Mysticism, and Talmudic Tradition* (Jewish Theological Seminary of America, 1960), pp. 72 and 95.

55. J. A. Wilson, "Egyptian Hymns and Prayers," in Pritchard (ed.), *Ancient Near Eastern Texts,* p. 381.

56. *The Common Background of Greek and Hebrew Civilizations* (W. W. Norton & Company, Inc., 1965), p. 86.

Mithras, who among other symbols is represented as the sun, and was advocated as the champion of truth and justice, was referred to in some parts of the Roman Empire as he who "hunts against the powers of evil." [57]

The gods may commission human agents to mete out justice. The bas-relief on the Code of Hammurabi shows Shamash commissioning the writing of the law code. The king, as earthly representative of Shamash, shepherds the people by commission of Marduk.[58] It is my contention that "hunting" and "shepherding" here are nearly indistinguishable in meaning, similar to the synonymous use of the two metaphors in John 21:3 ff., 15-16. According to C. H. Gordon, Hammurabi was for Mesopotamia what Moses and Minos were for Eastern Mediterranean culture.[59]

Men-Fishing in Cultic Context. Various kinds and forms of ritual were designed to reenact periodically the benefit that the hunting of one god by another had for mankind. Benevolent or malevolent gods wield their nets for good or ill. At the "House of the Net," an Egyptian temple at Kemennu dedicated to Hermes Thot, a scene was annually reenacted showing how Thot with his sacred net left his temple on a barge to go fishing in the Nile for the limbs of Osiris.[60] The result of his catch brought saving power to those seeking relief from disease, for Thot was one of eighteen healing deities in Egypt, similar to Nebo, his Sumerian-Babylonian counterpart.[61] The beneficial effect of Thot's fishing is transmitted through charms, spells, and other catching devices employed in healing exorcisms. The netting agent is ultimately the divine power itself which men call upon directly or with the help and mediation of priests.

The priestly mediation of the divine fishing power is particularly clear in the water exorcisms of the Ea cult at

57. M. J. Vermaseren, *Mithras, the Secret God* (Barnes & Noble, Inc., 1963), pp. 94, 185.

58. T. J. Meek, "The Code of Hammurabi," in Pritchard (ed.), *Ancient Near Eastern Texts,* Prologue (i), pp. 30 f., 50; Epilogue (xxxv), pp. 80 f.; (xxv), p. 90; Epilogue (reverse, xxiv), pp. 10 f.

59. *Common Background,* p. 279.

60. Eisler, *Orpheus,* p. 45, n. 2; p. 21, n. 3.

61. Jayne, *Healing Gods,* p. 125.

Eridu in the delta region of the Euphrates.[62] Ea priests are represented with fish masks, symbol of the *ichthuōn bios,*[63] and with line and hook [64] or with the mythical net *usurtu,*[65] fishing the faithful, that is, healing them with water exorcism rites. Ea is known as the most important of a dozen or more healing deities in Babylonia and Assyria.[66] Amulets showing figures cloaked in fishskins were popularly worn for protection against calamities incurred from getting caught in evil nets, and for assurance of remaining caught in the sacred net, of which the net named Nert, which belongs to the goddess Neith as shown on the Shuttle amulet,[67] may be a good example. A gem with an engraved fish-masqueraded figure, dating from the patristic period,[68] may have served the same purpose. The underlying notion is that physical or mental illness can cover a person like a net,[69] and that certain gods, such as Marduk with his powerful net and spells, can free a person from the evil net, or bag the ferocious animal pursuing the sick.[70] Whatever, if any, connections might exist between the Mesopotamian cultic men-fishers and the functionaries in Mandaean baptismal and exorcistic rites, we do well to heed the warning against hastily connecting the two.[71]

The same warning also pertains to the alleged connec-

62. On Near Eastern water rites in general, see J. Thomas, *Le Mouvement Baptiste en Palestine et Syrie* (Gembloux: Duculot, 1935), pp. 289–309.

63. Eisler, *Vorträge der Bibliothek Warburg,* II, pp. 112–123.

64. Pritchard, *Ancient Near East in Pictures,* p. 215, Fig. 658, and p. 328.

65. E. A. W. Budge, *The Book of the Dead,* 6th ed. (London: Routledge & Kegan Paul, Ltd., 1953), pp. 121 f. On priests of the Babylonian moon sanctuary in Harran entering the temple wrapped in nets, see Eisler, *Orpheus,* p. 74.

66. Jayne, *Healing Gods,* p. 118.

67. E. A. W. Budge, *Amulets and Superstitions* (London: Oxford University Press, 1930), pp. 149 f.

68. H. Leclercq, *"Pêcheur," Dictionnaire d'Archéologie Chrétienne et de Liturgie,* Vol. XIII:2 (1938), cols. 2877–2882, Fig. 10026.

69. R. H. Pfeiffer, "Akkadian Observations of Life and the World Order," in Pritchard (ed.), *Ancient Near Eastern Texts,* p. 435. Cf. G. Widengren, *The Accadian and Hebrew Psalms of Lamentation as Religious Documents* (Uppsala: Almquist, 1936), pp. 123, 238 f.

70. Pfeiffer, "Akkadian Observations," *loc. cit.,* p. 437; Jayne, *Healing Gods,* pp. 123–125; C. J. Gadd, *Ideas of Divine Rule in the Ancient East* (London: Oxford University Press, 1948), p. 11, n. 5.

71. K. Rudolph, *Die Mandäer* (Göttingen: Vandenhoeck, 1960), Vol. I, pp. 215 f.

tions between Mesopotamia and Egypt. While the techniques of priestly ritual may be the same in both cultures, for instance, the use of charms and incantations of spells, either by the believer in direct contact with the saving deity or more likely, with the help of priests, the scope of the fishing of men may be quite different. Drawing on the power of Marduk, the evils that plague people can be eliminated, which meant largely freedom from bodily or mental illness. Eisler saw in the designation of Marduk or of other gods as hunters or fishers a reflection of the priestly functions of the *retiarius* or net hunter who, in ritual sacrifices, serves as "the hunter, guardian, and finally the killer of the sacred beast." [72]

By contrast, the men-fishing in Egypt, which has its share of fishing men from the nets of illnesses, is primarily preoccupied with fishing in the sense of getting man to participate in the full divine life after death. This aspect of men-fishing as the expression of eschatological salvation is more fully explored in the following section. But here in connection with fishing as cultic concern we must show how even in the Egyptian interpretation of men-fishing the cultic, ritual context prevails. *The Book of Gates* shows [73] how in Egyptian mythology, and in the corresponding priestly reenactment of the mythical action in ritual, the casting of nets and the reciting of incantations are used by a group of gods, and by the priests as their earthly ministers, to immobilize the serpent Āapep and the crocodile Sessi, which block Afu Ra's way through the ninth of the twelve regions of Tuat, that is, of "the other world." The fishing of the divine crocodile, identified as "the great and mighty fish," and often linked with the Leviathan motif in Jewish mythology, has crucial importance for man's escape from the evil net and for attaining salvation. *The Book of the Dead* prescribes the incantations of the magical names of the fishing gear (besides the net are mentioned rope, cordage, pole, slaughtering

72. *Orpheus the Fisher,* pp. 27 f. In quite a different sense does Paul in Rom. 15:16 understand his office as "priestly service."

73. E. A. W. Budge, *The Papyri of Ani* (G. P. Putnam's Sons, 1913), Vol. I, pp. 158 f.

knife, weights, and other articles) which, if rightly used, assure man the eschatological rescue from all evil.[74]

Another example of the use of fishing metaphors in the context of magical ritual is the amulet of Batra Giwargis,[75] preserved in Ethiopian Christian tradition, which depicts the *Marbeta Salomon,* the Net of Solomon. The amulet provides us with one more tangible evidence of the continuation of the magical aspect of men-fishing in both Jewish and Christian circles. Solomon's wisdom is understood here to have given him, and all who use the Net of Solomon as a charm, the "authority over all the fiends of hell." As in other religious traditions, so here in Judaism and Christianity, the catch intended may be either the immediate freedom from illness and the benefit of health or the ultimate freedom from death and assurance of immortality.

Of a different kind of men-fishing in a cultic context are the ritually induced and structured raptures or ascension to heaven and paradise familiar to Greek [76] and Rabbinical as well as to Hellenistic-Jewish Christian traditions, such as Paul's experience in II Cor. 12:2-4.[77] Such raptures or seizures must have been subject to different interpretations as to their meaning. In Christian, especially Gnostic, circles, they may well have been taken as anticipations of the eschatological catch that brought full participation in the eternal life. In some religious traditions that have incorporated Near Eastern wisdom traditions, it is the good or bad word or deed that catches men for good or ill at the time of the eschatological catch. With their emphasis on powerful net-spirits luring and rapturing men, syncretistic gnostic traditions carry on within and alongside of Judaism and Christianity what was intimated or known in Near Eastern traditions long ago. It is negligible for our immediate purpose here how these net-spirits were identified, whether as zodiacal cosmic powers and their corre-

74. Budge, *The Book of the Dead,* CLIII, A and B.

75. Budge, *Amulets and Superstitions,* p. 192, and figure on p. 190. Cf. E. Lohse, art. "*Solomōn,*" in *TWNT,* Vol. VII, (1964), pp. 462 f.

76. In the Phaëthon myth, and the travels in the chariot of the sun-god Helios. See Astour, *Hellenosemitica,* pp. 268–271 for Semitic background.

77. Scholem, *Jewish Gnosticism,* pp. 14–19.

sponding virtues and vices,[78] or in the mythologized form of such forces as desire, ignorance, and the like,[79] or as deceitful lust, power to contrive evil, and the like.[80]

Men-Fishing as Eschatological Salvation. The net-spirits can be controlled through ritual, magical rites or some form of religious, ethical life specified differently in each religious cultural tradition. There appear to be two ways in which this control is realized to keep man from evil fishers, and to assure him the netting by the good fishers, for the benefit of his life now and in the world to come. One way is through incantations, the cultic form of men-fishing outlined above. The other way is through association with a specified superhuman divine fisher of men, who gives aid and assurance in the quest for ultimate salvation. To avoid the net-spirits, Greek tradition advocates traveling by "the road of Zeus" (*Dios Hodos*),[81] while Near Eastern traditions recommend the use of a ship, which in Jewish esoteric tradition is replaced by "the chariot of Elijah."

Traveling on foot and unaided, as all unrighteous must do,[82] is fraught with dangers of getting trapped by the malevolently fishing forces. Satan or Belial, and "the angels of destruction" that serve them, represent in Jewish and Christian tradition what Ur, the giant son of Ruha, is in Mandaean theology. The net or nets used by Belial correspond, however vaguely, to Ur's net (*silita*) by which unbelievers are brought to ruin. The serpent Āapep and the crocodile Sessi, and the brood of vipers that serve them, are the Egyptian counterpart to Jewish and Mandaean traditions.

The Egyptian *Book of the Dead,* which Eisler[83] called

78. Eisler, *Vorträge der Bibliothek Warburg,* II, pp. 86 f.

79. R. M. Grant (ed.), *Gnosticism* (Harper & Brothers, 1961), p. 67, on the Gospel of Mary.

80. *Ibid.,* p. 217, on the Hermetic Tractate (I, 25) of Poimandres. For a modern psychological interpretation of "Gnostic Symbols of the Self," see C. G. Jung's essay under that title in his *Collected Works* (cited above, n. 3), pp. 184–221.

81. Eisler, *Vorträge der Bibliothek Warburg,* II, pp. 124 f.

82. E. S. Drower (ed.), *Diwan Abatur* (*Studi e Testi,* 151; Città del Vaticano, 1950), p. 10.

83. *Orpheus the Fisher,* p. 291.

"an other-worldly guide-book of similar purpose to the Orphic Hades-literature," was designed specifically for people striving to escape the net of "the fowler, whose fingers are hidden." [84] Scenes of fishing, fowling, or hunting on sarcophagi or fresco walls of tombs from ancient Egypt [85] to Roman imperial times [86] may have been copied in early Christian sepulchral art.[87] The use of the music of pipes (*auloi*) besides nets and hounds in the Etruscan tradition of boar and stag hunt, as Aelian reports in his study *On the Characteristics of Animals* (XII, 46), may be the clue for the interpretation of flute players on the walls of Etruscan tombs. If the fishing or hunting quality of flute-playing is applicable here, we would then have here a seemingly unlikely parallel to the fisherman symbol in Christian catacomb art. More important, however, than formal similarity is the interpretation of the meaning of the symbol. How taxing the hermeneutical problem can be, especially if literary sources are lacking, is evident in the debate over the proper interpretation of the jar from Grotta Ferrata. Goodenough sees in the scene of the diving man, some fishes, and the angler only "a pagan cinerary urn," whereas Eisler sees in it symbols of either Christ or Peter as "fishers of men." [88]

A clear case of men-fishing as eschatological salvation appears in the Hermetic tradition,[89] in Samaritan, Mandaean, and Manichaean eschatologies. In the fifth chapter of the *Kephalaia* of Mani,[90] the founder of Manichaeism, a third-century rival of Christianity, man is depicted as subject to two sets of four fishers, each with his own ship, net, even a sea, peculiar to each. Commission to fish men

84. Budge, *The Book of the Dead,* CLIII, A:6 f.

85. On the juxtaposition of fishes and their shepherd, see H. Goedicke, "Eine Variante des 'Hirtenliedes,'" *Wiener Zeitschr. f. d. Kunde d. Morgenlandes,* Vol. 54 (1957), pp. 46–50. Cf. Eisler, *Orpheus,* p. 285.

86. Eisler, *Vorträge der Bibliothek Warburg,* II, pp. 123 f., 173 f.

87. W. Lowrie, *Art in the Early Church,* rev. ed. (Harper Torchbooks, Harper & Row, Publishers, Inc., 1965), pp. 55–57, *passim.*

88. Goodenough, *Jewish Symbols,* Vol. I, p. 100.

89. Grant (ed.), *Gnosticism,* pp. 209–233, esp. pp. 217 f. employing the shepherd and guide motif, rather than that of fisher or hunter.

90. Carl Schmidt (ed.), *Manichäische Handschriften der Staatlichen Museen Berlin* (Stuttgart: Kohlhammer, 1935), Vol. I.

is given by the rival powers of light and darkness. As with earlier and contemporary Rabbinic tradition, working with models of four,[91] three fishers of men are said to have worked in the past, while the last is yet to come. According to Manichaean tradition, the first three fishers of men had been: (1) the Primordial Man, prototype or *archē* of all subsequent fishers of men; [92] (2) the so-called "third emissary"; and (3) Jesus, who used "his wisdom" (*sophia*) [93] as the net, his *ekklēsia* as his ship, to catch men. The fourth fisher to come, "the Great Thought" himself who commissioned the first three, fishes with "his living Spirit" which will "rescue and free from all bonds and fetters" at the time of the dissolution of the cosmos when the last fisherman gathers up himself.[94]

The four evil fishers of men are correspondingly: (1) "the king of the realm of darkness," using as net "his fire and his desire"; (2) "the evil mind"; (3) "desire" (*epithumia*); and finally, (4) "the spirit of darkness," which keeps men caught and enslaved by false teaching (*planē*). Polotsky [95] called attention to the seemingly contradictory aspect of this men-fishing as involving both a passive and an active element simultaneously. Fishing men is to "call" them; to be caught or let oneself be caught is to "hear the call." We have a basically similar setup in Mandaean and Samaritan eschatology.[96]

According to G. Widengren,[97] we have to distinguish between two different fishers of men in Mandaean thought, each fisher receiving his commission from another authority. There is *Ptāhil,* or "Gabriel the Apostle," who receives

91. See below, pp. 109 f.

92. Schmidt, *Manichäische Handschriften,* p. 43, lines 34 f.

93. Cf. U. Wilckens, art. *"sophia,"* in *TWNT,* Vol. VII (1964), pp. 510–514.

94. Schmidt, *Manichäische Handschriften, Kephalaia,* Ch. LXXI, on the method of gathering.

95. C. Schmidt and H. J. Polotsky, *Ein Mani-Fund in Ägypten* (Sonderausgabe aus den Sitzungsberichten d. Preuss. Akademie d. Wiss., Phil.-hist. Klasse 1933, No. 1; Berlin: de Gruyter, 1933), p. 79.

96. J. MacDonald, *The Theology of the Samaritans* (The Westminster Press, 1964), p. 369, *passim.*

97. *The Ascension of the Apostle and the Heavenly Book,* Vol. III, *King and Saviour* (Uppsala Univ. Arsskrift, 1950:7), esp. pp. 59–76, on Mandaean literature.

his commission from the "father of the Uthras" to descend to *tibil,* the earth, to proclaim Jesus, "the word made flesh," as universal salvation. There is also the figure of *Dēnānuxt,* a fictitious human being favored by God, who in the company of one of the Uthras, called *Din-Mlikh,* ascends to the highest heavens to receive there his commission, by *Din-Mlikh* and not the supreme God, "to proceed into the world, [to] call the call of life, and [to] teach disciples." [98] He descends to earth to carry out his mission, after which he ascends again at last to receive his eschatological rewards.

Men-Fishing as Messenger or Interpreter. The mythological tradition provides the following examples for this category which, to my knowledge, has neither been identified yet as a distinctive idiom nor been applied to the discussion about the meaning of fishers of men. In the Mesopotamian tradition we have the obscure reference to "the fisherman of the gods" in the *Inscription on the Statue of King Kurigalzu.*[99] Whether in *Inanna's Descent to the Nether World* [100] the messenger Ninshubur,[101] who accompanies Inanna (Ishtar in Akkadian), is also such a "fisherman of the gods" can only be conjectured. In the Greek tradition we have Hermes, the messenger of the gods who is represented as fisher either alone or in the company of Poseidon and Herakles.[102]

The Ugaritic tradition provides us with further clues. The fisherman who accompanies Lady Ashera is called by the double name *Qadesh wa-Amrur* (Holy and Blessed),[103] who appears once as emissary of Baal,[104] another time as

98. *Ibid.,* p. 66.

99. Kramer, "Sumerian Myths and Epic Tales," in Pritchard (ed.), *Ancient Near Eastern Texts,* fragment A (viii).

100. *Ibid.,* pp. 52–57, esp. lines 28 f., 169 f., 298 f.

101. On other messenger gods in ancient Mesopotamia, such as Bunene, Isimu, Ishum, Mummu, Namtar, Nishbur, Nusku, Papsukkal, see D. O. Edzard, "Botengötter," *Wörterbuch der Mythologie,* edited by H. W. Haussig (Stuttgart: Klett, n. d.), I Abteilung, p. 46.

102. Eisler, *Orpheus,* p. 45, n. 2; also Figs. XXVI and LXII.

103. H. L. Ginzberg, "Ugaritic Myths, Epics, and Legends," in Pritchard (ed.), *Ancient Near Eastern Texts,* p. 132 (tablet II AB, ii, 30–37). On double names in the Near East, see Gordon, *Common Background,* pp. 237 f.; on p. 194 he interprets *Qadesh wa-Amrur* as two persons.

104. Ginzberg, "Ugaritic Myths," *loc cit.,* p. 138 (tablet V F).

Asherah's spokesman, displaying what Plato in his *Sophist,* in analogy to fishing, called the rhetorical "art of persuasive hunting." [105] Lucian's rhetorical skills are symbolized in the role of the Fisherman who is also accompanied by a partner. That interpreters or messengers were sent out in pairs is also documented in Jewish and Christian traditions.[106] The role of the counselor or wise man in the courts of gods or earthly kings [107] may in some form be related to this kind of men-fishing.

Men-Fishing as Wisdom-Teaching. The mythological tradition attributes to Ea, among other functions, that of guarding and dispensing wisdom. Ea is the Lord of all wisdom and master over "the house of wisdom." Similarly Orpheus, the divine fisher and shepherd, is known as teacher of wisdom.[108] The same applies to Oannēs, "the fish or fish-god as lord and teacher of all wisdom." [109] The seven primordial wise men (*Abgal* or *Apkallu*) of the Sumerian creation myth were represented clad in fish masks, as was Oannēs, who in some yet indeterminable way seems related to them. Eisler's fanciful philological argument brings even John the Baptist in connection with Oannēs-Hani, but only in the later syncretistic form of the Baptist movement. The content of this wisdom could range from the esoteric cosmological speculations to the concrete political and personal counsels given by the professional wise men or magicians. The form which this teaching of wisdom took could range from priestly cultic or ritual patterns to magical craftsmanship. Palestinian Judaism, even

105. *Ibid.,* tablet II AB (iv).

106. Talmud *Yebamoth,* 62b, attributes to Rabbi Akiba twelve thousand pairs of disciples. For a general survey, see J. Jeremias, "Paarweise Sendung im Neuen Testament," in *New Testament Essays: Studies in Memory of Thomas Walter Manson,* edited by A. J. B. Higgins (Manchester: Manchester University Press, 1959), pp. 136–143.

107. P. A. H. Boer, "The Counselor," *Wisdom in Israel and in the Ancient Near East,* H. H. Rowley, *Festschrift,* edited by M. Noth and D. W. Thomas, *Vetus Testamentum,* Supplement to Vol. III (Leiden: Brill, 1955), pp. 42–71; O. Betz, *Der Paraklet* (Arbeiten zur Geschichte d. Spätjudentums und Urchristentums, II; Leiden: Brill, 1963), esp. pp. 36 ff.; McKane, *Prophets and Wise Men.*

108. Eisler, *Vorträge der Bibliothek Warburg,* II, p. 141.

109. Eisler, *Orpheus,* p. 45. On Glaucos as one of several Greek counterparts to the Sumerian Oannēs, see Astour, *Hellenosemitica,* pp. 255 f.

before its alleged Hellenization, also contained these elements, not only in scribal, rabbinical circles, but also among priests long after the Deuteronomic reform.

The distinction we seem to be advocating here between men-fishing as wisdom-teaching and men-fishing as magic or cultic practices to assure health or eternal salvation is admittedly artificial, if not indeed misleading. For the variety of forms and contents of wisdom teachings, designed to catch men for the benefit of a better life, existed side by side, sometimes by chance in one and the same person thus engaged in the fishing of men. This interrelation between cultic and magical teaching, and between school- and temple-centered education is characteristic, in varying degrees to be sure, of ancient Near Eastern traditions. This is true also of Judaism, Biblical and post-Biblical, and even for New Testament Christianity, where the magical aspects, though marginal, are nevertheless preserved.

But to stop with this observation, as psychologists, sociologists, phenomenologists, and historians of religions have all too often done, is to fall short of the most crucial aspect of all, namely, the critical discernment of the different norms operative in each religious tradition. Wisdom and witchcraft, word and wonder, meditation and miracle, mental intuition and magical incantation, rational speech and ritual spells, are not mutually exclusive; neither are they of equal value or significance. Wherever all or some of these means are employed in religion or culture to fish men by divine decree, the critical examination of the validity and proportion of one form of men-fishing over against another becomes indispensable. It is the merit of Van der Leeuw's phenomenology of religion to have called attention to this perennial task of a hermeneutical theology.[110]

Other Uses of the Fishing Metaphor. Familiar to Near Eastern wisdom traditions is the warning that people in

110. G. Van der Leeuw, *Religion in Essence and Manifestation,* 2 vols. (Harper Torchbooks, Harper & Row, Publishers, Inc., 1963), Vol. 2, Epilegomena. See also the essays of J. Daniélou and M. Eliade in *The History of Religions: Essays in Methodology,* edited by M. Eliade and J. M. Kitagawa (The University of Chicago Press, 1959).

using carelessly spoken words, especially oaths and other legally binding oral commitments, get trapped and caught. Equally familiar is the warning against sexual license and prostitution, though the designation of a prostitute as a "fisher of the night" [111] may be somewhat unusual. Even more unusual seems to be the application of the fishing metaphor to acts of generosity or shrewdness on the part of an Egyptian Chief Steward who in helping certain orphans and widows (presumably among his tenants) turned them into "timid fish" and "fat fowl," which must mean that they became unconditionally subservient to the steward. A tenant farmer who is reported to have applied for help from the steward, no doubt with the help of a professional scribe who may have authored the metaphor, alludes to this catch.[112] The Biblical Job, himself reputed to be a fisher of men, is accused by Eliphaz of having refused help to orphans and widows (Job 22:6 ff.). The steward of Jesus' parable (Luke 16:1-13) may be a close analogy, for he acted prudently or shrewdly also by catching or obligating people, or as Luke puts it, making friends for himself "by means of unrighteous mammon" (Luke 16:9).

The Fishing Metaphor in Biblical Judaism

Yahweh as Men-Hunter. This is a misleading distinction insofar as Yahweh is the principal agent in men-hunting, even if it is carried out by his delegates. For three reasons, it is nevertheless justifiable to speak of Yahweh as men-hunter separately. For one, the use of the fishing or hunting metaphors is so general, or they appear applicable to such universal conditions of men, that one can no longer identify a concrete national or political situation. Secondly, the metaphoric fishing situation, that is, the God-man relation, is of such an intimately personal or private nature that it would be appropriate to speak of mystical, ecstatic experiences or of miraculous, magical events.

111. Eisler, *Orpheus,* Plate LXIII.

112. J. A. Wilson, "Egyptian Didactic Tales," in Pritchard (ed.), *Ancient Near Eastern Texts,* p. 408, papyrus B 1, 60 f.

Thirdly, the men-fishing activity of Yahweh is associated with events in nature rather than in history.[113] The miraculous events accompanying Israel's exodus from Egypt, especially the flood by which Yahweh, the "man of war" (Ex. 15:3), captures the Egyptians, were taken in Rabbinic interpretation as examples of God's second major men-hunt in history after his first at the time of the first flood.

The focus in all of these uses of the fishing metaphor is on Yahweh and the vindiction of his true nature, that is, a kind of theodicy. When used synonymously with military and legal terminologies in their metaphoric sense, Yahweh's men-hunting appears as an expression of the inevitable execution of retributive justice, a conviction familiar to the ancient Near East. But more characteristic of Israel's religion is the idea that Yahweh establishes here the final, i.e., valid, vindication of his covenant loyalty and Torah righteousness. To say of Yahweh that he whets his sword or prepares deadly weapons, making his arrows fiery shafts (e.g., Ps. 7:12 f.), is identical in meaning with saying that he hunts with bow and arrow or that he uses the hunting, fishing, or fowling net (s).

Furthermore, Yahweh, the hunter who takes a person into his net (e.g., Job 10:16; 19:6) and closes his net around the victim, is in the same context compared to a witness who puts the accused or defendant "in the wrong." When Job 10:16 f. speaks, in strict parallelism, of Yahweh hunting Job like a lion and of renewing his witness against Job, the juxtaposition of the hunting and trial metaphors is quite in order, as shown frequently in prophetic literature (e.g., Hos. 7:2 f.; Ezek. 17:19-21), and does therefore not require the suggested emendation hastily proposed by M. Pope.[114] The combination of the two metaphors may be of pre-Israelite origin. What is peculiar to Israel is the use to which this combination is put when it sets forth its saving message of Yahweh's covenant and Torah.

113. See P. Tillich, *Systematic Theology,* 2 vols. (The University of Chicago Press, 1951), Vol. I, pp. 118–120, on "Nature as a Medium of Revelation."

114. *The Anchor Bible,* Vol. XV, edited by W. F. Albright and D. N. Freedman (Doubleday & Company, Inc., 1965), pp. 77 and 79.

Gerleman's brief study of the terminology of the chase in the Old Testament brought to light that even such terms as "being, or getting, hemmed or hedged in" (e.g., Job 1:10; 3:23; 19:8; Hos. 2:6; Lam. 3:7, and others), or references to "fear," are taken from the battue style of hunting employed metaphorically to speak of Yahweh's (or his opponents') way of dealing with man in general, or with Israel in particular. The introduction of messengers or angels of Yahweh (or of his opponents), who take the place of the image of the divine (or demonic) power pursuing men directly, has been explained in two ways. It can be interpreted either in the light of the growing tendency of delegating the fishing functions to authorized agents, or in the light of the growing theological concern to preserve the transcendental character of the divine, as well as of the demonic, powers at the very times they are experienced as fully manifest in nature or history.

Even the earliest of Israel's classical prophets conceived of Yahweh's all-transforming intervention in Israel's affairs more and more in apocalyptic terms, although, as in Isa. 13:14 f., for instance, the hunting metaphor applied to Yahweh's action is expressly related to Assyria's invasion. In light of our later observation about men-fishing in Rabbinical and apocalyptic Judaism, and in order to avoid misinterpretation, it is important to realize that the eschatological fishing of men, attributed to Yahweh himself, is clearly and deeply rooted in the Old Testament itself. That Yahweh himself hunts after men is found, first, in those instances where the critical distinction is announced between the divinely appointed fishing tool (whether as representative of Israel's religious institutions, or as non-Israelite political and cultural dynamics) and the divine fisher or fishing purpose that transcends the immediate historical situation, though manifesting itself in it. The profound theological issue that emerges as a consequence of this distinction is whether God, by revoking his one-time commission to someone as fisher of men, thereby discredits his divine word or faithfulness, or more pointedly, whether there is injustice on God's part (see Rom., chs. 9 to 11).

Growing emphasis on Yahweh's own men-fishing is

found, secondly, in the redaction of the works of the classical prophets by the addition of apocalyptic material. One of the most influential texts for the interpretation of the fishing metaphor in Biblical and post-Biblical Judaism is Isa. 24:17 f., which may be of preexilic origin. A variation on the same theme, though no longer related to the role of Israel as a whole, or that of its institutional leaders on behalf of Israel, is found in Israel's wisdom literature. Proverbs, Ecclesiastes, Job, not to mention many psalms, clearly reflect God's men-fishing action in the execution, not just of Torah righteousness, but of retributive justice in all of man's cultural and social pursuits (e.g., Job 20:23 f.). Another aspect of Yahweh's ultimate fishing activities in Messianic times is the catch of Leviathan, symbol of all power able to transform man.

Textual criticism provides us with still further evidence of the growing distinction between Yahweh-appointed fishers of men and Yahweh's own fishing. In Ezek. 32:3, for instance, the Masoretic text speaks of "the many peoples," i.e., the united armed forces of the Babylonian conqueror, and *their* nets which are cast over Israel, while later Greek and Latin versions alter the text to read that it was God and *his* net that caught Israel. See also Wisd. of Sol. 19:4 where God himself drags (*helkein*) Egypt to its doom. The Masoretic text of Job 19:6, which referred to God's "net," is changed by the Septuagint to God's "stronghold." [115]

The destructive aspect of men-fishing attributed to false gods or idols is but the other side of the same coin described above in terms of Yahweh's own men-fishing activity. Throughout the centuries of cross fertilization with the cultures of Assyria, Babylonia, Egypt, Persia, and then Hellenistic culture of the Roman era, concern over idolatry grew as reflected in the speculation about the three nets of Belial, and the snaring net spirits of the magical traditions in post-Biblical Judaism. But canonical Judaism had set the precedent by seeing in Solomon's harem and the religious elements it injected into Israel's religion, or

115. H. W. Heiland, art. *"ochurōma,"* in *TWNT*, G. Friedrich (ed.), Vol. V (1954), pp. 590–591.

in the intermarriage with residents of the land conquered by Joshua, "a snare and a trap [Septuagint has here plural forms] . . . , a scourge on . . . [Israel's] sides, and thorns in . . . [its] eyes" (Josh. 23:13). Judges 2:3 explicitly identifies cultural cross fertilization between Israelites and resident Canaanites and other Semites as the source of idolatry (cf. Jer. 18:15; Ps. 106:34-39). Hosea's reference to the treacherous bow of idolatry (ch. 7:16; cf. Ps. 78:57) also belongs to this context.

Yahweh's Men-Fishing Commission. We propose to deal with the material applicable to this section under two separate headings in order to do justice to two different categories of men-fishers appointed by one and the same authority, but each with a different purpose and function. To clarify this is important for the assessment of the degree of the substantive reinterpretation of the fishing metaphor in the New Testament. The first category of divinely appointed fishers of men consists of non-Israelite, political, military agents as they appear in the course of the cultural turmoil of ancient Near Eastern history in the last millennium B.C. The main fishing agents appointed by Yahweh are the Assyrians (see Amos 4:2; Hos. 7:2 ff.; Isa. 10:5 f.; 13:15; 37:29 and its parallel in II Kings 19:28; and possibly the prediction in I Kings 14:15), and the Babylonians (Jer. 16:16; Hab. 1:6 ff.; Ezek. 12:13; 19:8 f.). By the Egyptian invasion of Judah, the Arab conquest of Moab, and the Persian campaign against Babylon, men are caught up in the nets of those commissioned by Yahweh to do his work. In Ezekiel's prophecy about Gog-Magog (ch. 38) all attention rests so much on Yahweh's action, and so little is known about the agent Yahweh commissioned to do his work, that we see again the intimate connection between the one who authorizes the fishing and the ones who, like Galilean or Egyptian tenant fishers, go out and do the actual fishing.

The second category of divinely appointed fishers of men consists of the heads of Israel's various cultural and religious institutions. These men, no less than the commissioned non-Israelites, engage in men-fishing as an extension of Yahweh's own dealing with men. The men-fishing functions of king, wise man, or judge, are not the same as those of the priest, prophet, or magician. Moreover, Israel's cultural developments brought about modification and change within each type of religious leadership. When divinely commissioned fishers of men are criticized at times for having neglected their charge, it is important to recognize the specific historical, cultural context. Jeremiah's critique of prophet, priest, and wise man is not the same as the charges that Jerusalem leaders and the Qumran Teacher of Righteousness exchanged. The men-fishing, which is the substance of the distinctive literary genre of the "songs of lament," is not the same in the Biblical psalms as that in the Qumran Hymns. And yet, the crucial hermeneutical task is the same in each case, namely, to check and test the criteria by which divine, i.e., properly executed, men-fishing can be distinguished from demonic or improperly executed men-fishing.

We are therefore dealing here with three separate yet interrelated problems: (1) the nature of revelation, or Yahweh's fishing activity in history; (2) the medium (s) of revelation, or the delegated authority and function of divine fishing in terms of cosmic, natural, or historical, human mediums; and (3) the demonic distortions of revelation. Underlying all three problems is the hermeneutical problem of the criteria or critical principles by which revelation, mediated in and through processes of nature and history, can be tested or verified as to whether or not it was or is authentic, genuine, or true; in other words, whether or not a given revelation is God's eschatological revelation that reveals man's eschatological existence, i.e., his faith existence.

Tillich saw clearly that one had to distinguish not only between a formal and material criterion in facing the hermeneutical issue, but also between the abstract critical principle operative in the critical theological inquiry and the concrete norm as it materialized in history and human experience.[116] Applied to our inquiry, we must distinguish between the abstract principle of God's commission to his

116. *Systematic Theology,* Vol. I, pp. 47–52.

servant, his anointed, his son, his people, his rod, his net, and numerous other symbols, and the concrete norm as realized in history which above all others is the person of Moses, with David, the Patriarchs, and others far behind as alternatives. But the more concrete the norm was experienced to be, the more subject it was and remained to historical, cultural changes.

The commission that Yahweh can give to a non-Israelite power to intervene in the life of another nation and change it radically is often referred to in the Old Testament with more than one metaphor, of which those derived from fishing, hunting, or fowling interest us here most. For ever since early patristic exegesis it has been customary, and after that unchallenged, to see in these prophetic references to men-fishing the primary resource for Jesus, and after him for the early church, to have understood and used the "fisher of men" idiom. But how did Israel's prophets understand the fishing metaphor applied to Yahweh's action in history? Moreover, how different, if at all, was their understanding from that which Israel's rivals had, whether in ancient Greece or Mesopotamia, for they also conceived of the god-man relationships in terms of fishing or hunting metaphors?

To seek fresh answers to these questions is the purpose of this study. We can begin with the traditional observation that the fishing metaphor in the prophetic understanding is interchangeable with accounts of literal warfare. The divinely commissioned fishers of men were in historical, political reality military aggressors and conquerors who imposed the standards of another culture and religion and new norms of identity on the conquered. Philological and archaeological sources led us to see that ever since the middle of the third millennium the fishing or hunting metaphor was used to depict a person's or a group's complete enslavement and the loss or radical transformation of the identity of the one caught. Thus the first and seemingly primary meaning of the fishing metaphor appears to be that of bringing men to the destruction of their old self-identity and with it of their personal and cultural self-understanding.

This is indeed the one and only sense in which Israel's prophets conceive of Yahweh's delegated men-fishing directed at Israel's neighbors (Assyria, Babylonia, Moab, Egypt, and the cryptic Magog), and also, but with the notable restriction, to only certain individuals within Israelite society. It is important that we distinguish such individual victims of Yahweh's men-fishing from that which involves Israel as a whole. This distinction has not been brought to bear on Yahweh's men-fishing activity as understood by the Old Testament prophets. Examples of individuals who get caught in the net of Yahweh's commissioned men-fishers are king Jehoahaz and his successor Eliakim, renamed Jehoiakim, who each engaged in metaphoric men-hunts of their own which were contrary to their Yahweh-appointed duties (II Kings 23:31 ff.; Ezek. 19:3 ff.). Yahweh therefore orders them caught in nets and with hooks to be taken into Babylonian exile where he will "enter into judgment with . . . [them] for the treason . . . committed against . . . [him]" (Ezek. 17:19-21). Again, the fishing or hunting metaphor stands for destruction, and is synonymous with the pronouncement of the verdict of guilt at the end of the trial in Yahweh's court, resulting in the execution of the sentence. Yahweh's men-fishing in this sense means execution of divine judgment. But to say, as many exegetes still do, that this is the substance of the Old Testament understanding of the fishing metaphor, which Jesus then took over, is superficial exegesis at best.

Before focusing on the full scope of men-fishing in the Old Testament, let us look briefly into the two reasons that are given repeatedly for Yahweh's decision to authorize fishers of men to do their critical, destructive work. So stereotyped are the reasons given that one suspects here an established tradition which may be, I conjecture, even of non-Israelite origin. Even a once divinely commissioned fisher of men, as Assyria or Babylonia, or a leader of Israel's covenant people, can become subject to Yahweh's men-fishing activity if he is found to be misusing his authority by committing: (1) social, political evils (e.g., oppressive taxation, as in Ezek. 19:3; or living in luxury as lovers of pleasure, as in Hab. 1:16); and (2) idolatry (e.g., II Kings 23:32, 37; 24:3 f.; Isa. 47:6-15; Ezek. 13:18 ff.). Pharaoh is brought to ruin because he made himself like god,[117] just as the "wicked man" in Job 15:25 f., who defies the Almighty, or like the Qumran Teacher of Righteousness in his charges against the wicked priest. Ezekiel's comparison of Pharaoh with the dragon to be fished and destroyed seems traditional (cf. Ps. 74:13 ff.; 87:4; Ezek. 29:3) and may have been inspired by the legend of the catch of Leviathan.[118] When a fisher of men commissioned by Yahweh fails to catch or abuses his charge, he is not quietly dismissed. He stands to suffer the consequences as everyone else does who violates God's standards.[119] What are these standards or principles which alone give full content and scope to the fishing metaphor?

Another dimension of the divinely commissioned men-fishing emerges from a closer examination of the contexts in which fishing metaphors are used in the Old Testament. With respect to Assyria's commission to fish Israel (Amos 4:2), the prophet reveals that it is the last of many preceding "acts of God" whose purpose it was to bring Israel to return to the Lord (Amos 4:6 ff.). In getting caught, Israel should be prepared "to meet . . . [her] God" (Amos 4:12). In Hosea's prophecy the Assyrian conquest of Israel and the deportation of ten of the twelve tribes is designed to convict Israel of her pride, but also to make Israel "return to the Lord . . . [and] seek him" (Hos. 7:10). The fishing action is thus more like an educational chastisement (ch. 10:10) rather than mere punishment or execution of the victim. This theological perspective is characteristic also of the Deuteronomic school of theology in seventh-century Judah. By man's standards, men-fishing in terms of retributive justice and vengeance always and only means destruction, but not so with God (Hos. 11:9; cf. Isa. 10:6 f.), who, though authorizing As-

117. See Strack-Billerbeck, *Kommentar,* Vol. II, pp. 463, 542; Vol. IV, p. 445. McKane, *Prophets and Wise Men,* p. 77, n. 2, offers a different interpretation.

118. Eisler, *Orpheus,* p. 28.

119. Cf. McKane, *Prophets and Wise Men,* p. 68, *passim,* on the doctrine of "instrumentality."

syria to catch Israel, as he permitted Satan to take Job into his power, nevertheless does not issue the commission with the intent of destroying the fish to be caught (Hos. 11:9; Job 1:12; 2:6; Isa. 10:6 ff.).

Isaiah's commission to prophesy (ch. 6:1 ff.) does indeed include the fatal word of Yahweh's irrevocable judgment (ch. 6:9-12), but it includes, however faintly, or in terms of literary composition secondarily, the assurance of a stump to be left as holy remnant who, because of his understanding that it was Yahweh who fished, leans upon and returns to the Lord (ch. 10:20 f.). The fish that must be dragged out of its element, the Holy Land, and thus seemingly be disinherited, is assured of being gathered again out of exile and to live in its proper milieu (Isa. 11:11 ff.). The fishing that Assyria does on God's behalf for the good of Israel is to turn Israel back on the way by which she came (Isa. 37:29; II Kings 19:28). Jeremiah saw his own commission of announcing Babylon as divine fisher both as critical function, which is "to pluck up . . . break down, . . . destroy . . . overthrow," and as likewise eschatological function, to build and to plant (ch. 1:10).[120] Deutero-Isaiah also knew that the application of the divine net (which, following Isa. 51:22, Rabbinic tradition later equated with the divine cup and bowl) included Israel's radical renewal. Hence, his recourse to creation myth and the exodus tradition.

It is my contention that this second aspect of the divine fishing action in history as new creation, or as Yahweh's self-vindication as merciful and faithful creator and covenant partner, is brought out most clearly in the shepherding metaphor which, as indicated above,[121] is closely related to the fishing or hunting metaphor. As paradoxically as Israel can be shepherded with a rod of iron, so also can she be fished with more than judgmental vengeance. I do not claim that the metaphoric uses of shepherding and fishing are simply synonymous. But I do claim that the

120. R. Bach, "Bauen und Pflanzen," in *Studien zur Theologie der alttestament. Überlieferungen,* edited by R. Rendtorff and K. Koch (Neukirchen, 1961), pp. 7–32.

121. See p. 78.

theological interpretation of the meaning of Yahweh's mighty acts in history draws on both metaphors to reveal the dialectic nature of Yahweh's eschatological power. Ezekiel is still another witness. He reflects the dialectic of God's saving and judging relation to Israel by saying (ch. 12:16) that Yahweh will let some fish escape from the net in which all, without exception, are caught by the Babylonian invasion. The purpose of letting these fish escape is the same as that of the leftover stump in Isaiah's vision. In a parable, elements of which Jesus later echoes in one of his own (Mark 4:31 f.), Ezekiel (ch. 17:22-24) declares that Yahweh's intention in getting Israel caught by a fisher of men is to "bring low the high tree" (i.e., to bring judgment), but to "make high the low tree" (i.e., to bring about "new creation").

This second aspect is no more within the capacity of any of Yahweh's delegated fishers of men than is the first or judgmental aspect. For historical, political catastrophes or natural disasters can no more of and by themselves signify divine action than can the escape from them or from their effects. Whether or not a divinely ordained fishing of men did take place is only God's doing and will be known only if experienced as God's doing rather than as mere historical accident, inscrutable fate, or even demonic curse.

Israel's multiform institutional religious leadership is the other medium, besides non-Israelite mediums, through which Yahweh executes his own fishing of men, with Israel as the symbol of the ultimate scope of Yahweh's dealing with all men. But is there enough evidence to support the thesis that Israel's religious leadership provides examples of divine men-fishers? I believe there is. First of all, we have to consider all fishing, hunting, or fowling metaphors applied positively or negatively to descriptions of the functions of Israel's religious leaders. Secondly, we must pay special attention to the "songs of lament," the literary genre that more than any other is saturated with hunting metaphors which reflect tensions and rivalries between Israelite leaders or official covenant members. Thirdly, and formally related to the "songs of lament," we find the most explicit use of the "fisher of men" metaphor in the Qumran Hymns where it also alludes to religious leaders.

Two recent studies of the literary genre of the "songs of lament" [122] have clarified the literary tradition which, besides that of the prophets, is the other main source for the use of the fishing or hunting metaphors in the Old Testament. What sets the "songs of lament" apart from other literary traditions in which the fishing metaphor is used is that men-fishing alludes to relationships between members of the same religious or cultural community. Thus the hunter is, or is seemingly, as religious as the hunted. Psalm 55:13 f. speaks of his pursuer as formerly his equal, his companion, his familiar friend with whom he "used to hold sweet converse together and to walk in fellowship in God's house."

In following Westermann's distinction between three types of laments,[123] that of the individual, of the mediator, and of the people, we can eliminate the latter, because here the opponent is the political enemy or foreign aggressor with which we dealt earlier. The application of the fishing metaphor to fellow Israelites suggests to Westermann "the process of the gradual disintegration of the people of God." [124] It suggests to me something more positive. I see in the men-fishing contest among Israelites the social expression of the hermeneutical crisis provoked by the claim peculiar to Israel that Yahweh's eschatological revelation was historically mediated. As inquiring historian, one cannot help assuming that both sides in this contest were motivated by what each thought sincerely would serve the best interests and highest ideals that Israel stood for. This would be true of the men-fishing contest between the

122. Widengren, *Accadian and Hebrew Psalms of Lamentation;* C. Westermann, "Struktur und Geschichte der Klage im Alten Testament," in *Forschungen am Alten Testament* (Theologische Bücherei, No. 24; Munich: Kaiser, 1964), pp. 266–305, which is a reprint of an article written in 1954.

123. "Struktur und Geschichte der Klage," *loc. cit.*, pp. 280–290, 269, and p. 290, n. 77, and pp. 273–279, respectively.

124. *Ibid.*, p. 290. Cf. also H. W. Hertzberg, "Die 'Abtrünnigen' und die 'Vielen,'" in *Verbannung und Heimkehr*, W. Rudolph *Festschrift* (1961), pp. 97–108.

Jerusalem hierarchy and the Qumran leadership, as between Jesus and Israel's leaders.[125]

The parties in this men-fishing contest can be identified with a variety of metaphors besides those of fishing, fowling, or hunting. The most frequent are predatory animals, of which lions [126] and eagles [127] are the most preferred metaphors, and the metaphoric use of dogs as part of the battue style of hunting.[128] Other metaphors used are those of offensive or defensive warfare, and certain court proceedings. With this general orientation we can now turn to the examination of specific men-fishers of Israel in terms of five representative types of religious leadership.

The king was one such representative or medium of Yahweh's revelation to Israel and, through them, to the nations.[129] The shepherding and fishing functions of the king as chief executive and supreme commander resemble those of other Near Eastern kings, notably Hammurabi. According to Prov. 20:26 the men-fishing functions of the king in executing justice can be likened to winnowing the wicked and driving the wheel over them. In the appointment of the shepherd boy David to the royal authority of shepherding Israel we have the closest analogy to the New Testament account of Galilean fishermen being called to be fishers of men.

The king, who is charged with what Paul later called the authority from God as God's servant (*diakonos*) or minister (*leitourgos*) to execute God's wrath on the wrongdoer (Rom. 13:1-7), can lose his commission. Meta-

125. Jeremias, *The Parables of Jesus*, pp. 166 ff.; Dodd, *Historical Tradition*, pp. 382–385.

126. The man-hunting lion of the cryptic logion 7 in the Gospel of Thomas could belong to this context. Cf. also the theriomorphic images applied to false prophets in The Revelation to John (ch. 19:20, *et passim*). On I Cor. 15:32, see now R. E. Osborne, "Paul and the Wild Beasts," *Journal of Biblical Literature*, Vol. 85 (1966), pp. 225–230.

127. On Matt. 24:28 par. Luke 17:37, see Jeremias, *The Parables of Jesus*, p. 162, n. 46.

128. That "dog" need not be derogatory in meaning as in Phil. 3:2 is evident in the self-designation of heresy-hunting "Hounds of the Lord" by the medieval Dominicans. Cf. also Isa. 56:10 f., and O. Michel, art. *"kuōn,"* in *TWNT*, Vol. III (1938), pp. 1100–1103.

129. C. Feucht, *Untersuchungen zum Heiligkeitsgesetz* (Theol. Arbeiten, No. 20; Berlin: Evg. Verlagsanstalt, 1964), pp. 89–91 and 230–232.

phorically speaking, he becomes a fox,[130] that is, a "wicked ruler" (Ps. 94:20-23), who acts like a roaring lion (Zeph. 3:3) and devours men (Ezek. 19:6; II Kings 24:4; Test. of Judah 21:7). Israel's kings lost their men-fishing commission as readily as did the kings of Assyria and Babylonia due to failure in executing properly Yahweh's wrath in terms of the specific men-fishing function of administering retributive justice. Two traditions could be cited for explaining the combination of the fishing metaphor with retributive justice. One is that of Near Eastern and Greek wisdom and mythology. The other might be called the tradition of universal experience brought into focus by ritual and later secularized drama. In Israel's Leviathan tradition the notion is preserved that Yahweh ultimately vindicates his righteousness and establishes justice no matter what the obstacles.[131]

When a king fails to execute Yahweh's work in the shepherding and fishing of the people, he brings ruin to himself and to the people. Order is replaced by chaos when even among the covenant members everyone lies in wait for blood, "and each hunts his brother with a net" (Micah 7:2; Isa. 19:2). The newly established eschatological community should be free from all such destructive, vindictive men-hunting (Damascus Doc. 20:11; I Cor. 6:6; cf. Matt. 5:21-26). In Matt. 10:35 f. and its parallel in Luke 12:53, the coming of Jesus newly provokes radical transformation of established human relationships with allusion to Micah 7:2 but now in another sense.

Besides the king and his officials (*archontes*), as Zeph. 3:3 f. calls them, we have a second type of men-fisher in Israel, the judges (*kritai;* less often used is the synonym *dikastai*). It seems that Job was such a judge who took his seat in the square where he "broke the fangs of the unrighteous, and made him drop his prey from his teeth"

130. Cf. Luke 13:32. On the prophet as fox, see Ezek. 13:2 ff.

131. C. Müller, *Gottes Gerechtigkeit und Gottes Volk* (Forschungen zur Rel. und Lit. d. A. und N. T., No. 86; Göttingen: Vandenhoeck, 1964), esp. Ch. 4 on "Rechtsstreit-Gedanke und *Dikaiosunē Theou*"; P. Stuhlmacher, *Gerechtigkeit Gottes bei Paulus* (Forschungen zur Rel. und Lit. d. A. und N. T., No. 87; Göttingen: Vandenhoeck, 1965), pp. 102–184.

(ch. 29:17). He was then confident that his bow would ever be new in his hand (ch. 29:20). Not unlike the king's own shepherding function, the judge's commission was to "winnow the wicked." But more than that, he was also an instructor and teacher of people (Job 4:3 f.). This educational aspect not only brings judges (Hebrew, *sopherim*) and wise men (Hebrew, *hakamim*) together,[132] but also reveals in Israel what possibly earlier appears in classical Greek as the close connection between men-fishing and education,[133] for those who follow the teacher "avoid the snares of death" (Prov. 13:14; 14:27).

When the judge fails to do his God-appointed work, again the evil connotation of men-fishing appears. Social evils break out. The innocent are murdered; the orphans and widows are crushed; the poor are seized. These are like refrains in the "songs of lament" (cf. James 2:6 f.; 5:6). Verbal agreements, contracts, and oaths, which put a man in his neighbor's power to begin with (e.g., Prov. 6:2), are broken and exploited by evil men-fishers, the unrighteous judges. Plato had criticized the Sophists for engaging in men-fishing only for personal profit. Job's friends level the same charges (Job 20:19; 22:6-9). The reputation of an unrighteous judge who neither fears God nor regards man (Luke 18:2, 6) is in Rabbinic and New Testament literature practically identical with that of the tax collectors.[134] Jeremiah 5:26-28 gives a detailed description of men-fishing (*zōgrein*) in terms of social and economic injustices. But justice will ultimately prevail.[135] Only the faithful fishers of men receive the reward of judging also the twelve tribes of Israel in the eschatological future (Matt. 19:28). The tradition that all faithful members of the New Israel shall be rewarded with the privilege of judging the world and even the angels (I Cor. 6:2 f.) is a further extension.

132. McKane, *Prophets and Wise Men*, pp. 102 ff.

133. See above, pp. 69–71.

134. Strack-Billerbeck, *Kommentar*, Vol. II, p. 239.

135. On the popular maxim of how the trapper gets trapped, see Ps. 7:15; 9:15 f.; and often. Job 18:8; Eccl. 10:8; Prov. 1:17 f.; 5:22 and often. Also, I QH 2:29.

A third class of divinely commissioned fishers of men are the prophets who, like their Gentile counterparts,[136] announce the life-transforming power of the Word of God. In Amos' announcement of the men-fishing commission that Yahweh gives to Assyria (ch. 3:2 ff.), the hunting metaphor stands for Yahweh's own critical intervention or transforming revelation through the medium of Assyria. But it also stands for what the prophet does who brings into language Yahweh's revelation (Amos 3:4 f., 8).[137] What the prophet does is far more than merely state a fact or predict a future event. The confrontation with, and engagement in, political actions as initiated and controlled neither by Assyria nor by Israel but solely by Yahweh is the call to hear the Word of God. The prophetic word becomes a language event.[138] To represent Yahweh revealed or speaking in historical events the prophet engages in a task different from that of other religious officials by injecting a note of critical discernment, especially in contesting with rival prophets, priests, and wise men. Compared with the priestly or scribal understanding of Yahweh's *memra*,[139] the prophetic idea of Yahweh's revelation mediated through the particular prophet was at once more concrete and offensive.

False prophets, according to Hos. 9:8, are like "a fowler's snare" to themselves and all their ways, and to those whom they were to serve. Ezekiel 13:17-19 denounces Jewish female prophets in Jerusalem or in Babylonian captivity for hunting down souls belonging to Yahweh's people and for catching, or keeping, them alive for personal profit. The "songs of lament" complain of men-hunters who use flattery, smooth speech, arrogance, and insolence in baiting their prey.[140] From a passing remark in Jer. 23:9 it ap-

136. See above, p. 74.

137. H. G. Reventlow, *Das Amt des Propheten bei Amos* (Göttingen: Vandenhoeck, 1962); R. E. Clements, *Prophecy and Covenant* (Studies in Biblical Theology, No. 43; London: SCM Press, Ltd., 1965).

138. See E. Fuchs, *Studies of the Historical Jesus* (Studies in Biblical Theology, No. 42; London: SCM Press, Ltd., 1964), pp. 207–212, "What is a 'language-event'?"

139. On the Targumist's interpretation of Isa. 8:14 f., see Strack-Billerbeck, *Kommentar,* Vol. II, p. 325; Vol. III, p. 276.

140. Cf. Ps. 5, 10, 12, 52, 55, 59, 69, 140, and others.

pears that false prophets relied on the proverbial truth in wine to engage in men-fishing which resembles the Dionysian cultic men-fishing. Jeremiah's threat that Yahweh will catch the wine-bibbing prophets by giving them poisonous water to drink (ch. 23:15) may allude to the method of fishing with poison, which tradition is still preserved in Hellenistic *halieutica* literature [141] and may also be reflected in the reference to deadly pestilence in Ps. 91:3.

The true prophetic fisher of men is one who would have turned Israel from its evil way and from the evil of its doings (Jer. 23:22). This the false prophet does not do. His whole way of life and his message do not concretize what abstractly he may have in common with Jeremiah or Habakkuk. This is the same conflict we see again provoked by the ministry of the Qumran Teacher of Righteousness, and later by John the Baptist. But the lives of these two men did not suffice as universally acceptable norm either, because both remained restricted in their men-fishing activity exclusively to Israel. Only in the prophet from Nazareth are the concrete norm and the universal principle matched perfectly when God stands fully revealed in the medium of the Man of Sorrows as his eschatological prophet.[142]

A fourth type of divinely commissioned fisher of men in Israel are the priests who, like their Gentile counterparts,[143] administer the transforming power of God through sacrifices, rites, and ceremonies, as well as through teaching (Deut. 33:10; Zech. 7:2 ff.). The Teacher of Righteousness at Qumran, who felt called by God to be a fisher of men in Israel, was a priest. In Eichrodt's estimate [144] the "most important channel of priestly influence" was the priestly ministry of ethical teaching and paraenetic counseling, which was different from the prophetic teach-

141. See above, Ch. I, n. 58.

142. F. Hahn, *Christologische Hoheitstitel* (Forschungen zur Rel. und Lit. d. A. und N. T., No. 83; Göttingen: Vandenhoeck, 1963), pp. 351–404.

143. See above, pp. 67 f. and 78 ff. Cf. E. O. James, *The Nature and Function of Priesthood* (London: Thames & Hudson, Ltd., 1955).

144. W. Eichrodt, *Theology of the Old Testament* (The Westminster Press, 1961), Vol. I, pp. 395 f.

ing [145] and from that of the wise men. Scott outlined four different kinds of Torah that the priests taught and thereby brought or kept Israel under the power of Yahweh's covenant reality and justice. Convinced of the real presence or immanence of Yahweh in the world, the priests sought in their men-fishing ministry to bring men back to the full dynamic of the divine life. The priestly men-fishing ministry was designed to serve those in sin and error by catching them through the purification, sanctification, healing, and enlightenment of body, mind, and soul.

But this ministry becomes "an appalling and horrible thing" when "the priests rule at their direction" (Jer. 5:30 f.), when in the execution of their men-fishing ministry they become ungodly (Jer. 23:11). They become a snare and a net in which Israel gets caught (Hos. 5:1). Filled with "the spirit of harlotry" (Hos. 5:4), the priests make Israel become like a stag that gets "caught fast till an arrow pierces its entrails" (Prov. 7:22 f.), for idolatry, to which false priestly men-fishing leads, is like "a deep pit" or "a narrow well" (two images related to hunting), and like a robber lying in wait (Prov. 23:27 f.), which alludes to the literal manhunt). According to Ps. 69:22, the priestly or Levitical men-fishing functions become a snare and a trap to the commissioned fishers themselves. For the divine men-fishing if neglected cannot be merely ignored or become harmless play. Its only alternative is to become demonic men-fishing. It becomes an opium for the people and for the men-fishing ministers alike.

A fifth class of men-fishers in Israel are the wise men who, like their Gentile counterparts,[146] bring men under the critical and life-transforming power of the divine wisdom. McKane distinguishes between two kinds of wise men, each kind fully developed before Israel adopted each for its own religious, political, and cultural life. One kind serves as teacher or tutor of statesmen, diplomats, and ad-

145. *Ibid.*, pp. 416 f. See also J. Begrich's essay of 1936, now reprinted in *Ges. Studien zum Alten Testament* (Theol. Bücherei, Vol. 21; Munich: Kaiser, 1964), pp. 232–260 on priestly *torah.*

146. See above, pp. 69 ff. and 86 f.; cf. Isa. 47:9 ff. and Ezek. 13:17 f.

ministrators.[147] Besides teaching, they serve as secretary, advisor, counselor, or scribe at royal courts,[148] which in our time would be equivalent to serving as Secretary of State, as member of the resident's cabinet, or as political, cultural, and technical adviser, including speech-writing and foreign-language interpretation.

The other type of wise man also teaches and functions in public affairs and as consultant, not only to private individuals, but primarily to palace and temple officials. But the men-fishing wisdom tools this type uses are exclusively those of "specialized occult techniques," and "spurious esoteric knowledge," [149] gained by dream interpretation, astrology, augury, and the like, and applied through incantations, charms, spells. Israel appears to be familiar with this second type (Isa. 3:2 f.; Ex. 7:12, *passim*) at least as early, if not earlier, than with the first type. Aaron and Moses, Joseph and Solomon, Daniel and the magician sons of one of the high priests (Acts 19:14), not to speak of the traditions associated with the men-hunting angels, sons of God, or mighty men of Gen., chs. 6 and 10, are all examples of the second type. Even the gospel tradition about Jesus' exorcistic activity and of his teaching as whispering secrets to his disciples (Matt. 10:27; par. Luke 12:3) [150] also belong to this tradition.

In the syncretistic milieu of post-Biblical Judaism, as in Manichaeism, the working of this second type of wise man became associated with a strongly dualistic world view, in which divine fishers of men compete with their demonic counterparts. Evil net-spirits are constantly seeking to frustrate the soteriological men-fishing experiences. In a midrash on Num., ch. 12, it is claimed that Ps. 91:3, with its petition for deliverance from the snare of the fowler

147. McKane, *Prophets and Wise Men,* p. 17.

148. On mythological parallels, see above, pp. 85 f.

149. McKane, *Prophets and Wise Men,* pp. 94–101, on "Wisdom as Esoteric Knowledge." Cf. G. Delling, art. "*magos,*" in *TWNT,* G. Friedrich (ed.), Vol. IV (1942), pp. 360–363.

150. H. Conzelmann, art. "*skotos,*" in *TWNT,* Vol. VII:8/9 (1964), p. 442. See also G. Widengren, "Tradition and Literature in Early Judaism and in the Early Church," *Numen,* Vol. X (1963), pp. 42–83, esp. pp. 56 ff., on the relation between esoteric knowledge and written revelation.

and deadly pestilence, was used by Moses on the occasion of his ascent to Mt. Sinai to ask for protection against snaring demons (*mazzikin*).[151] Israel's arsenal of defensive tools and measures against evil men-fishing agents consisted of the reading or recitation of the Word of God, Torah obedience, the use of amulets, prescribed incantations, and ascetic exercises, besides prayer for direct intervention by God himself or by his angels.[152] It is important to recognize the soteriological function of this magical form of men-fishing through wisdom-teaching to which must belong also the cryptic origin of the tradition of Merkabah mysticism.[153]

The application of fishing, fowling, or hunting metaphors to the pragmatic and esoteric wisdom-teaching suggests that man's engagement in the cultural and religious life of his time means contact with transforming powers for good or evil. To denounce all so-called magic as witchcraft, and to initiate periodic witch-hunts in the name of religious orthodoxy,[154] can be as uncritical as the summary denunciation of all religion as opium for people, or as nothing but psychological projection. Wisdom, whether pragmatic or magical, no less than prophecy and the work of the legislative and executive branches of civil government, must be and remain subject to the critical test whether or not the access to and use of transforming power is related to truth. If the wise man happens to be, as often in Israel, a priest or scribe, this hermeneutical test is all the more indispensable so that both people and leaders, both the fishes and the fishermen, know that it is the liberating truth of God which is at work among them as mediums of his revelation, giving each the will and the power to achieve his purpose (Phil. 2:13).

151. See Strack-Billerbeck, *Kommentar,* Vol. IV, pp. 529 and 501. Cf. Scholem, *Jewish Gnosticism,* pp. 73 f., on the snaring *succubus.*

152. Strack-Billerbeck, *Kommentar,* Vol. IV, pp. 527–533.

153. See above, p. 81.

154. Hengel, *Die Zeloten,* pp. 191 f.

The Fishing Metaphor in Rabbinic Tradition

Eisler's study of the sources for the Christian understanding of the fishing metaphor called attention to the contributions of apocalyptic Judaism. But like others since, Eisler failed to account for the theological diversity in post-Biblical Judaism, or the "schisms" as Josephus called them. The so-called sectarian Judaism—in itself a mixture of various traditions—was essentially apocalyptically oriented, whereas another group, also a composite of rival factions—the Pharisaic and Sadducean "schisms," here in this study labeled together as Rabbinic Judaism—was seemingly antiapocalyptic, though both of these schisms within normative, middle-of-the-road, Rabbinic Judaism also knew, of course, of God's apocalyptic fishing activities.

Together with the relatively short-lived but intensive Zealot movement, which Josephus calls the third schism in Palestinian Judaism of New Testament times, we may in fact have three alternative interpretations of the fishing metaphor to consider as background for the Christian usage: (1) The nationalistic, zealotic, radical left-wing Pharisaic group engaged in men-fishing or men-hunting, often all too literally so, as an activity of "this age," which was essentially non-Messianic or at best anticipatory of the Messianic age as preceding "the age to come." (2) By contrast, the sectarian fishers of men acted in the belief that the divine net, ax, sickle, bow, scales, or plumb line, or the whole arsenal of weapons for the final war of the sons of light against the sons of darkness was now commissioned to be used by the appointed human or angelic fishers, harvesters, soldiers, judges, or other metaphoric expressions for the agents of God's final intervention in, and transformation of, history. (3) Different from both of these, the middle-of-the-road Pharisees and traditional Sadducees saw the fishing of men essentially as an activity of "the present age." But instead of carrying on "a [zealotic] worldly war" (II Cor. 10:3), they used as the fishing tools and tackle "the law [as] the embodiment of knowledge and truth" (Rom. 2:20).

Fishing in the Present. An example of the Rabbinic reinterpretation of God's fishing of men in history can be found in the interpretation of Ps. 11:4-6. On the one hand, these verses, which speak of God's mighty acts in history as continued "tests" [155] running throughout Israel's history, are interpreted now to apply to all people on earth, to both wicked and righteous, and not just to Israel. On the other hand, there is a significant change in v. 6. The original Hebrew text which spoke of God's casting his nets (plural) over the wicked has been changed in the Septuagint version to God's raining coals of fire and brimstone on the wicked, which the rabbis took as an allusion to the Sodom- and Gomorrah-like Last Judgment. In the Hebrew literary pattern of using synonymously two different metaphors in parallels, Ps. 11:6 identifies then the drinking of the cup with getting caught in the divine nets.

With the extension that Hellenistic Judaism gave to the divine "tests" or *paideia* as directed at all people the divine casting of nets is removed from the historical to the apocalyptic dimension. This shift in emphasis is again noticeable when the rabbis interpret other Biblical references to divine nets as occasionally referring to one of the seven place names of the underworld where the departed souls were kept.[156]

More characteristic, however, of the Rabbinic understanding of fishing metaphors is the schematization of divine fishing activities into certain periods of history, of which the apocalyptic period is always one. An example of this schematization is the fourth-century A.D. teaching of the four good cups matching the four evil cups which God gives Israel, or mankind, to drink,[157] or the fourfold out-

155. See also Heb. 12:3 ff., where instead of "tests" we have the familiar concept of divine *paideia* (see above, pp. 15 f.), characteristic of Rabbinic Judaism. See Strack-Billerbeck, *Kommentar,* Vol. II, pp. 193–197, 274–282.

156. Strack-Billerbeck, *Kommentar,* Vol. IV, p. 1091. On net-spirits in Jewish tradition, see pp. 106 f. On underworld as place of retribution, see p. 72.

157. Strack-Billerbeck, *Kommentar,* Vol. I, p. 837; Vol. II, p. 618; Vol. III, p. 833; Vol. IV, pp. 57 f. See J. Jeremias, *The Eucharistic Words of Jesus,* rev. ed. (Charles Scribner's Sons, 1966), pp. 59 and 206, on the relation of the four cups of comfort to the four Passover cups.

pouring of good spirit matching the four outpouring of evil spirit.[158] This fourfold pattern resembles the Manichaean tradition of the four good fishers or hunters of men who are cast into balance against the four evil fishers or hunters.[159]

Getting caught in the divine nets seems to spell ruin. But what appears to be the punishment of a vindictive judge is in reality the "educational" *paideia* or soteriological dimension of the divine fishing activity in history. It is for Abelson nothing but "a pledge of God's merciful interest in [the sinner], urging him to abandon his evil course." [160] For Buber it reveals that "God is ever concerned to bring the man who strives against Him to his senses." [161]

Rabbi Akiba gleaned from Scripture five major manhunts of God in history.[162] Three happened in the past: the hunting of the generation of the great Flood; the hunting of Job; and the hunting of the Egyptians of the exodus generation. Two manhunts were yet to come: the prophecied hunting of Gog-Magog, and the hunting of the godless Gentiles and the faithless Jews at the end of history. The decisiveness and power of the final fishing activity of God will be manifest then [163] in the fishing of Leviathan, the mythical sea monster whose flesh will be given as food to the righteous of the end-time.[164] But until that time arrives, the fishing activity of God and of his representatives remains the same as it always was: the teaching and appli-

158. Strack-Billerbeck, *Kommentar,* Vol. II, p. 615.

159. See above, pp. 83 f.

160. J. Abelson, *The Immanence of God in Rabbinic Literature* (London: Macmillan & Co., Ltd., 1912), p. 31. Similarly, Betz, *Der Paraklet,* p. 111; O. Michel, art. *"skorpizō,"* in *TWNT,* Vol. VII (1964), p. 420:34 ff., on the scattering of Israel in the Dispersion as act of divine mercy; cf. J. A. Baird, *The Justice of God in the Teaching of Jesus* (The Westminster Press, 1963), p. 42.

161. M. Buber, *Two Types of Faith* (London: Routledge & Kegan Paul, Ltd., 1951), p. 84.

162. Strack-Billerbeck, *Kommentar,* Vol. II, p. 19; Vol. IV, p. 1079.

163. In previous times God manifested his power in such signs as the slaughter of the firstborn of the Egyptians, the appearance in the whirlwind, and the like.

164. See above, p. 91. Cf. Strack-Billerbeck, *Kommentar,* Vol. IV, pp. 1159–1161. Goodenough, *Jewish Symbols,* Vol. V, pp. 35–41.

cation of the Law and the covenants.[165]

Men-Fishing as Torah-Teaching. Scheftelowitz pointed out [166] that in Rabbinical traditions the meaning of the religious symbol of fish and fishing is twofold. According to one meaning, all Israelites since birth and incorporation into the saving covenant can be compared with fish who need water, which is Torah observance and faithfulness to the covenant, as the indispensable medium for living. Fishing here has a soteriological meaning, but differently conceived from what Mánek proposed. According to the other meaning only students of the Law, the disciples of a rabbi, were likened to fishes. This is evidenced by the first-century A.D. document of Rabbi Nathan, who transmits the following saying of Rabban Gamaliel, with whom the later apostle Paul was associated as one of his students or "fish." [167]

> On the subject of disciples, Rabban Gamaliel the Elder spoke of four kinds: an unclean fish, a clean fish, a fish from the Jordan, a fish from the Great Sea. [The unclean fish is] a poor youth who studies Scripture and Mishnah, Halakha and Agada, and is without understanding. [The clean fish is] a rich fish who studies Scripture [etc.] and has understanding. [The fish from the Jordan is] a scholar who studies Scripture [etc.] and is without the talent for give and take. [The fish from the Great Sea is] a scholar who studies Scripture [etc.] and has talent for give and take.[168]

Whether a poor youth was to be admitted to study the Law, i.e., considered worthy to be fished, was apparently a matter of dispute between the schools of Shammai and

165. On the alleged "lack of historicity" in this view of God's revelation, see D. Rössler, *Gesetz und Geschichte* (Wissenschaftl. Monogr. z. A. und N. T., No. 3; Neukirchener Verlag, 2d ed., 1962), pp. 12–42.

166. *Archiv für Religionswissenschaft,* Vol. XIV, pp. 1 ff.

167. J. Goldin, *The Fathers According to Rabbi Nathan* (Yale Judaica Series, Vol. X; Yale University Press, 1955); Strack-Billerbeck, *Kommentar,* Vol. II, p. 637, ask "what class [of fish] Gamaliel might have assigned to his most famous disciple, the apostle Paul."

168. Goldin, *The Fathers,* p. 166. Cf. also the reference to "big fish" in the Gospel of Thomas, logion 8, and "large fish" in Artemidorus, *Onicriticon,* II, 14 (see above, p. 70). On teacher-student relationships, see M. Arzt, "The Teacher in Talmud and Midrash," *Morcedai M. Kaplan* Jubilee Volume (Jewish Theological Seminary of America, 1953), pp. 35–47.

Hillel, with the former maintaining that "one ought to teach only him who is talented and meek and of distinguished ancestry and rich," whereas the latter advocated "higher education for every man." [169]

It is an open question whether it was from prophetic and wisdom traditions of the Old Testament, and Jewish apocalyptic traditions, or from the Hellenistic tradition outlined above, that rabbis of the time of Jesus and Paul derived the comparison of their own disciples with fish, and, by implication, themselves as fishers of men. We have already had occasion to remark on the similarity between Hellenistic and Rabbinic school education, with "fishing" as metaphor for the "sophistic" teaching activity of the educator or for the persuasive approach of the rhetorician or politician. Paul has such Rabbinic "fishing" of men in mind when he speaks of these Rabbinic "fishers" as guides, lights, correctors, and teachers (Rom. 2:19 f.).

If Sadducean or Pharisaic scribes, occasionally called "sophists" in Josephus, did indeed consider themselves the successors and heirs of the prophets and wise men of the Biblical period, then a case could be made for their interpretation of the metaphor of the fishing and fishers of men as a composite of both Jewish sapiential, prophetic, apocalyptic material and Hellenistic traditions. The mixture of Biblical and Hellenistic traditions is characteristic also of logion 8 of the Gospel of Thomas [170] which likens the Gnostic teacher to

> a wise fisherman who cast his net into the sea; he drew it out of the sea when it was full of little fishes. Among them the wise fisherman found a large good fish. The wise fisherman cast all the little fishes down into the sea [and] chose the large fish without difficulty.[171]

169. Goldin, *The Fathers,* p. 26. On the social and economic factors behind Rabbinic school debates and decisions, see Ginzberg, *On Jewish Law and Lore,* pp. 102 f. Cf. also Finkelstein, *Akiba* (Meridian Books, The World Publishing Co., 1962), pp. 114 f.

170. For interpretations, see H. Montefiore and H. E. W. Turner, *Thomas and the Evangelists* (Studies in Biblical Theology, No. 35; London: SCM Press, Ltd., 1962), p. 55, n. 3; J. B. Bauer, "The Synoptic Tradition in the Gospel of Thomas," *Studia Evangelica,* Vol. III:2 (Berlin: Akademie-Verlag, 1964), pp. 315 f.

171. Translated by B. M. Metzger, in *Synopsis Quattuor Evangeliorum,* edited by K. Aland (Stuttgart: Württembergische Bibelanstalt, 1964),

"Little" and "big" fish were also mentioned in connection with the teaching activity of the Sophists.[172]

Men-Fishing as Mission. Georgi has recently outlined Jewish missionary activities in the historical and literary context of the religious and philosophical propaganda of the Hellenistic age.[173] One by-product of this study is the light that is shed on the large extent to which missionary men-fishing methods were held in common by the rival missions of the various religions or philosophical movements, let alone by rival factions within the same religion or school. How much Paul's own men-fishing missionary activity (e.g., I Cor., ch. 9) was shaped by Rabbinic "missionary maxims" has been demonstrated by D. Daube.[174] The two main Rabbinic missionary maxims were: (1) accommodation, i.e., "the idea that you must adopt the customs and mood of the person you wish to win over," [175] and (2) service and humility,[176] i.e., "the idea that to be a successful maker of proselytes you must become a servant of men and humble yourself."

Though Schlier had rejected it,[177] Schlatter's suggestion that the familiar phrase in Mark 8:36 and its parallels "to gain (*kerdainein*) the whole world" had its roots in Judaism's missionary men-fishing gained new support by Daube's analysis of the Hebrew equivalents to the Greek *kerdainein*.[178] Daube concedes that Rabbinic interest was primarily and narrowly in the winning back of sinners,

---

p. 518. See above, n. 168. For a different interpretation, see Jeremias, *The Parables of Jesus,* p. 201.

172. See above, p. 70.

173. D. Georgi, *Die Gegner des Paulus im Zweiten Korintherbrief* (Wissenschaftl. Monogr. z. A. und N. T., No. 9; Neukirchener Verlag, 1964), pp. 83–187.

174. *The New Testament and Rabbinic Judaism* (University of London School of Oriental and African Studies, Athlone Press, 1956), pp. 336–351.

175. *Ibid.,* pp. 336–346.

176. *Ibid.,* pp. 346–351. On *kalopoiein* as missionary motif, see H. Braun, art. *"poieō,"* in *TWNT,* Vol. VI (1959), pp. 475 f. See also W. C. van Unnik, "Die Rücksicht auf die Reaktion der Nicht-Christen als Motiv in der altchristlichen Paränese," *Beihefte z. Zeitschr. f. d. Neut. Wiss.,* Vol. 26 (1960), pp. 221–234. Cf. above, p. 88 on the charitable acts of the Egyptian Chief Steward as "fishing."

177. H. Schlier, art. *"kerdos,"* in *TWNT,* Vol. III (1938), p. 672.

178. Daube, *The New Testament and Rabbinic Judaism,* pp. 352–361, "A Missionary Term."

i.e., of "Israelites condemned and reprieved." Lucian's *The Fisherman* was similarly interested in winning back and bringing back to life the estranged philosophers.[179] The rabbis were interested in the making of proselytes.[180] No doubt there was a difference between mission proper, i.e., the winning over of Gentiles, and the winning back of lax or disloyal Israelites. This distinction "had practical consequences even in the earliest Rabbinic period." But, Daube argues, "two types of mission" do not warrant one to "expect two separate vocabularies for [each type]." [181]

To win back, to gather, or to fish a Jew meant to bring him back under the wings of the Shekinah, which is another way of saying that the omnipresence of God was to become a living, life-shaping reality to him again.[182] "Sinners," that is, Israelites, who had become lax, disloyal, nonpracticing Jews, or who followed false teachers (not necessarily Gentile or Christian teachers), are likened to the man who gets trapped by "the woman whose heart is snares and nets, and whose hands are fetters" (Eccl. 7:26).[183] Only the righteous, that is, the one who follows the true teachers, can escape her, i.e., the false teacher. This aspect of the fishing of the "insiders" with the purpose of bringing them back to full life again is as characteristic of the Rabbinic use of the fishing metaphor as it is of certain parts of the New Testament.[184] According to J. Munck, this same tradition applies to Paul's reference to himself as "one untimely born" (I Cor. 15:8) who, through Christ's man-fishing Damascus appearance, is brought to full life.[185]

With respect to the one type of Jewish men-fishing that he calls winning back lax or disloyal Israelites, which can be synonymous with the New Testament phrase "to call

179. See above, pp. 73 f.

180. Cf. K. G. Kuhn, art. *"prosēlutos,"* in *TWNT,* Vol. VI (1959), pp. 727–745.

181. Daube, *The New Testament and Rabbinic Judaism,* pp. 359 f.

182. Abelson, *The Immanence of God in Rabbinic Literature,* pp. 90 f.

183. See Strack-Billerbeck, *Kommentar,* Vol. I, p. 160.

184. For example, I Cor. 5:9-13; II Cor. 12:21; 13:2; and others.

185. "Paulus tamquam abortivus (I Cor. 15:8)," in *New Testament Essays: Studies in Memory of Thomas Walter Manson,* edited by A. J. B. Higgins (Manchester: Manchester University Press, 1959), pp. 180–193.

sinners,"[186] Daube observes that this was a somewhat problematic activity because there existed, with all the major schisms in the Judaism of New Testament times, "various degrees of membership . . . , some in closer, some in vaguer contact with the centre."[187] But the truer Daube's observation for post-Biblical Judaism, namely, "that the organization of a faith was quite generally not too rigid," all the more unavoidable the hermeneutical problem becomes. For in the definition of what goes on when men, especially with the conviction of a divine commission, go fishing after other men, the hermeneutical issue comes to focus simply by raising the question, What is meant by "the centre" that Daube mentioned? Furthermore, who defines what the center is, in relation to which Israelites have close or vague contact? This issue had appeared once before in the study of the fishing metaphor in the Biblical "songs of lament." The same issue will reappear forcefully in the study of competitive men-fishing between Qumran and Jerusalem. In our present context the hermeneutical issue becomes explicit in the Rabbinic controversies over false or heretical teachings.

Other Metaphoric Uses of Fishing and Hunting. This section is a collection of a variety of usages of the fishing or hunting metaphors that appear in Biblical and post-Biblical Judaism largely due to the influence of Near Eastern and Hellenistic traditions.

Unexpected historical or political events or natural catastrophes can be spoken of as entangling (*sagēneuein*) men in the meshes of panic like a draft (*bolon*) of fishes.[188] The same Hellenistic tradition is evident in Eccl. 9:12. Comparing men with fishes and birds which are senseless enough to get themselves caught in nets, it is taught, as part of the secular Near Eastern wisdom tradition, that all men are prone to get caught in an "evil net" when "evil times" suddenly fall upon them. The occasional Rabbinic

186. Mark 2:17, par. Matt. 9:13 and Luke 5:32; II Clem. 2:4; Barnabas 5:9; Justin, Apol. I, 15:8. Cf. I Tim. 1:15. See J. Jeremias, *The Parables of Jesus,* p. 121, on Mark 1:17 and 2:17.

187. Daube, *The New Testament and Rabbinic Judaism,* p. 359.

188. Philo, *On the Life of Moses,* Book II:250.

interpretation of "evil times" as synonymous with Last Judgment is obviously secondary. "Evil time" of the proverbial tradition, traces of which can also be found in the New Testament reference to "the evil day" (Eph. 6:13), does not refer to the time of God's eschatological judgment, but to any critical time when a person for a while is "given over to Satan," or Satan's power, as in the case of Job, or as in the cryptic case of I Cor. 5:5 where the man-fishing consists not in the forgiving, but in the retaining of sins. In the Rabbinic tradition of the excommunication of a sinner, the person is handed over "to Satan for the destruction of the flesh." [189] That every "evil time" or evil net has its corresponding good net is well-established Rabbinic teaching.[190]

The mythological tradition of three demonic "nets of Belial," which serve as antitype to the three divine nets gleaned from Isa. 24:17 with its references to "terror, . . . pit, and . . . snare," was reinterpreted in Rabbinic teaching as the catching effect that fornication or idolatry, wealth, and the defilement of the sanctuary have for Israel. This triple net of Belial may be related to another tradition current in post-Biblical Judaism about the three deadly sins.[191] This tradition may be the background for II Cor. 12:21 and Eph. 5:3-6 with their triads of immortality, impurity, and covetousness or idolatry. That the wicked, sinful, idolatrous person gets himself eventually ensnared in his own sin or idolatry could possibly be part of the age-old tradition of retributive justice mentioned earlier, which would make it synonymous with reaping or harvesting what one has sown.

The careless, thoughtless use of words can also get a person "caught." When Prov. 6:3 speaks of this as being

189. See Strack-Billerbeck, *Kommentar,* Vol. III, p. 358, on I Cor. 5:5; and Vol. III, p. 617, on Eph. 6:13. It is a different tradition when in Rom. 1:25, 28, God himself in his wrath gives up (*paradidonai*) men.

190. Strack-Billerbeck, *Kommentar,* Vol. III, p. 686, to Heb. 3:17. See also above, pp. 109 f.

191. R. H. Charles, "The Fragments of a Zadokite Work," in *The Apocrypha and Pseudepigrapha of the Old Testament* (Oxford: Clarendon Press), Vol. II (1913), p. 809; H. Kosmala, "The Three Nets of Belial," *Annual of the Swedish Theological Institute,* Vol. IV (Leiden: Brill, 1965), pp. 91–113.

brought into the power of one's neighbor, it must mean being held to verbal or written legal contracts, and the like.[192] Indiscretion is but a variation on the same theme of hunting people with their own words.[193] In the tradition of Rabbinic school debates, the Gospels speak of Pharisees and Herodians attempting to entrap Jesus in his talk (*agreuein logō*), or to entangle him in his talk (*pagideuein en logō*), or simply "take hold of what he said" (*epilambanesthai autou logou*).[194] In this context belongs also Saul's cunning which lays a snare for the spiritualist of Endor by consulting her in disguise, though he himself had outlawed seances (I Sam. 28:9).

As a person, especially when young, can get "caught" by exposing himself to the ideas a teacher professes in school, so likewise can exposure to "bad company ruin good morals" (I Cor. 15:33). Israel's wisdom tradition contains the warning:

> Make no friendship with a man given to anger,
> nor go with a wrathful man,
> lest you learn his ways
> and entangle yourself in a snare.
> (Prov. 22:24 f.)

Other warnings are directed at the snaring effect of flattering another person (Prov. 29:5), and at prostitution or sexual folly (Prov. 7:8 ff.; 22:14; *passim*).

Men-Fishing as Competitive, False Teaching. Psalms 22 and 31 referred to pursuers of the righteous in the tradition of the "songs of lament." When these psalms appear on the lips of Jesus on the cross (Mark 15:24, 34; Matt. 27:35, 46; John 19:24; Luke 23:46), those who first used Old Testament *testimonia* for the interpretation of the ministry of Jesus in the early Christian gospel tradition thereby implied that Israel's present religious leaders were pursuing Jesus, as their predecessors had done with other

192. See above, p. 72.

193. Sirach 27:20. Cf. p. 88 on a parallel in the Egyptian sapiential tradition.

194. The three references are to Mark 12:13; Matt. 22:15; and Luke 20:20 respectively. See also Luke 11:54 where Pharisees are reported to be out "to catch at (*thēreuein*) something [Jesus] might say."

righteous men before him, such as the Teacher of Righteousness or John the Baptist. Of the five subjects [195] that Rabbinic tradition had come to associate with the lament of Ps. 22, only two interest us here. It was held that at the end of history, just prior to God's final intervention for the vindication of his covenant loyalty and promises to Israel, demonic fishers of men would pursue or devour all Israelites who were faithful to the Law, i.e., who remained "fish." Moreover, these fishermen would go after the Messiah himself.

Rabbi Joshuah ben Nehemiah of the fourth century A.D., in his midrash on Ps. 7, derived from his teacher Rabbi Chanina ben Jichaq, saw in David's persecution by Saul (I Sam., chs. 18 ff.) a reference to Rome's persecution of Israel. This midrashic tradition had its antecedent in the interpretation of Nimrod and Esau, two other Biblical characters associated with hunting. Genesis 10:8 f. refers to Nimrod as one reputed to be "a mighty hunter before the Lord," who was "the first on earth to be a mighty man" who seemingly survived the great Flood besides Noah, for "the mighty men" were the offspring of the union between "the sons of God" and the daughters of men (Gen., ch. 6). What role this offspring played in the tradition of Jewish esoteric knowledge and magical practices has been reviewed earlier.

Ginzberg cites Rabbinic traditions and the Pseudo-Clementine Homilies (IX: 4-6) that identify Nimrod with the historical Zoroaster.[196] But Philo saw in Nimrod the model of the impious men (*ho asebēs*). By changing the Scriptural text from "hunter before the Lord" to "hunter against the Lord," Nimrod became for Philo the symbol of "the enemy and foe who stands against [literally, around] God," the ruler and leader of "everyone who is a great sinner." [197] Quite similar is the Rabbinic tradition about Esau who, according to Gen. 27:41 ff., took to hunting his twin brother, Jacob. In Genesis Rabba 63, Esau the hunter has become the symbol of all false teachers who hunt men

195. Strack-Billerbeck, *Kommentar,* Vol. II, pp. 574–580.
196. Ginzberg, *Legends of the Jews,* Vol. V, pp. 200 f.
197. Philo, *Questions and Answers on Genesis,* Book II:82.

with their own words. The rabbis took Esau's persecution of Jacob [198] as one example among others of literal and historical man-hunts. Another Biblical example is Haman's persecution of Mordecai (Esth., ch. 3).

The men-fishing of Nimrod, Esau, Haman, and others was done, the rabbis taught, either by way of political rule or by means of idolatry. Practitioners of idolatry capture and lead astray [199] the victims of their hunting which they pursue with cunning and deceit.[200] Midrashic texts on Genesis and Deuteronomy identify the men-hunting of Esau-Rome as catching its victims by words from their mouth, which can be taken to mean the insidious cross-examinations in court or as court trials with guile. This would fit in with such texts as I Peter 3:9-17, and also with the idolatry charges against Christianity to which Christian apologists, from the second century on, respond in a manner patterned at least in part after works of earlier Jewish apologists.

The Rabbinic interpretation of Nimrod's and Esau's hunting of men in terms of tyrannical rule [201] could be taken as an example of the Hellenistic Jewish tradition of the metaphoric interpretation of hunting derived from Plato's interpretation of tyrannical conquest and rule as examples of "coercive fishing" in a digression of his dialogue on *The Sophist*. While Esau becomes in Rabbinic tradition a favorite symbol of Imperial Rome, Nimrod is usually compared to one of the earlier conquerors, such as Nebuchadnezzar, Cyrus, Alexander the Great, and only occasionally was taken to symbolize Roman imperial rule.

Another contributory influence in the "fisher of men" tradition in pre-Christian Judaism, and related to "fishing" as false teaching as well as the passing on of esoteric teachings and magical practices, is the Rabbinic tradition

198. Ginzberg, *Legends of the Jews,* Vol. IV, p. 402; Vol. I, pp. 345 f. On "fishing" in the sense of "humbling someone," see use of *tapeinoun* in Septuagint.

199. Cf. *apagein* in I Cor. 12:2. On Ephraim's shibboleth interpreted as addiction to idolatry which gets him "caught," see Ginzberg, *Legends of the Jews,* Vol. II, p. 138; Vol. VI, pp. 203 f.

200. Ginzberg, *Legends of the Jews,* Vol. I, p. 326.

201. *Ibid.,* Vol. I, pp. 318 f.; Vol. V, pp. 199 f., p. 278, n. 51.

about Gen. 6:1-4. This cryptic Biblical passage records how angels, or "sons of God" chased after the daughters of men. The offspring of the sexual union are "the mighty men," a phrase first applied to Nimrod as mighty hunter then again as a stereotype designation of the enemy in the Biblical "songs of lament," and carried over into the hymns of the Qumran Teacher of Righteousness for designating his rival fisherman. What motivated the angels or "sons of God" to pursue the daughters of men is not as clear as it may appear at first, for as with the story of Eve's temptation of Adam the sexual aspect is secondary. According to scribal traditions preserved in Jubilee 4:15, Enoch 7:1 ff.; 8:1 ff., the angelic hunters engaged in their chase by divine order to teach men to "do judgment and righteousness on earth." [202] The actual effect, however, of this hunting of men was the corruption of mankind due to the received and developed teaching of "charms, conjuring formulas, how to cut roots, and the efficacy of plants." The transmission of exorcistic and healing knowledge reflected here is clearly the Jewish parallel to, or adoption of, the Babylonian tradition of the primordial seven wise men [203] and the Greek tradition of Chiron the Centaur.[204] If knowledge, science, culture, are powers, their abuses become demonic powers.

Another ancient Biblical tradition, in the form of the poetically stylized last will, or testament, of Jacob to his twelve sons (Gen., ch. 49), characterizes some of the twelve patriarchs by means of metaphors derived from hunting (depicting predatory animals [205]) or from warfare (depicting fierce warriors [206]). These metaphoric attributes, preserved and further reflected in the intertestamental document of The Testament of the Twelve Patriarchs, and in

202. D. S. Russell, *The Method and Message of Jewish Apocalyptic* (The Westminster Press, 1964), pp. 249 ff., on "Fallen Angels and the Origin of Evil."

203. See above, p. 86. Cf. McKane, *Prophets and Wise Men,* p. 96, n. 4.

204. See above, pp. 68 f. On the centaur as fisherman at Dura-Europos, see below, p. 125.

205. Gen. 49:8 ff., Judah as a lion's whelp; Gen. 49:16-18, Dan as serpent or viper; Gen. 49:27, Benjamin as ravenous wolf.

206. Gen. 49:5-7, Simeon and Levi use swords as weapons of violence.

the apocalyptic literary tradition about the symbols on the banners carried by the tribes of Israel, must have a positive meaning, and cannot have the derogatory meaning associated with the predatory reputation of Nimrod and Esau. This is the contention of O. Betz in his essay devoted to the interpretation of the two Gospel metaphors "fishers of men" and "sons of thunder,"[207] as applied to certain men among the Twelve which Jesus is reported to have called to represent the New Israel. According to Betz, Simon Peter, the fisher of men, thus inherits Simon Judah's traditional characterization as preying lion and skillful hunter. Regardless of what one may think of the details of Betz's argument, it is to his credit that the search for the origin of the fishing metaphor has been enlarged to include the soteriological dimension of the final reconstitution of Israel, freeing our research from the fixation with a few prophetic texts reiterated since early patristic times.

As "heresy" or false rival teaching became an increasingly acute problem even in Palestinian Judaism, and as "orthodoxy" developed as the guardian of the true Israel, "the centre"—partly because of the rise of Christianity, partly due to what Scholem misleadingly calls "Jewish Gnosticism"[208]—it became necessary to spell out the norm by which fisher and fished alike could determine whether the fishing of men was "of God or of men" (*ex ouranou ē ex anthrōpōn,* Mark 11:30). The difference between the Baptist movement and the sectarians of the Judean desert on the one side, and the Pharisaic and Sadducean "center" on the other side, was not that the former combined the teaching aspects of the fishing of men with the soteriological vision of a repentant and reconstituted twelve-tribe Israel, while the rabbis were concerned only with the teaching of the Torah. Rather, the difference was that both sides had mutually exclusive conceptions of how man is to participate in the transforming power of God, which is another way of saying that they disagreed on their understanding of the historicity of revelation, or, in Tillichian

207. *Revue de Qumran,* Vol. III (1961), pp. 41 ff.

208. *Jewish Gnosticism, Merkabah Mysticism, and Talmudic Tradition.*

terms, their interpretations of New Being.

Fishing in the Future. The change we observed in the Septuagint translation of Ps. 11:6 substituting "coals of fire and brimstone" for "nets" is part of a larger pattern in the Rabbinic interpretations of Biblical hunting metaphors. References to "snare," "pit," and the like, are taken not as pointing to historical events as past or present vindications of God, or of his commissioned hunting agent, but to the Last Judgment at the end of history which would not spare even the angels. Such inclusion of angels among the victims of the divine hunt led F. Nötscher to conclude that "therefore the mighty ones [i.e., the righteous of the eschatological community] will not be executing agents, but themselves be object of the divine judgment." [209] But this confuses two separate though related ideas. On the one hand, we have, for instance, the Teacher of Righteousness at Qumran who can say of his mission that he was appointed "for judgment and a counsel of truth"; on the other hand, he can pray that his rival, the wicked priest, have coals of fire and brimstone rain on him. The same tradition still operates in the teaching of Jesus who pronounces the Sodom- and Gomorrah-like Final Judgment on the cities that are unresponsive to his ministry.[210]

We must distinguish, therefore, between (1) the "fishing" that is the soteriologically motivated gathering and sifting or judging of the whole world, including Israel and the angels, which is executed by the divinely commissioned human agents,[211] and (2) the "fishing" that is the testing by fire to which the "fishers" themselves will be subjected (e.g., I Cor. 3:13 f.). It is not always clear to which of the two aspects of the apocalyptic "fishing" of

209. *Zur theologischen Terminologie der Qumran-Texte* (Bonner Bibl. Beiträge, No. 10; Bonn: Hanstein, 1956), p. 159.

210. Matt. 11:20-24, par. Luke 10:13-15. In Luke 9:54 the sons of Zebedee want to "bid fire come down from heaven" to bring the Final Judgment, the wrath of God, upon the inhospitable Samaritans (cf. Gen., ch. 19). Isaiah 24:17 is quoted in Luke 21:34 f. to express that Jerusalem will get "caught" because it did not respond to the divine visitation.

211. Cf. I Cor. 6:2 f.: "Do you not know that the saints will judge the world? . . . [and] that we are to judge angels?" See also the Q logion in Luke 22:28-30, par. in Matt. 19:28. Cf. also II Tim. 2:12; Mark 10:37, par. in Matt. 20:21; Rev. 3:21; 20:4; 22:5.

men the Rabbinic traditions refer when they interpret the hunting metaphors in terms of the apocalyptic doom, or as symbols of Gehenna, from which there is an escape provided [212] either by God directly or by the "fishers" commissioned by him, of which John the Baptist or the Qumran Teacher of Righteousness are representative examples.

In any case, Rabbinic tradition interpreted the apocalyptic fishing of men as prefigured in the ongoing fishing in the variety of traditional ministries of teaching, ruling, and judging Israel, living righteously, and acting charitably, all of which was carried on daily in home, school, synagogue, local and regional Sanhedrin, and the Temple. By contrast, the sectarians of the Judean desert, the Baptist and his movement, and Christianity conceived of the "fishing of men" as a radically new manifestation of God in history which would not vindicate the old, but create or reconstitute an altogether new covenant, New Israel, new creation.

Synagogal art confirms the Rabbinic interpretation of the fishing metaphors. One of the best examples to date is a mosaic from the synagogue of Hammam Lif in Tunisia [213] which shows four sea creatures, two ducks, one large fish, and one dolphin. Though "representations of seascapes with fish in the water are very common in the mosaics of North Africa, many of them showing fishing scenes, [there is] none in a form at all comparable to [that of Hammam Lif]." [214] From the mouths of the fish and of the dolphin hang what looks like long tongues. One interpretation suggests that these are "ropes or cords of some sort by which [they] have been caught." [215] The peculiar jagged object protruding from the top of the picture has been tentatively identified as "a conventionalized hand of God." [216]

212. Such as John's baptism of repentance, or esoteric wisdom, magic, and mysticism.

213. Goodenough, *Jewish Symbols,* Vol. III, Figs. 887 f. and 897 ff.; Vol. II, pp. 89–100, on Hammam Lif in general; Vol. V (1956), pp. 4 f. on the fish-catch mosaic.

214. Goodenough, *Jewish Symbols,* Vol. V, p. 4.

215. *Ibid.,* Vol. II, p. 95; Vol. V, p. 4.

216. *Ibid.*

Goodenough sees in the fish and dolphin, caught by hooks and ropes, Jewish "adaptations of some fishing, where Eros rides the back of a dolphin while he catches it with rod and line by the mouth." [217] Elsewhere Goodenough claims that this motif of Eros catching a dolphin does not so much symbolize a specific deity, in this case Eros, as it represents "divine power generally." [218] He also hypothesizes that the Hammam Lif mosaic originally had an Orpheus the Fisher standing on the shore fishing for the dolphin and the great fish, and that "later Jewish iconoclasts deliberately cut out" the mythological Orpheus figure.[219] E. J. Bickerman [220] contends against Goodenough that it was not mere borrowing, but deliberate Judaizing of Orphic theology that went on.

Over against F. M. Biebel's and H. Leclercq's interpretation of the Hammam Lif mosaic as "largely decorative," Goodenough suggests a symbolic approach. Equally divided is the interpretation of the meaning of the two divers on a Jewish (?) funerary jar from Sheikh Abreiq.[221] Goodenough sees in the Hammam Lif design "a series of signs of heaven and of [eschatological, Messianic] salvation." [222] He takes the large fish as Leviathan, which, according to legendary tradition,[223] was to be caught by the Messiah during his reign prior to the final victory of God over death and sin.

Next in importance to the Hammam Lif mosaic are the

217. *Ibid.,* Vol. V, p. 4.

218. *Ibid.,* p. 25, n. 160 (on the recent discovery of mosaics from Antioch). On the sepulchral significance of dolphins as carriers of the souls of the departed to the islands of the blest, see Lowrie, *Art in the Early Church,* p. 56. On Nabataean parallels, see N. Glueck, *Deities and Dolphins* (Farrar, Straus and Giroux, 1965).

219. Goodenough, *Jewish Symbols,* Vol. V, p. 4. For details on Moses as Orpheus, see R. Eisler, "Das Orpheusbild in den jüdischen Grabgemälden der Vigna Randanini"; on David as Orpheus, R. Eisler, "Das Orpheus-Davidbild in der alexandrinischen Bibelillustration"; and on Adam as Orpheus, R. Eisler, "Orpheus-Adam unter den Tieren," in *Vorträge der Bibliothek Warburg,* Vol. II, pp. 3–11, 11–23, 23–32.

220. "Symbolism in the Dura Synagogue," *Harvard Theological Review,* Vol. 58 (1965), pp. 127–151.

221. See above Ch. I, n. 56.

222. Goodenough, *Jewish Symbols,* Vol. II, p. 97.

223. *Ibid.,* Vol. V, pp. 31–61.

twenty-one ceiling tiles from the Dura-Europos synagogue in eastern Syria, near the Euphrates River. Each of the twenty-one tiles shows a centaur with a fish caught in one hand.[224] If it were the familiar zodiacal centaur, we would expect the *sagittarius,* or hunter with bow, whose favorite game are the hare or the panther. Kraeling has to admit that it is unknown in what context the zodiacal centaur was also conceived of as fisherman.[225] It might be of interest here to compare a figure from Sumerian-Babylonian mythology whose zodiacal representation was the *sagittarius*-centaur. I am referring, of course, to Marduk who in overcoming Tiamat uses a net besides other hunting and warfare gear.[226] In view of the symbolic value of the centaur in the synagogue at Capernaum [227] and Chorazin,[228] Goodenough feels sure that the Dura-Europos centaur also is "a token of salvation," for which the fish is an emblem.[229] Though Bickerman concedes that the ceiling tiles are primarily decorative, he goes farther than Goodenough when, besides the "specific function" of the tiles to express "the hope for individual salvation," he sees in them a means of "warding off the evil eye." [230]

Two points emerge in conclusion. First, many of the artistic representations of man getting "fished" are clearly inspired by Hellenistic traditions. They reflect the syncretistic milieu in which the fishing metaphor came to be interpreted in Rabbinic no less than in apocalyptic sectarian Judaism. Secondly, there is no doubt that the understanding of the meaning of man's salvation as the result of having been or going to be "fished" and "caught" was good orthodox early Rabbinic teaching continued in later Rabbinic literary and iconographic traditions. But no matter how syncretistic in New Testament times Jewish repre-

224. C. H. Kraeling, *The Synagogue,* The Excavations at Dura-Europos, Final Report VIII, Part I (Yale University Press, 1956), pp. 42 f., Plate IX, 3. For the reconstructed ceiling, see Plate VII.

225. *Ibid.,* p. 43. But see above, p. 120.

226. See p. 76.

227. Goodenough, *Jewish Symbols,* Vol. I, p. 185.

228. *Ibid.,* pp. 194–196.

229. *Ibid.,* Vol. IX (1964), p. 54.

230. "Symbolism in the Dura Synagogue," *loc. cit.,* pp. 144 f.

sentations of fishing and fishers as "tokens of salvation" appear to have been or become, the theological interpretation of the metaphors remained inseparably connected with the salvation of Israel as indispensably instrumental for the salvation of mankind. In the apocalyptic literary interpretations more so perhaps than in the Rabbinic school debates, one can see signs that within Judaism itself, as later on also in Jewish Christianity, this traditional hermeneutical framework did not remain uncontested.

The Fishing Metaphor in Qumran Literature and John the Baptist

Qumran. The historical setting of the Qumran interpretation of the fishing of men is the late second century B.C.,[231] the time of great cultural changes and the resultant Hellenization or syncretization of Judaism as well as Judaism's version of Near Eastern resistance to Hellenism.[232] It is the time when the dualistic world view, so characteristic of the second type of "wise men" tradition as outlined above, became fully developed in Rabbinic school tradition as in esoteric and apocalyptic literary circles of priests, wise men, or scribes. At the climax of "the present evil age" (Gal. 1:4), in which Esau and his fellow hunters of men and Belial, or Antichrist, and their messengers, or men-fishers, are active,[233] the vision of the final divine counteroffensive, or the theodicy problem, became a theological obsession. Through human [234] or angelic [235] mediums Yahweh is expected to reveal himself as superior to all other forces in nature and history through the events of the Messianic age, which is conceived of as either im-

231. J. Carmignac, "Les éléments historiques des 'Hymnes' de Qumran," *Revue de Qumran,* Vol. II (1959), pp. 205–222.

232. Eddy, *The King Is Dead,* esp. Chs. VIII and IX.

233. Russell, *Jewish Apocalyptic,* Ch. X.

234. Among them were such figures as the Messiahs from the houses of David and of Aaron. On "the Son of Man" as corporate or individual human agent, see Russell, *Jewish Apocalyptic,* pp. 324 ff.

235. See Matt. 13:49; Rev. 7:1 ff., *et passim.* On the mythological aspects of the "Son of Man" tradition, see Russell, *Jewish Apocalyptic,* pp. 345 ff.

mediately preceding or actually part of "the age to come," the "new creation," the eschatological covenant, or the like.

Judaism's theological engagement with the culture of its days was conducted at Qumran in a way different from that used by the leading Sadducean or Pharisaic priests and scribes of the temple, the synagogue, or the Pharisaic communes. The Priestly author of the Qumran Hymns, or Hodayot (I QH),[236] the so-called Teacher of Righteousness, or "the true teacher," reflects the historical tension between different theological schools of Palestinian Judaism. It has become customary in some quarters of modern scholarship to speak of one school of thought as orthodox and of the other as sectarian. But this is misleading. But the tensions and schisms within Palestinian Judaism were nevertheless very real. "The congregation of those that seek smooth things" (I QH 2:32), that is, the members of the Pharisaic communes, and further characterized as spokesmen of lies, seekers of deceit, and, in the tradition of Gen., chs. 6 and 10, as "the mighty" (I QH 2:35; 5:7), are said to be engaged in a manhunt of their fellow Israelites. "Envy" is seen as one of their motivations, as characteristic also of the Zealots, the radical wing of Pharisaism, and of the opposition to Jesus (Matt. 27:18) and the first apostles (Acts 5:17), as well as later Christian opposition to fellow believers (I Clem. 4 f.). Moreover, the sometimes literal man-hunt was conducted as a service to God (I QH 2:33; cf. John 16:2). This feature is particularly interesting, since it shows that both parties in this men-hunting contest were convinced that each had received God's authorization for this task which ultimately was to vindicate God's truth as judgment on unbelievers, but as salvation for the faithful remnant.[237]

In I QH 3:24 ff. the Teacher of Righteousness describes the activity of his rival "fishers" as the work of the "dis-

236. The translations here quoted are from M. Mansoor, *The Thanksgiving Hymns* (Studies on the Texts of the Desert of Judah, Vol. III; Leiden: Brill, 1961).

237. J. Becker, *Das Heil Gottes* (Studien zur Umwelt des N. T., No. 3; Göttingen: Vandenhoeck, 1964), pp. 58–74; Nötscher, *Zur Theologischen Terminologie der Qumran-Texte,* p. 185. Cf. also Betz, *Der Paraklet,* pp. 69–72.

semblers" (Ps. 26:4) or similar terms taken directly from the Biblical "songs of lament." The opponents act in "wickedness," "great oppression," and with "calamitous destruction." They open "all the snares of the pit," spread "all the traps of wickedness and the nets of the tyrants." They dart "all the arrows of the pit," let "the [measuring] line fall upon judgment, and the lot of anger [fall] on the abandoned ones." The Qumran Teacher felt at times that "deadly pangs surrounded him with no escape."

Besides alluding to the tradition of the "songs of lament," the Teacher employed metaphors from the kind of apocalyptic and mythological tradition (e.g., I QH 3:29-33) that later characterizes the preaching of John the Baptist and Mandaean theology. This language reflects not so much the emotional intensity of the men-fishing contest as the uncompromising claims exerted by each party. If, as Mansoor suggests, the Teacher's enemies are Jerusalem Pharisees, then it follows that they, likened as they are to Belial, were fishing with the three nets of Belial that in the Damascus Document 4:13-18 are identified with fornication or idolatry, with wealth, and with the defilement of the sanctuary. This could be a reflection on the vices of Alexander Jannaeus (104–78 B.C.), though similar stereotype charges were later made against Jesus.

The Teacher's rivals are referred to as "young lions whose teeth are like a sword and their fangs like a sharp spear," and as venomous vipers (I QH 5:9 f.). John the Baptist referred to Pharisees and Sadducees (Matt. 3:7) as predatory vipers, while Luke 3:7 applies the same metaphor to the people.[238] Betz,[239] followed by Mansoor, understands the hunting vipers to refer to false teachers, as evidently also in Rom. 3:13 and I Cor. 15:32. Though the Qumran Teacher felt for a while as "in the den of lions who sharpened their tongue as a sword" (I QH 5:13), God vindicated him by clamping "their teeth shut," making them withdraw their tongue (v. 14; cf. Dan. 6:22). This

238. Cf. H. Conzelmann, *The Theology of St. Luke,* p. 21 and p. 146, n. 2.

239. "Die Proselytentaufe der Qumransekte und die Taufe im Neuen Testament," *Revue de Qumran,* Vol. I (1958), pp. 213–234, esp. p. 223.

divine action, however, came through none other than the Teacher himself, through whom God acted "mightily" with powerful signs and wonders (I QH 5:15). In the heat of this smelting process [240] of religious factionalism or schisms, the dross was consumed so that those who were genuine would become manifest (cf. I Cor. 11:19).

God's own counterfishing ultimately will be or already has been vindicated in the ministry of the Qumran Teacher and in the community life he heads. After his rescue from the pit (I QH 5:6), the Teacher felt commissioned to have been "put in the midst of lions" where God established him "for judgment and a counsel of truth" (vs. 8 f.). When he adds that this commission came "in terror," it could mean that he for a while, or all the time, felt more hunted than hunting. And it is not at all clear what it means that the fishing commission came to him during or after his staying "in a place of exile." That his commission to fish men was essentially a constructive, positive, or soteriological function, and not exclusively judgmental, has been emphasized among others by G. Jeremias.[241] As Priestly teacher, in the tradition of his Old Testament counterparts, the Qumran leader and the community that followed him (the "many fishermen" of I QH 5:7 f.) represented the true Israel, true Torah obedience, true covenant loyalty, and all the other symbols traditionally used of the eschatological community. This makes him and his followers seemingly indistinguishable from the Baptist and his followers, and from Jesus and his disciples. It is therefore all-important to identify the distinctive feature and method of the men-fishing activity of each of these three eschatological figures and of the communities that formed around them.

We have already observed that the Qumran Teacher employed metaphors and symbols derived from esoteric mythological traditions, and from those of the "songs of lament." But so also did Jesus, or at any rate the early gospel tradition. It must therefore be said that neither the

240. On the relation between fishing and smelting or refining metaphors in I QH 5, see above, Ch. II, n. 61.

241. *Der Lehrer der Gerechtigkeit* (Göttingen: Vandenhoeck, 1963).

Qumran Teacher nor Jesus produced the fishing metaphor out of the creative depths of poetic or theological genius. Both drew on the Biblical and extra-Biblical traditions of the metaphor then current in Palestinian Judaism. What remains is the all-important question of how each interpreted the fishing commission and how it was understood subsequently in the community and tradition associated with each leader.[242]

The Qumran Teacher, as later John the Baptist, differed from the Jerusalem-centered religious leaders of Israel in the important point that their respective ministries were part of the inaugurated Messianic times,[243] while the Jerusalem leadership had no comparable eschatological conceptions.[244] In two points does the men-fishing activity of the Qumran leader and of his community members differ from that of the prophetic Biblical idea of the Assyrians or Babylonians as fishers of men, and from the men-fishing activity of priestly and scribal Torah teaching. One point is that the Qumran fishers of men were not to be succeeded by other fishers, as Babylonia succeeded Assyria, or as priests and scribes had their successors. Like John the Baptist later, the Qumran fishers of men understood themselves to be the immediate predecessors of the Messiah, and therefore as executors of the eschatological fish catch, harvest, battle, sentence of the Final Judgment, or whatever other metaphors were used for the unique passage from "the present age [or world]" to "the age [or world] to come." The Jerusalem "orthodoxy" did not recognize such a caesura in present history. Eschatological "newness" for them remained a chronologically futuristic reality. This alone made them "seers of error" or false fishers of men (I QH 4:20) in the eyes of the Qumran Teacher.

The other point on which the Qumran fishers of men differed from their rivals among Jerusalem's Pharisees,

242. *Ibid.*, pp. 319–353.

243. Cf. N. A. Dahl, "Eschatologie und Geschichte im Lichte der Qumrantexte," in *Zeit und Geschichte,* Bultmann *Festschrift* (Tübingen: Mohr, 1964), pp. 2–18.

244. See A. Finkel, *The Pharisees and the Teacher of Nazareth* (Arbeiten z. Gesch. d. Spätjud. u. Urchristentums, Vol. IV; Leiden: Brill, 1964). Cf. D. Rössler, *Gesetz und Geschichte.*

scribes, and priests, was that the Qumran community claimed possession of a superior knowledge of the man-catching mysteries of God. They claimed for themselves a special illumination which enabled them through spiritual, i.e., allegorical, exegesis of Scriptural texts to receive and to impart full enlightenment about the mystery of Israel's ultimate salvation,[245] much the same way in which Paul proceeds in Rom., chs. 9 to 11. This method of men-fishing puts the Qumran community in proximity to the esoteric wisdom tradition of the men-fishing wise men.[246] In both cases the tools for their men-fishing activity were the sacred texts plus the sacred esoteric written traditions along with the Biblical text, comparable to the scribal "tradition of the elders" complementing the Torah. But the difference between the Qumran and the Rabbinic method of fishing was that the Qumran method was esoteric exegetical, whereas the Rabbinic method was a pragmatic wisdom-teaching which was socially and economically oriented, and thus explicitly missionary in outlook.[247] The traditions from which such texts as II Tim. 2:24-26; 3:14 to 4:5 were derived are closer to the Qumran idea of bringing men to salvation through the teaching of the spiritual sense of Scripture than to the Rabbinic understanding of the pedagogical men-fishing through Torah teaching.

John the Baptist. In view of the patristic literary and iconographic sources which identify men-fishing with baptism, it is necessary here to comment briefly on Eisler's thesis that the movement associated with John the Baptist was a contributary to the Christian understanding of the fishing metaphor.[248] By putting the Baptist and his movement in the context of syncretistic Judaism, Eisler rightly

245. Cf. O. Betz, *Offenbarung und Schriftforschung in der Qumran-sekte* (Wissenschaftl. Unters. z. N. T., No. 6; Tübingen: Mohr, 1960).

246. See above, p. 106. Cf. also J. M. Robinson, "*Logoi Sophōn,*" in *Zeit und Geschichte,* Bultmann *Festschrift,* pp. 77–96.

247. See Georgi, *Die Gegner des Paulus,* pp. 168–182; R. M. Grant, *The Letter and the Spirit* (London: S.P.C.K., 1957), pp. 31–40; Ginzberg, *On Jewish Law and Lore,* pp. 77 ff. and 127–150.

248. Eisler, *Vorträge der Bibliothek Warburg,* II, p. 107, n. 6; and *Orpheus,* pp. 139–191.

perceived, though often based on fanciful evidences, that the immediate resources from which Jesus and the early Christians gained their understanding of the men-fishing metaphor was not the canonical Old Testament, but the esoteric wisdom tradition and the apocalyptic Rabbinic reinterpretation of Scripture. The key text for Eisler's thesis that the fishing metaphor was known and used in the Baptist tradition is Ezek. 47:9-10. It is postulated that Ezekiel's vision of the Dead Sea being again filled with fish in Messianic times was applied by the Baptist to the meaning of the baptism he offered.

The principal objection is that nowhere in Biblical and post-Biblical Judaism is there a trace of a tradition that associated the fishing metaphor with baptism, nor does the New Testament seem to associate men-fishing with baptism. But John's baptism is unique, if not as rite, at least in its theological interpretation.[249] For the novelty of the Baptist's own ministry was the combination of the sacramental with the eschatological, or better, of the cultic act with the eschatological teaching that made the rite a veritable sacrament. To be baptized was to receive the full benefit of God's forgiveness of sins, which in turn assured the baptized person of the escape from the wrath to come (Luke 3:7).

Only in a formal sense does John's baptismal Jordan water,[250] into which he "cast men as sheep are cast before the shepherd," [251] resemble the metaphoric use of water in Rabbinic tradition as the milieu in which the righteous live. To fish men by baptism meant for John that men were taken out of the old aeon and transferred to the new by denouncing the old and leaving the world to itself, that is, to judgment. In this respect the desert communities at Qumran and elsewhere along the Jordan valley show affin-

249. J. Thomas, *Le Mouvement Baptiste,* pp. 85–88; H. Thyen, "*Baptisma metanoias eis aphesin hamartiōn*" in *Zeit und Geschichte,* Bultmann *Festschrift,* pp. 97–125.

250. On the theological traditions associated with Jordan, see K. H. Rengstorf, art. "*Iordanēs,*" in *TWNT,* Vol. VI (1959), pp. 608–623.

251. A Mandaean saying quoted in Eisler, *Orpheus,* p. 142, n. 3. Cf. also E. Segelberg, *Masbūtā, Studies in the Ritual of the Mandaean Baptism* (Uppsala, 1958).

ities with the Baptist movement, but in their understanding of the actual execution of the men-fishing ministry the two groups differ as radically from one another as each does from the Rabbinic men-fishing.

If the account in John 1:35 ff. has any historical merit [252] in associating the Galilean fishermen Andrew and Simon Peter with John the Baptist prior to Jesus' call, and if therefore these two disciples had knowledge of the "fish-symbolism connected with [John's baptism]," [253] it would then follow that the designation of the first disciples as "fishers of men" would be completely in context. D. Flusser now claims that Jesus' call of the disciples to their eschatological office, of which the task of men-fishing was a part, was patterned not so much after Qumran as after John the Baptist and the eschatological community that gathered around him.[254] The problem we face, then, is not that of finding a suitable context in which Jesus and his disciples could have understood the fishing metaphor, but rather that of determining the way in which Jesus', and then his disciples', understanding of men-fishing differed from that previously known and practiced by the Baptist. We also have to ask whether the Christianization of the Baptist and the adaptation of baptism as initiatory Christian rite, contributed to or was the result of the loss of any distinctive difference in the conception of the men-fishing ministry as practiced by John and the later Baptist movement, and that of Jesus and the church? [255]

252. See Dodd, *Historical Tradition*, pp. 276–278. Cf. Thyen, *"Baptisma metanoias," loc. cit.*, p. 103.

253. Eisler, *Orpheus*, p. 182.

254. "Qumran und die Zwölf," in *Initiation*, Supplement to *Numen*, Vol. X, pp. 134–146.

255. For a suggestive answer, cf. Thyen, *"Baptisma metanoias," loc. cit.*, p. 200, n. 2.

CHAPTER IV

The Fishing Metaphor in Christian Tradition

Methodological Considerations

FOR A LONG TIME students of the New Testament have puzzled over the fact that the phrase "fishers of men" is used so little in the New Testament, less than almost any other metaphor attributed to Jesus. Until the end of the second century it is nowhere attested to in early Christian literature, and then eventually at first only in the commentaries. The first three centuries of Christian art and iconography reveal metaphoric representations of fishing and fishermen that were likely derived from sources other than the canonical Old Testament and the emerging new canon. Philological studies of the variety of fishing metaphors employed in Patristic Greek make one account for their appearance in terms of influences other than that of the Septuagint and the New Testament. Outstanding, then, as the singular use of the phrase "fishers of men" may be in the New Testament, it is hoped that the material presented in the preceding chapter is convincing enough evidence for "the interplay of tradition and novelty" also with respect to this metaphor.[1] To say that the gospel metaphor of the fishers of men has "no real parallel in earlier literature" [2] is too ambiguous, if not misleading.

Even if one were to conclude (which I do not) that the

1. See A. N. Wilder, "Eschatology and the Speech-Modes of the Gospel," in *Zeit und Geschichte,* Bultmann *Festschrift,* pp. 19–30, esp. pp. 22 ff., on convention and novelty.

2. F. W. Beare, *The Earliest Records of Jesus* (Abingdon Press, 1962), p. 47.

metaphor "fishers of men," like "pillars" in Gal. 2:9 or the novel metaphors in the Gospel of Thomas, is a secondary product of the gospel tradition, the decisive theological question would still be what criterion or hermeneutical norm was used or implied for the proper interpretation of the metaphor. A primarily linguistic orientation can only list this metaphor along with others and conclude that Jesus used it explicitly for some elsewhere yet to be defined task of his disciples, and implictly for speaking of his own mission.[3] Like countless exegetes ever since patristic times, most modern commentators never do come right out and say what the theological meaning of this metaphor is.[4]

Even farther afield lead those considerations which seek in the literal meaning of fishing a clue to the theological interpretation. Part One of this study has shown that new insights can indeed be gained from a critical study of the fishing traditions in Roman Palestine. This portion of the study was to present the evidence that the call of Jesus to become fishers of men was directed at people who were anything but the idyllic and naïve fishermen of Galilee's lower proletariat. When G. W. Buchanan,[5] however, puts Zebedee's fishing business on the same economic level as that of the wealthy tax collectors, he goes too far. The image part of a metaphor, in our case, fishing, must be distinguished from the material or substantive theological part of the metaphor.[6]

The image of fishing is immediately intelligible even to those who are not fishermen themselves. But what is substantively to be communicated by this image is the divine revelation or, in this case, the participation of certain men in mediating the eschatological revelation. The metaphor serves as analogy, but not in the sense in which the school

3. J. Jeremias, *The Parables of Jesus,* pp. 121 f. and 216 f.

4. H. Riesenfeld, "The Ministry in the New Testament," in *The Root of the Vine,* edited by A. Fridrichsen (Philosophical Library, Inc., 1953), pp. 96–127, esp. pp. 117 f., 121 f. See below, pp. 148 f. on W. D. Davies, K. H. Schelkle, and others.

5. "Jesus and the Upper Class," *Novum Testamentum,* Vol. VII (1964), pp. 195–209, esp. p. 206.

6. E. Fuchs, *Hermeneutik* (Bad Cannstadt: Müllerschön, 1954), pp. 211 ff.; also, *Studies of the Historical Jesus,* pp. 125 f.

of form critics understands it.[7] Form criticism can appreciate metaphors solely as formal literary entities which then are treated in the way familiar since classical rhetorics. Only recently have we become aware of the misleading effect this approach has had on the interpretation of the gospel metaphors and parables.[8] If one takes the fishing metaphor here as a picturesque mode of speech about something that could be referred to also directly and without illustrative images, one is bound to run into trouble when faced with the question, In what sense is the task which the disciples are to undertake analogous to fishing? [9] To hunt for clues and confirmation of one's interpretation of the metaphor by turning to other and related metaphors—in our case, the closest parallel is the parable of the dragnet (Matt. 13:47-50)—leaves the theological interpretation as unresolved as in Jeremias' approach.

The same criticism would apply to my own work if the material gathered in the previous chapter on the fishing metaphors in non-Christian traditions were to be used to establish a certain meaning or meanings and to conclude that Jesus or the early church took this over. Literary and archaeological parallels from the history of religions to Jesus' use of the metaphor can at best confirm what A. Ehrhardt, for instance, claimed with respect to Greek proverbs, namely, that "even Jesus himself was not opposed to the use of [already established metaphors]." [10] But more than that, such parallels confirm that even the preaching of Jesus,[11] with all its alleged uniqueness, was in its technical linguistic dimension part of the syncretistic

7. E.g., R. Bultmann, *The History of the Synoptic Tradition,* translated by J. Marsh (Oxford: Basil Blackwell & Mott, Ltd., 1963), esp. pp. 166 ff.

8. E. Jüngel, *Paulus und Jesus* (Hermeneutische Untersuchungen z. Theologie, No. 2; Tübingen: Mohr, 1962), pp. 87–139, especially his critique of Jülicher on pp. 88–102. See also R. Funk's essay quoted below, n. 80.

9. Beare, *Earliest Records of Jesus,* p. 47.

10. "Greek Proverbs in the Gospels," *Harvard Theological Review,* Vol. 46 (1953); now in *The Framework of the New Testament Stories* (Harvard University Press, 1964), pp. 44–63. Similarly, W. D. Davies, *The Setting of the Sermon on the Mount* (Cambridge: Cambridge University Press, 1964), pp. 457–460.

11. H. Koester, "Häretiker im Urchristentum als Theologisches Problem," in *Zeit und Geschichte,* Bultmann *Festschrift,* p. 67.

phenomenon which Christianity represents as a historical movement. Neither the traditions nor the image of the fishing metaphor give us a clue to its theological interpretation in the Gospels. For the theological criterion for such an interpretation can only be the historical Jesus whose ministry is more than mere presupposition of New Testament theology as in Bultmann, but rather the origin and hermeneutical norm of theology.

The understanding of the New Testament fishing metaphor which fully takes into account the form- or tradition-critical research but which goes beyond it confronts us on three levels. There is, first of all, its understanding in the context of the ministry of Jesus and of his disciples before Easter. The second level is provided by the formation of the gospel tradition in all its complexity.[12] It is on this second level that the metaphor becomes associated with the pericope of Jesus' call to discipleship. On the third level we find the fishing metaphor in the theological compositions of the Gospel-writing Evangelists. This will be the outline of this chapter to which is appended a brief review of the understanding of the fishing metaphor in early Christian art and in early Christian literature other than the gospel tradition.

Men-Fishing in the Ministry of Jesus and His Disciples

One could be led to understand the fishing image in terms of the actual fishing techniques according to which there are three distinctive steps involved (see above pp. 36–45). First, there is the preparation of the fishing tools and bait, and the finding of the fish. This part resembles the farmer's sowing (*speirein*). Then comes the actual fishing, the toil (*kopian, ergazesthai*) of letting down (*chalan*) the nets and hauling in the catch (*helkuein*).[13] This part resembles the harvesting (*therizein, synagein*),

12. See E. Hennecke, *New Testament Apocrypha*, 2 vols., edited by W. Schneemelcher, translated by R. McL. Wilson (The Westminster Press), Vol. I (1963), pp. 69 ff.

13. Cf. Luke 17:7, *arotrian* and *poimainein*.

the winning of a battle or the winning of a sentence in court. Thirdly comes the sifting (*syllegein*), the selling for profit and the taking in of the reward for all the labor. This part resembles the agricultural sorting that follows the harvest or the shepherd's sorting of the sheep at the end of the day's or season's work. It is comparable to the successful refinement of pure metal from ores or to prosecution and vindication in court.

The metaphor in the preaching of Jesus is not, however, a veiled, symbolic statement of the timetable or sequence of eschatological events. R. A. Cole suggests that of all the "homely metaphors" Jesus used, such as "farmer," "fisher," and others, "each describes a different aspect of our common obligations to our Lord and our fellow-men." [14] But he does not go far enough, for he tells us nothing about the way in which fishing is different from farming; nor does he show how the different aspects of these "our common obligations" relate to the work and word of Jesus, if at all they do. M. Meinertz lists the fishing metaphor together with others used in the preaching of Jesus and takes them all as expressions of Jesus' "at once compassionate and authoritative salvation activity." [15] This is certainly a different interpretation from that of R. M. Grant who sees in the fishers of men "representatives of God's wrath" in the alleged traditional Old Testament sense,[16] but he adds that fishing also implies "telling men how this wrath is to be avoided by repentance," [17] without qualifying whether, if at all, this fishing differed from the Baptist's and that of his disciples.

Smith's study of the metaphor [18] never quite makes up

14. *The Gospel According to Mark* (Tyndale New Testament Commentaries; Wm. B. Eerdmans Publishing Company, 1961), p. 60.

15. *Theologie des Neuen Testamentes* (Die Heilige Schrift des Neuen Testamentes, edited by F. Tillmann; Bonn: Hanstein, 1950), Vol. I, p. 173, "Fürsorgende und gleichzeitig authoritätsbewusste Heilstätigkeit." See also *ibid.*, p. 72.

16. So in J. Schmid, V. Taylor, and other commentaries. See above, p. 94.

17. *A Historical Introduction to the New Testament* (Harper & Row, Publishers, Inc., 1963), p. 317.

18. C. W. F. Smith, *Harvard Theological Review*, Vol. 52 (1959), pp. 187 ff.

for what is lost by the misleading premise with which he operates that Jesus or the primitive tradition could never have used "well-known figures [such as "fishers of men"] in an entirely new sense." Jesus' use of the parabolic speech mode teaches us otherwise. This is the merit of Betz's study [19] which puts the metaphor in the context of Jesus' "holy war." [20] By calling his first disciples "sons of thunder" and "fishers of men," Betz, like Grant, claims that the originally threatening meaning of executing God's wrath became transformed in the mind of Jesus to a soteriological meaning. Jesus and his disciples make war on Satan. G. Bornkamm had spoken of the soteriological meaning which Jesus had given to the metaphor *zuerst,* that is, "primarily." But when his translators take *zuerst* in the sense of "for the first time," [21] then a totally different judgment, a historically, not theologically, oriented one is suggested which, as Chapter III demonstrated, cannot be substantiated.

Like Betz, though in a different way, Mánek [22] and Lohmeyer [23] interpret the metaphor soteriologically, with Mánek resorting to "old cosmogonical myths" as framework for the interpretation that man is to be "rescued from the chaotic waters of darkness." By identifying this men-fishing with baptism, Mánek makes common cause with P. Carrington, who sees Jesus as working in the water. "His nets were out; he was catching men in the water." [24] When Carrington goes on to relate this men-fishing not only to the baptism of John which Jesus is said to "carry on" but also to the Sacrament of Baptism in Christian catacomb art, it becomes painfully obvious then that a critical theological interpretation is called for but not offered. No answer is given wherein we should see the

19. Betz, *Revue de Qumran,* Vol. III (1961), pp. 41–70.

20. "Jesu Heiliger Krieg," *Novum Testamentum,* Vol. II (1958), pp. 116–137.

21. *Jesus of Nazareth,* translated by I. and F. McLuskey with J. M. Robinson (Harper & Brothers, 1960), p. 149.

22. *Novum Testamentum,* Vol. II (1958), pp. 138–141.

23. E. Lohmeyer, *Das Evangelium des Markus* (Meyer Kommentar, 11th ed.; Göttingen: Vandenhoeck, 1951), p. 32.

24. *According to Mark: A Running Commentary on the Oldest Gospel* (Cambridge: Cambridge University Press, 1960), p. 48.

distinctive nature of Jesus' men-fishing, if only compared with that of John the Baptist who through baptism, teaching, prayer, and ascetic conduct of life is engaged in men-fishing as he builds the highway in the desert (Luke 1:76), turns "the hearts of the fathers to the children, and the disobedient to the wisdom of the just" (v. 17). For John also gave "knowledge of salvation . . . in the forgiveness of . . . sins"; he gave light to those in darkness as well (Luke 1:77, 79) and made a prepared people ready for the Lord (v. 17).[25]

These recent interpretations of the men-fishing metaphor in the preaching of Jesus had all been anticipated in Eisler's work, for he argued the case that the already established soteriological meaning of the fishing metaphor was given by Jesus still another new and soteriological connotation. Eisler imagined this to have taken place in a sermon Jesus preached right after he himself had submitted to John's baptism. This sermon allegedly made reference to Jer. 16:16 and Ezek. 47:9 f. And though his listeners supposedly had hitherto understood the metaphor only in "the bad sense of ensnaring people by cruel violence, or by sly deceit," through Jesus it became "a transparent Messianic metaphor." [26] In three respects Eisler's argument is still valid. First, Jesus, like the Baptist before or beside him, applied a soteriological connotation to the metaphor which in popular Jewish tradition was used only in a bad sense, but which elsewhere (this for Eisler meant the ancient Near East and Hellenistic syncretism) had a positive meaning. Secondly, Eisler saw this new meaning which Jesus gave to the already soteriologically understood metaphor as something that was "in no way connected with the idea of a spiritual rebirth or with the rite of baptism." [27] Thirdly, Eisler saw how the Baptist and Orphic models came to alter the interpretation of the fishing metaphor in early Christian art and literature. The gnosticizing interpretation in the Gospel of Thomas (logion 8) has

25. On Baptist traditions in Luke, chs. 1 and 2, and John, chs. 1 through 4, see Thyen, *"Baptisma metanoias," loc. cit.*, pp. 114–121.

26. Eisler, *Orpheus*, p. 126.

27. *Ibid.*

further substantiated Eisler's perspective.

The criterion for the interpretation of the fishing metaphor in the preaching of Jesus is derived from, as it is confirmed by, the interpretation of the ministry of the historical Jesus as distinct from the gospel traditions and compositions about the gospel of Jesus as the Christ. The three-dimensional aspect of the fishing image presented earlier is filled with theological content, that is, with metaphoric meaning, by the historic ministry of Jesus in which some of his followers were asked to participate as partners. Men were fished by yielding to the call to repentance, issued by the fishers of men who proclaimed the nearness of the Kingdom of God for which there were empirical "signs" that testified to or proved the reality of the divine imminence, or the dynamic of the divine revelation. But does it matter whether one is fished by Jesus and his disciples or by the Baptist and his associates? What difference is there, if any, between Jesus' and the Baptist's way of seeing the transforming power of God related to the present?

The answer to this question will be all the more significant as historical-critical studies lead one to conclude that concern for eschatological salvation was the core of the Baptist movement, of the communities to which we owe the Dead Sea Scrolls, and of the ministry of Jesus. In each case there was realized and inaugurated eschatology, imminent Parousia, and even Parousia delay.[28] In each of these three movements, among others in post-Biblical Judaism, man was conceived of as both actively involved in God's imminent vindication of himself as God before man, and also passively involved through faith in suffering and joy. In each case, however, the crucial question is, How was that faith to be made and kept active in its participation with the work of God? By what criterion was one to judge whether the claimed participation in God's work was really God's, and not demonic, as the Qumran Teacher of Righteousness and John the Baptist challenge by their public denunciation of even certain Pharisaic forms of priestly and scribal leadership?

28. See Dahl, "Eschatologie und Geschichte im Lichte der Qumrantexte," in *Zeit und Geschichte,* Bultmann *Festschrift,* pp. 3–18, esp. p. 14.

Men-Fishing Under Eschatological Auspices. Neither the Qumran Teacher, nor the Baptist, nor Jesus can fully be understood in their eschatological ministry in which their respective communities, followers, or disciples shared unless one sees each in terms of the appeal that is issued for active participation in the rediscovered dynamics of revelation as salvation. In each case, but peculiar to each, there was a gift associated with the appeal to active participation. What was that gift or bait with which these fishers of men set out to fish, and by which men were caught? At Qumran it was the Teacher's gift of spiritual exegesis that called for the immediate realization of the new covenant community in the light of the exegetically discerned imminence of God's vindication. For John the Baptist it was the gift of teaching the knowledge of salvation and the forgiveness of sins sealed by baptism and signified by a concrete life of repentance and ascetic discipline.[29] What the Jerusalem opposition—the wicked priest or the men of lies in Qumran literature, the brood of vipers in John—objected to and denounced was not the gift that each claimed, but the appeal to active participation that was issued on the basis of it. Not orthodoxy but orthopraxy was at issue. For his ascetic way of life, the Baptist (presumably also his disciples) was denounced as "having a demon" (Matt. 11:18, par. Luke 7:33). For his association with outcasts as his way of actively participating in the gift of God, Jesus was denounced as a "glutton and a drunkard" (Matt. 11:19, par. Luke 7:34).

To speak of Jesus' disciples as partners in the eschatological ministry of their master, through whom "wisdom is justified," requires a clarification. Imminent, inaugurated, or realized as eschatology is in each case, whether at Qumran, with John or Jesus, and proved by the "signs and wonders" that accompany each and their respective disciples, it is of great importance that we avoid identifying the "signs" of "the end" with the Kingdom itself. For the relation between the eschatological present and "the end," that is, the coming of God, remains in all three his-

29. On the religious significance of abstinence or renunciation in the ministry of the Baptist and in Jesus' avowal of abstinence at the Last Supper, see J. Jeremias, *The Eucharistic Words of Jesus,* pp. 212–218.

torical instances still hidden. Yet in spite of the hiddenness, the "delay" of the Parousia, or the secret (*mystērion*) of the Kingdom, there is nevertheless a relation between the present and the future; there is neverthless understanding of "the mystery," made possible by the Teacher at Qumran, or by John or Jesus. To use, as Cullmann does, the term *Heilsgeschichte* for this time element is not very helpful, for the nature of this time, or rather its content, is yet to be interpreted.

The few and often-quoted verses in support of "realized eschatology" or the Kingdom of God as present in the ministry of Jesus and his disciples [30] do not identify the Kingdom with present history. That God reveals himself in present history and that the "signs" of the Kingdom are evident in the present is not the same as saying that the present is the Kingdom. To distinguish the two, and to insist that such an affirmation as "God was in Christ" is not the same as "Jesus was God," is a critical theological reflection that has nothing to do with Arianism, adoptionism, or other Christological heresies. A reputable Catholic exegete, R. Schnackenburg, in the very chapter that deals with "the salvific work of Jesus as a sign of God's reign," rightly distinguishes between God's revelation in Jesus as divine power from the "not yet complete manifestation of [God's] glory." He amplifies this by saying that "it would be too much to look upon this present and active reign of God [in Jesus' and his disciples' ministry] as fully realized or as institutional. It still points like a sign to the fully realized kingdom of the future and at once guarantees and calls for it." [31]

The stumbling block of the eschatological ministry of Jesus and his partners lay not so much in what he said about himself (e.g., Messianic claims and titles), or what the disciples had to say when they confessed him as the

30. N. Perrin, *The Kingdom of God in the Teaching of Jesus* (The Westminster Press, 1963), pp. 74–78; J. Jeremias, *The Parables of Jesus,* pp. 115–124; R. Schnackenburg, *God's Rule and Kingdom,* translated by J. Murray (Herder & Herder, Inc., 1963), pp. 114 ff.; G. E. Ladd, *Jesus and the Kingdom* (Harper & Row, Publishers, Inc., 1964), pp. 145–213.

31. *God's Rule and Kingdom,* pp. 125 and 127 respectively. R. H. Fuller, *The Foundations of New Testament Christology* (Charles Scribner's Sons, 1965), speaks of the "proleptic presence of the future kingdom."

Messiah designate, but in the demand Jesus and the disciples made on their hearers for a life of active participation in the work of God for which not Moses or the Torah but Jesus himself gave assurance that it was for real and approved by God. This was "the faith of Jesus," that is, the faith Jesus himself had,[32] and the disciples' faith in Jesus, which was at work in their men-fishing activity and there to be tested in the accompanying passivity of their suffering, rejoicing, and waiting or hoping for the Kingdom by meeting persecution as Jesus himself met death.

The "mystery" element in realized eschatology is not a metaphysical puzzle or apocalyptic secret. It is the same mystery that accounts for "the parables of Jesus as self-revelation." [33] His Messianic "secret" and "the secret of the kingdom" (Mark 4:11) are but synonyms for what Schnackenburg calls "the concealed reign" of God, the experience of which is analogous to Paul's experience of the power of God in weakness, which C. H. Dodd once identified as "Paul's second conversion." [34] The power of the Kingdom experienced and mediated by the disciples in their partnership with Jesus materialized at first in the public and widespread success they had which was similar to Jesus' own initial public success. But the understanding of the secret of the Kingdom's success as power, and of its continuation and consummation not in but of history, came only in the second period of their partnersip with Jesus.

Just when this second period began is for theological reasons assessed differently by each Evangelist and in each gospel tradition. The climax of the first period is the return from, and rejoicing in, the success of "the eschatological ministry" [35] whose purpose, according to Greig, due

32. Fuchs, *Studies of the Historical Jesus,* p. 60; G. Ebeling, "Jesus and Faith," in *Word and Faith* (London: SCM Press, Ltd., 1963), pp. 201–246.

33. The title of J. J. Vincent's essay in *Studia Evangelica* (Texte und Untersuchungen, No. 73; Berlin: Akademie Verlag, 1958). See also Ladd, *Jesus and the Kingdom,* pp. 214–238.

34. Quoted by T. W. Manson in *Studies in the Gospels and Epistles,* edited by M. Black (The Westminster Press, 1962), p. 163.

35. Title of C. G. Greig's essay in *The New Testament in Historical and Contemporary Perspective,* Memorial to G. H. C. Macgregor (Oxford: Basil Blackwell & Mott, Ltd., 1965), pp. 99–131.

to his understanding of the nearness of the Kingdom as "chronological proximity rather than mere existential challenge," [36] was to establish "a Fabian underground movement." [37] In the tradition of A. Schweitzer's Consistent Eschatology, Greig sees the whole second period of the disciples' partnership with Jesus as subject to the experienced Parousia delay, which brought "the seeds of Christian institutionalism [that] lay in the minds of John the Baptist and Jesus themselves" [38] to a fruition which "is quite irrelevant for us" today.[39]

Forceful and provocative as Greig's essay is, its premise, however, is what Fuchs called "the *'proton pseudos'* [of accommodating] the *nature* of the Basileia within a secondary temporal context of phenomena." [40] There is no trace of failure in the texts that report the disciples' return to Jesus after their mission. Not adjustment to the Parousia delay is the clue for the interpretation of the various gospel traditions about discipleship, but the learning and making intelligible of why the participation in Jesus' ministry as mediator of the resurrection powers of God's eschatological revelation meant partnership also in suffering, in waiting upon the Lord, and in the faith and prayer of Jesus.

It is the merit of Strobel's study [41] to have called attention to the pattern of constructive theological ideas associated with the tradition of Parousia delay since at least seventh-century B.C. prophetic preaching. These theological ideas took account of the dialectic of faith, of mediatorship, and of the very dynamic of divine revelation. The

36. *Ibid.*, p. 115.

37. *Ibid.*, p. 114. Cf. also Dodd, *Historical Tradition*, p. 217, n. 2, on "the quasi-political aspect" of Jesus' mission.

38. Greig, "The Eschatological Ministry," *loc. cit.*, p. 127.

39. *Ibid.*, p. 130.

40. *Studies of the Historical Jesus*, p. 123. Cf. J. Knox, *Jesus: Lord and Christ* (Harper & Brothers, 1958), p. 90: "There are other kinds of immediacy besides temporal immediacy." See also O. Cullmann's restatement of his position in *Heil als Geschichte* (Tübingen: Mohr, 1965), pp. 188 ff., esp. pp. 196 f.

41. A. Strobel, *Untersuchungen zum eschatologischen Verzögerungsproblem, Novum Testamentum*, Supplement to Vol. II (Leiden: Brill, 1961).

account could be given in Messianic or apocalyptic idiom, or in seemingly nonapocalyptic or even antiapocalyptic terms on the polarity of divine judgment and mercy, best represented in the Pharisaic conception of the *middot* of God,[42] or as almost gnosticizing speculation of Rabbinic traditions on the polarities to which man, as all life, is subject, including the polarity of historical and eschatological time.

Participation in the eschatological, men-fishing ministry of Jesus means more than going forth as emissary of Jesus' faith in the imminence of the Kingdom. It means also to teach what Jesus teaches in his parables, and what newly with or after Easter he commissioned also his partners to teach: the mystery of the Kingdom, the yoke of the Kingdom, the meaning of the Parousia delay, or the meaning of immediacy in terms other than mere temporal immediacy.[43] Kümmel,[44] Knox,[45] and others—notably Cullmann—do us a service by insisting that there is a temporal element in what Jesus is saying and doing about the Kingdom. But little is served by either leaving this temporal element then uninterpreted or resorting to Schweitzer's solution which for the teaching of Jesus is as unsatisfactory as for Paul's alleged error on, and later adjustment to, the Parousia delay.[46] Only the problem is properly marked, but no solution or interpretation yet proposed, if, with J. Knox, one says that there was a temporal dimension but that for Jesus "there are other kinds of immediacy besides temporal immediacy" or if, with R. M. Grant, the Kingdom's this-worldly vs. its otherworldly character is to be seen as analogous to Jesus' view of himself as Messiah as over against that as Son of Man.[47] Not mere synthesis of

42. Buber, *Two Types of Faith,* pp. 152 ff. Cf. H. Loewe, "The Ideas of Pharisaism," in *Judaism and Christianity* (London: Sheldon Press, 1937), Vol. II, pp. 23 f.

43. Ladd, *Jesus and the Kingdom,* pp. 239–257, and 258 ff.

44. W. G. Kümmel, "Die Naherwartung in der Verkündigung Jesu," *Heilsgeschehen und Geschichte* (Marburg: Elwert, 1965), pp. 457–470, also pp. 351–363.

45. *Jesus: Lord and Christ,* pp. 83–90.

46. See J. Bonsirven, *Theology of the New Testament* (The Newman Press, 1963), pp. 364–368.

47. *A Historical Introduction to the New Testament,* p. 338.

these poles is required, as Grant rightly warns, nor, for that matter, some form of dialectic (e.g., potentiality and realization, as in Grant), but a hermeneutic, which suggests an interpretation of the problem by also stating the criterion or norm to be used. One can, of course, choose between Dodd's idealist, Bultmann's existential, Tillich's phenomenological, or the traditional dogmatic version of the norm, and many other possible or available versions. But a deliberate choice and therefore announcement of the critical norm has to be made.[48]

The question of when Jesus' promise of "making you fishers of men" did actually materialize is, then, also a quest for more than mere chronological information. Similarly, there is more at stake than mere phenomenological analysis when the disciples of Jesus as his partners are compared with the Qumran Teacher and his "many fishermen," or with John the Baptist and his disciples who "chose to remain close to him in order to aid him in his ministry." [49] To aid him is their *heilsgeschichtliche* function, similar to that of Jesus' disciples.[50] But Scobie does not say what this ministry was, nor does he attempt to define any difference in perspective on the ministry of John's disciples before and after John's death, with which a new dimension of *Heilsgeschichte* emerged for John's disciples, as it did for Jesus' disciples with Calvary.

Interpretations of the distinctive character of the partnership with Jesus as compared with the Baptist and the Qumran Teacher have often been offered by pointing out that some of the similes which Jesus used to speak of his own involvement in doing the work of God were also used when speaking of the disciples' partnership work. Jeremias lists the following "figures and symbols" with "a thread of eschatological meaning running through all" of them: [51] shepherd, physician, teacher, householder, fisherman, architect, and king. But Jeremias does not distinguish the

48. See R. H. Hiers, "Eschatology and Methodology," *Journal of Biblical Literature,* Vol. 85 (1966), pp. 170–184.

49. C. H. H. Scobie, *John the Baptist* (London: SCM Press, Ltd., 1964), pp. 131, 141.

50. See Cullmann, *Heil als Geschichte,* pp. 199 ff.

51. *The Parables of Jesus,* p. 121, and pp. 216 f.

symbols of steward, messenger, servant, and son from the other symbols, thereby overlooking a category—that of mediator or medium—which is all-important for the critical interpretation of revelation, whether in the form of the ministry of Jesus [52] or that of his disciples' partnership with him.

Another purely descriptive, uncritical list of metaphors cited to facilitate the interpretation of the precise nature of the disciples' ministry is given by H. Riesenfeld.[53] Besides those listed by Jeremias, he also mentions the metaphors of gardener, sower, pilot, host, and bridegroom. In his attempt to gain "light on the ministry from the New Testament," [54] W. D. Davies also employs the metaphors and adds to the list of Jeremias and Riesenfeld the metaphors of deacon, high priest, and bishop. Schelkle's study of *Jüngerschaft und Apostelamt* [55] expands the list even further by including also the metaphors of father, herald, and leader. There is a merit in studying these metaphors synoptically, as B. Gerhardsson pointed out rightly in his critical review of the works of G. Klein [56] and W. Schmithals [57] by criticizing that the metaphor of messenger or apostle has for too long been analyzed in strict isolation from related symbols, similes, or metaphors which often influenced each other through changing combinations and different uses in different religious traditions of Judaism and Christianity.[58]

But when Davies concludes from the examination of the metaphors "that all ministry is His ministry," or when Riesenfeld's interpretation leads only to the emphasis on

52. See C. F. D. Moule, "From Defendant to Judge," *Studiorum Novi Test. Societas,* Bulletin III (1952), pp. 40–53.

53. "The Ministry in the New Testament," in Fridrichsen (ed.), *The Root of the Vine,* pp. 117 ff.

54. An essay by this title in *Christian Origins and Judaism* (The Westminster Press, 1962), pp. 231–245.

55. K. H. Schelkle, *Discipleship and Priesthood,* translated by J. Disselhorst (Herder & Herder, Inc., 1965).

56. *Die Zwölf Apostel* (Forschungen zur Rel. und Lit. d. A. und N. T., No. 77, Göttingen: Vandenhoeck, 1961).

57. *Das kirchliche Apostelamt* (Forschungen zur Rel. und Lit. d. A. und N. T., No. 79; Göttingen: Vandenhoeck, 1961).

58. "Die Boten Gottes und die Apostel Christi," in *Svensk Exegetisk Arsbok,* Vol. 27 (1962), pp. 89–131, esp. p. 126.

the continuity between Jesus and the disciples, then only one side of the issue has been made clear. This is fine and good as far as it goes, but it does not go far enough. As with the interpretation of charisma,[59] the criterion for a genuine ministry lies not in the mere fact of its association with the ministry of Jesus, but in the use to which it is put. This, however, is clearly subject to variation and alteration within the New Testament, both before and after Easter, and further underscored by the extracanonical gospel traditions on discipleship.[60] Manson's list [61] of "words and phrases characteristic of those sections of the teaching addressed to the disciples" reveals at a glance something of the complexity and urgency of this critical task.

Men-Fishing as Mission of Israel. The criterion by which this critical task is to be executed should be gained from the text itself. Historical and literary studies have made us aware of the secondary character of many of the texts, that is to say that many texts represent not facts only of Jesus' ministry, including the facts of authentic words of Jesus, but also interpretations. To separate not fact from interpretation, but one interpretation from another, e.g., the interpretation Jesus gave of his own ministry and of that of his disciples before Easter from the interpretation of the same as found in the gospel traditions and in the present Gospels, both canonical and extracanonical—this is the goal of all critical studies of Biblical texts.

In the ministry of Jesus and of his Twelve as Kingdom ministry we must distinguish two further points in order to bring into focus what men-fishing meant in the ministry of Jesus and his partners before Easter. One point concerns the restriction of the Kingdom ministry to Israel. The other point invites explanation of the reason (s) for Jesus' particularistic concern for Israel, for the Jerusalem-centered mission of Jesus and the Twelve, and also why the death and resurrection of Jesus in Jerusalem are indis-

59. See E. Käsemann, "Ministry and Community in the New Testament," in *Essays on New Testament Themes* (Studies in Biblical Theology, No. 41; London: SCM Press, Ltd., 1964), pp. 63–94.

60. See E. Hennecke, *New Testament Apocrypha,* Vol. I, pp. 71 ff.

61. T. W. Manson, *The Teaching of Jesus* (Cambridge: Cambridge University Press, 1963), pp. 320–323, Appendix I.

pensable for the proper understanding of the transition from particularism to universalism in the men-fishing ministry.

Jesus' historical mission and the share that his historical partners had in more than one mission of the kind typified in Mark, ch. 6, and parallels,[62] remained confined to Israel. But the significance of this observation escapes one if this confinement is understood only historically, or if Jesus' obsession with going to Jerusalem is taken as expression of his parochialism. The emerging typology of Jesus' and the disciples' ministry in the light of the Old Testament, and the use of Old Testament "testimonies" in the interpretation of the meaning and scope of that ministry, as well as Luke's reference in ch. 13:33 to Jesus' going to Jerusalem as necessary because every prophet did so—all these may indeed be secondary, but nonetheless significant theological interpretations of what was taken to be Jesus' understanding of his and his disciples' Kingdom ministry.

It is not enough to say with Hahn [63] that the Twelve were "at once put into Jesus' own service of proclamation and mighty works," and this "not merely [as] his messengers, [but as] his fellow workers." Like countless others, Hahn leaves unconnected what he calls the obvious observation "that the activity of the disciples, like that of their master, is concentrated on Israel," and the theological claim that "what is laid upon them is the same message directed to the eschatological salvation of the whole world." [64] How can such obvious restriction to Israel become equally obviously a universally directed salvation ministry? Why Jesus and the disciples concentrate on Israel is, then, not an obvious fact but a symbol or parable charged with theological content no less than the inscription on the cross or the Matthean and Lucan genealogies and infancy narratives.

62. Dodd, *Historical Tradition,* p. 404, says that "such missions [!] were a part of [Jesus'] strategy."

63. F. Hahn, *Mission in the New Testament* (Studies in Biblical Theology, No. 47; London: SCM Press, Ltd., 1965), pp. 40 f.

64. *Ibid.,* p. 41.

This theological content of the symbolic fact is perhaps brought into focus if I formulate my thesis that the mission of Jesus and the Twelve *to* Israel was designed, or what Dodd calls "part of Jesus' strategy," to recover the sense of the mission *of* Israel. The "mystery" of the Kingdom cannot be understood without understanding the mystery of Israel. It appears to me indispensable for an interpretation of the meaning of the men-fishing metaphor in the ministry of the historical Jesus that we recognize in the restriction of the Kingdom ministry to Israel not a mere accident of history, let alone a sign of Jesus' provincialism, but a significant symbol by which the meaning of Kingdom—the apocalyptic symbol of universal salvation—and the meaning of Israel—the symbol of mediumship and salvation history—become alternately clear by seeing each in the light of the other.

The most likely answer to the question of what Christians of the third or fourth generation found so difficult to understand in Paul's letters (II Peter 3:16) is Paul's eschatological scheme of the salvation of Israel in the context of Gentile mission (Rom., chs. 9 to 11).[65] How could men-fishing as Gentile mission be understood as a roundabout way of reaching Israel and thereby manifest "the truth of God" and "confirm the promises given to the patriarchs" (Rom. 15:8 f.)? Paul's relationship to James[66] and his devotion in collecting *sarkika* from his churches (RSV translates Rom. 15:27 as "material blessings") as an expression of the Gentiles' indebtedness for having come to share in the *pneumatika* of the saints at Jerusalem (RSV "spiritual blessings")[67] are two distinct historical problems, yet related to what is the essentially theological problem of Israel-Jerusalem for Christian theology. Rome's claim to have taken over the role of Jerusalem became as tragic for Christianity as the fatal error that "God had re-

65. H. J. Schoeps, *Paul* (The Westminster Press, 1961), p. 170, n. 1, and p. 271, sees it too narrowly with Harnack in "the most knotty justification . . . [of] universalism . . . [in terms of] the abolition of the law."

66. W. Schmithals, *Paul and James* (Studies in Biblical Theology, No. 46; London: SCM Press, Ltd., 1965).

67. D. Georgi, *Die Geschichte der Kollekte des Paulus für Jerusalem* (Theol. Forschung, No. 38; Hamburg: Reich, 1965), especially pp. 81–87.

jected Israel," or that Torah and Law were abolished.

In order to understand the symbolism of Jesus' calling the Twelve as partners from among a number of disciples, we must clearly distinguish two points. One point concerns the Twelve as over against the general call to discipleship. To this latter category belong now, that is, in their present context or rather form (pronouncement story or biographical apothegm), the "fisher of men" pericope (Mark 1:16-20 and parallels). The second point concerns the differentiation between partnership with Jesus, even in the specific sense of the Twelve as special partners (in contrast to other disciples, the serving women, the "strange exorcist," and other "true relatives" of Jesus), and the role of the church as a separate sect and organization. That there is this distinction is one of the more plausible reasons which one could cite to explain why the simile of the fisher never became a popular symbol for ecclesiastical office, unlike other similes Jesus used, such as those of householder, steward, shepherd, executive, emissary, and others. For the fishing metaphor, which, like other metaphors, serves as comprehensive symbol of the meaning of the mission or ministry of Jesus understood as the mission of Israel, resisted more successfully than others all attempts at becoming domesticated, that is, ecclesiasticized.[68]

If, then, the Twelve represent not a separate group, hence a sect or church either organized before or to be organized after Easter, but represent separateness—the way Israel represents not a chosen people as distinct race or national, cultural entity, but chosenness, holiness, or, as Schoeps puts it, the embodiment of the sovereignty of God on earth— [69] the same is also applicable to Simon as Peter. As Simon he is an individual disciple, brother of Andrew, and only one of the Twelve. But as Peter, the Rock, he is a symbol of Israel,[70] as the Twelve are. For Jesus to appear

68. For a medieval example of the Roman pontif as *piscator,* depicting the pope's tiara, symbol of his authority, as a wicker basket, see pp. 233 f. Not until the thirteenth century does the "fisher ring" become an exclusively papal symbol. See H. Lesêtre, art. *"pêcheur,"* in *Dictionnaire de la Bible,* edited by F. Vigouroux (Paris: Letouzey), Vol. V (1922), col. 16.

69. *Paul,* p. 214.

70. On the discussion of the role of Peter in modern exegesis, see

to Cephas and the Twelve (I Cor. 15:5) are but two ways of saying one thing. But to say this and leave it there would be no credit to critical studies, for the meaning of "Twelve" and "Peter" certainly came to be understood differently even within the New Testament, let alone in extracanonical traditions and patristic literature.

It is my contention that the designation of Simon as Peter [71] and as "fisher of men" are two separate yet synonymous symbols preserved in different traditions. The original meaning of these symbols in the men-fishing, Rock-laying ministry of Jesus was reinterpreted in the gospel tradition to such an extent that "fisher of men" eventually became synonymous with the executive power of the keys, which is a process similar to the application of such parable metaphors as those of steward, householder, shepherd, and the like, to ecclesiastical office.[72]

The question of exactly when Simon was appointed to be the "Rock" is identical with the question of exactly when he was to become the fisher of men, or when the Twelve were appointed. That the gospel traditions give different answers in each case is clear evidence that the church understood the charge to Peter and the Twelve primarily not from a chronological perspective, but as a theological category. And it is the different interpretations of the theological dimension of the meaning of "Rock," "men-fisher" and "Twelve," and not the chronology of when these symbols were first introduced, that interests us here. In that sense the study of the use and abuse of the different interpretations given to similes and metaphors or symbols used by Jesus is similar to what happened in the history of the interpretations of the parables of Jesus.

The historicity of the Twelve, and of the call to Simon as "fisher of men" and "rock," has been suspect on the grounds that the Kingdom ministry precluded any such

---

Kümmel, "Die Naherwartung," *Heilsgeschehen und Geschichte,* p. 290, nn. 5, 6; p. 301, n. 55. Nothing more than suggestive is Eisler's speculation that "Peter" has the same numerical (gematric) value as "net" (*Orpheus,* p. 119, n. 2).

71. On petra, Petros, Cephas, see H. Rheinfelder, *Der übersetzte Eigenname* (Munich: Hueber, n.d.).

72. J. Jeremias, *The Parables of Jesus,* pp. 53 ff.

confinement to a person or select group of persons, and that only a parochial Jewish Christianity could be responsible for creating and preserving such a tradition. Provided we leave the passage of Simon's endowment with the keys (Matt. 16:19) out of our present considerations, we can then say that the men-fishing appointments of Peter and of the Twelve are properly understood only if we recognize in "Peter" and "Twelve" two separate but complementary or synonymous symbols. As with the "purpose," that is, significance, of the symbolism of Jesus' parable teaching, the symbolism of Peter and the Twelve is a call *to* Israel in order to manifest the full scope of the call *of* Israel.[73]

Kümmel asks whether Jesus could have assigned to an individual human being, that is, Simon, or even to a group of individuals, the Twelve, "such a decisive role." The thrust of Kümmel's question is not directed at whether man can decide or mediate another man's participation in the Kingdom of God but whether Jesus conceived of this role of Peter and the Twelve as identical with their functions as church leaders, thus making decision over entrance into the Kingdom and over membership in the church synonymous. These two aspects, Kingdom and Israel, and church and Israel, have to be kept separate. If not, as often in Christian theology, and even in parts of the New Testament, then only confusion reigns.[74]

When Kümmel answers his question in the negative, he is right in view of the clear distinction between Kingdom and church, but he is wrong in view of the indissoluble connection between Kingdom and Israel. Israel is the symbol for salvation history, the symbol of what election and chosenness, what mediumship, means. Israel stands as

73. On the meaning of Isa. 6:9-10 in connection with Jesus' and presumably also the disciples' use of parables, see Manson, *The Teaching of Jesus,* pp. 75–80; J. Jeremias, *The Parables of Jesus,* pp. 15–18.

74. On the misinterpreted idea of Israel's rejection by God, see J. Munck, *Paul and the Salvation of Mankind* (London: SCM Press, Ltd., 1959), p. 259; and the complementary notion of Christianity as third race, see E. Peterson, *Frühkirche, Judentum und Gnosis* (Rome: Herder, 1959), pp. 51–63. On the significance of post-Biblical Jewish thought forms for the formation of early Christian traditions, see the works of L. Goppelt, J. Daniélou, G. Quispel, and others.

a warning against all attempts at equating God *in* history with history as revelation, or God *in* nature with nature *as* God. With Israel's call to mediumship began the quest for true, perfect, final mediumship, which is identical with the quest for final revelation.

The symbol that is Israel represents the human agent appointed to be the medium of God's eschatological revelation. What is overlooked in Kümmel's negative reply is not the fact but the significance of the fact that it was Jesus, and not God directly, who assigned this men-fishing ministry to Peter and the Twelve. What partnership or participation in the mediumship means for the disciples is wrapped up in the mystery of the symbol of Jesus as Israel,[75] as servant, king, prophet, priest, and other symbols. Jesus assigns, appoints, calls, chooses partners just as Moses appointed leaders, elders, and the like, or as Samuel anointed a king. The issue is not that authority is delegated, but what the nature of this authority is which is delegated, and whose authority it is.

Should Flusser[76] have succeeded in making plausible the idea that Jesus took over from John the Baptist not only the message of the imminent Kingdom, but also the symbolism of twelve disciples, the theological question of wherein, then, the two men and the two groups of twelve differed would again arise forcefully. The men-fishing function of the Twelve associated with Jesus is wrongly interpreted by Flusser when he sees in the Twelve an " 'ecclesiastical' institution of the Messianic Jesus community," which Flusser takes "in the deepest sense as ecclesial—'ecclesiologically,' that is, as both an organization and also an eschatological-mystical institution."[77] What Flusser calls "the esoteric aspect of the meaning of the Twelve" I take to mean the esoterism of the mystery of the revelation of which Israel itself is a symbol, which in historical perspective is but one among numerous other symbols es-

75. E. Schweizer, *Neotestamentica* (Zurich: Zwingli, 1963), pp. 244 f., speaks of the "tactics of Jesus" which "wanted the whole of Israel."

76. "Qumran und die Zwölf," in *Initiation,* Supplement to *Numen,* Vol. X, pp. 144 f.

77. *Ibid.,* p. 146.

tablished in the history of religions, let alone in nature and the variety of cultures, but which in theological perspective claims to be the supreme symbol in the Judeo-Christian tradition.[78]

Israel is the symbol of isolated, individualized, "elect" historical existence under God which corresponds to, or is typified by, the incarnation. Typology of the Old Testament as hermeneutical method [79] is legitimate as a phenomenology of this special form of historical existence. When R. Funk says that the parables are "the language event which brings the Kingdom near," [80] I want to say the same in other words when speaking of the mission of Jesus and the disciples *to* Israel as the recovery of the mission *of* Israel. The historical event that was Jesus and the Twelve was more than speaking parables; it was a parable. It was the symbolic confirmation of the mission of Israel. To say that this is borne out by the meaning of men-fishing in Biblical and post-Biblical Judaism would emphasize only one side, the element of continuity, which for Funk is the "spoken word" in a given language event. The crucial theological issue emerges only in the discontinuity, the newness, of the mission of Jesus and his Twelve, which corresponds to Funk's second language function, the "speaking word" as "medium of discovery." [81]

The original meaning of men-fishing was inseparably connected with the symbolism of Simon as Peter, the appointment of the Twelve, and the historical restriction to Jewish territory. It is no convincing counterargument to point out that Peter soon left Jerusalem, or that nowhere in Acts is Peter's priority explicitly justified as based on Jesus.[82] For Jerusalem remains a, though not the, center of

78. M. Goguel, *The Life of Jesus* (London: George Allen & Unwin, Ltd., 1933), p. 340, can strangely say both (1) that Jesus' choice of the Twelve had "quite transparent symbolic reasons," and (2) that "the number of twelve had no particular sacred character in his eyes"!

79. Cf. C. Westermann (ed.), *Essays on Old Testament Hermeneutics,* (John Knox Press, 1963).

80. "Saying and Seeing: Phenomenology of Language and the New Testament," *Journal of Bible and Religion,* Vol. 34 (1966), p. 207.

81. *Ibid.,* p. 201.

82. Kümmel, in *Heilsgeschehen und Geschichte,* p. 307. Cf. F. V. Filson, *Three Crucial Decades* (John Knox Press, 1963), pp. 57 ff. On Mary's

Christianity, even for the Antiochian Hellenists. And Peter's priority was not legalistically conceived, any more than the whole early Christian conception of apostolate was legalistically conceived as some contend in the light of the *shaliah* tradition. It is the fallacy of the Vatican Curia to conceive of the papacy primarily in legalistic rather than symbolic terms.

As former men-fishing disciples of John the Baptist, Simon knows, as does Jesus after submitting to John's baptism, what it is to be a "prepared people" (Luke 1:17) without, as in Qumran, getting separated as organized sect from the rest of Israel, dissociated from Temple and Jerusalem. Instead, Jesus and his men-fishing partners represent within Israel what the true Israel, the New Israel, the Israel of God (Gal. 6:16), should be, and always has been (not historically, but theologically, symbolically): the medium and means by which "knowledge of salvation" (Luke 1:77), light and life (v. 79), were to be spread to all.

When Israel adopts institutional forms, such as kingship, Temple, schools of wisdom, and the like, her status which was to be "light to the nations" (Isa. 49:6) becomes "like all the nations" (I Sam. 8:5, 20), and "the light of Israel . . . [becomes] a fire," that is, Israel is subjected to refinement (Isa. 10:17). The fisher of men himself gets fished. In the Israel-centered men-fishing ministry of Jesus and the Twelve more is at stake than mere mission to Israel. This "more" is not quantitative, as implied in the question whether Jesus did also and besides turn to Gentiles or worked in Gentile territory, but, rather, it is qualitatively more. It is "new": the newly conceived mission of Israel with a corresponding new key to the Scriptures (Luke 24:27, 32; cf. "according to the scriptures" in I Cor. 15:3 ff.) which quite early in Christian tradition became wrongly understood or applied.[83]

To account for the possibility that this newness of Jesus'

---

priority over Peter in interpreting the meaning and content of the apostolic commission, see "The Gospel of Mary," in Grant (ed.), *Gnosticism,* pp. 66–68.

83. Georgi, *Die Gegner des Paulus im Zweiten Korintherbrief,* pp. 265 ff.

mission, and with it the nature of "apostolic," men-fishing authority, may be misinterpreted, or at least variously interpreted allegedly commencing with Easter, is a task which properly belongs, not to the following section, but to this section on the historical Jesus. For it is my contention that the theological diversification in early Christianity is inadequately explained if the traditional perspective of the Tübingen school, or that of the "history of religions" school, is applied only to post-Easter primitive Christianity. To relegate all diversification to the subapostolic period, as Munck does, also is not fully convincing. It is my thesis that we must look for the cause of theological diversification in the very ministry of the historical Jesus and his Twelve. The symbolism of the appointment and partnership of the Twelve came to be interpreted as variously as the parables of Jesus, or as the meaning and mission of Israel came to be interpreted by each of the "schisms" in post-Biblical Judaism.

Recent critical studies on the nature and significance of gnosticism, rather than of its historical, cultural origins, have shown that gnosticism or syncretism was a complex phenomenon which grew in complexity to the degree that rabbi or priest, Qumran or Baptist member, Jesus or disciple, Paul or the rival "servant" of Christ, felt compelled to establish the identity and mission of the true Israel. To say with Koester that Jesus himself, and not merely the early church, was a thoroughly syncretistic phenomenon is an observation not so much of historical as of theological significance. This is true also of the significance of Goodenough's study of *Jewish Symbols in the Greco-Roman Period* for the understanding of contemporary Israel not merely as historical entity, subject to acculturation and engaged in apologetics, but also and primarily as religious body both sure of and in search of its true identity.

I would like to take Tillich's sentence, that "the telling of a parable [by] Jesus contains all the artistic potentialities of Christianity," [84] and modify it by saying that the "parable" of the historical ministry of Jesus and his

84. Tillich, *Systematic Theology*, Vol. III (1963), p. 201.

Twelve contains all the syncretistic potentialities of Christianity. The clear-cut division between church and gnosticism, still advocated in many quarters of scholarship, is indeed an anachronism. But to go on and sharply distinguish between the mission of the historical Jesus as eschatological, nonsyncretistic Kingdom ministry, and the early Hellenistic-Jewish Christian ministry as uneschatological and syncretistic seems just as anachronistic. I am not advocating a syncretistic milieu in which "all cats are gray." But I am insisting that we avoid for the study of the historical Jesus as over against the early church the same mistake we long made in pitching so-called normative Judaism against sectarian Judaism.

Scholem's studies have shown how anachronistic have been many of our conceptions of Rabbinical Judaism. To say that Jesus was a thoroughly syncretistic phenomenon means to me that *the* historical Jesus is as elusive as is *the* church of the New Testament period. The appearance of Antichrists, that is, of men-fishers who were guided by "another Jesus," a "different spirit," and a "different gospel" (II Cor. 11:4), is to me most plausible if, while fully conceding individual variation and distinct characteristics among early Christian "heresies," we consider as their source the actual ministry of the historical Jesus and the Twelve.

What does all this have to do with the interpretation of the disciples' task as men-fishing? The answer comes with the interpretation of the traditions of the mission charges preserved in three separate strands of the tradition, the Marcan (Mark 6:7-13; Luke 9:1-6), the Q source (Luke 10:1-12; Matt. 9:37 to 11:1),[85] and the Johannine version (John 4:35-38).[86] The purpose of this mission, the meaning of the commission given to the Twelve (or Seventy), and the interpretation of the meaning of the men-fishing metaphor are all part of the same question. As

85. Hahn, *Mission in the New Testament,* pp. 41–46. Cf. F. C. Grant, "The Mission of the Disciples," *Journal of Biblical Literature,* Vol. 35 (1916), pp. 293–314. See also Ladd, *Jesus and the Kingdom,* pp. 239–257, on "Jesus, Israel, and His Disciples."

86. Dodd, *Historical Tradition,* pp. 391–405.

with the call of the disciples and the either immediately (Mark 1:17; John 1:42; Luke 5:10) or soon following (Mark 3:13-19 and parallels) appointment to a task (fisher of men, apostle, "rock"), Peter and the Twelve are "most actively drawn into the service of [Jesus'] message and the proclamation of the kingdom's victory." [87] The crucial issue, however, is not the fact that Jesus permitted the Twelve to share in his mission,[88] but rather how this indubitable mission and partnership came to be interpreted not only after Easter, but even before then.

A. Schweitzer may have been wrong in the interpretation he advocated, but he was right in insisting that the call and commission of the disciples, like other "decisions of Jesus, were determined by dogmatic, eschatological considerations." [89] What they were after Easter as decisions of the Spirit or the Counselor is another matter. What they were before Easter depended entirely on the way Jesus not only made but personally enforced them. And here is where the full impact of the contention that Jesus himself was a syncretistic phenomenon lies. For emerging gospel traditions reflect, then, not merely some Western or Eastern Syrian against Galilean or Judean provenance, but also certain aspects of the historical Jesus and his partners. These aspects became differently interpreted or accentuated in each gospel tradition.

The fact that of the three or four *topoi*—that is, the stylized form, fixed content, and sequence—of the mission discourses of Jesus the first and/or concluding part, dealing with the disciples' commission, is the one "we can grasp with the least certainty" [90] should warn us that here, as in the important variations in the formulations of the Easter commissions,[91] the church has shown its heavy hand in in-

87. Bornkamm, *Jesus of Nazareth,* p. 149.

88. On Catholic interpretations, see D. M. Stanley, *The Apostolic Church in the New Testament* (The Newman Press, 1965), pp. 396 f.; R. Schnackenburg, *The Church in the New Testament* (Freiburg: Herder, 1965), pp. 126 f.

89. *The Quest of the Historical Jesus* (London: A. & C. Black, Ltd., 1945), p. 357.

90. Hahn, *Mission in the New Testament,* p. 43.

91. See below, pp. 193–96.

terpreting the meaning of the commission. The necessity for interpretation arose out of the contest of rival interpretations as to the correct or incorrect meaning of apostleship, of the mission of Israel, and with it of men-fishing. The possibility for divergent interpretations must be seen to have arisen not merely with the *kērygma* after Easter, but also with the historical Jesus. Jesus and his partners as teachers and preachers of the Kingdom in the various "forms" of sayings traditional to Israel's wise men, prophets, priests, and apocalypticists are no more and no less significant a new language event than when they act as exorcists, healers, or otherwise gifted charismatics, psychics, magicians, or the like. Whether by doing (*poiein*) or teaching (*didaskein*), in either case was it necessary to manifest the "speaking word" in the "spoken word," the "new" in the "old," its "true" Israel in the historical Israel.

What was the assurance of the Kingdom's presence in the person and conduct of the historical Jesus, which manifested itself in "signs and wonders" of both word and deed. that is, with authority, with newness, was later the assurance of the exaltation of Jesus as Lord which manifested itself in similar ways. It may be quite legitimate to distinguish between a Jesus *kērygma,* emphasizing the notion of Kingdom and the Parousia of Jesus as Son of Man, and a Christ *kērygma* with emphasis on exaltation, Lordship, and the like. But instead of deriving this difference, with all its conceded theological significance, from post-Easter gospel sources, we should see its basis in the historical Jesus, where both types of *kērygma* have their root. The independent sources for different types of Christology, soteriology, and their corresponding conceptions of men-fishing ministry, all feed on ultimately the syncretistic model of Jesus' historical ministry, on his and his partners' teaching and conduct in Israel.

Rewarding as it is to study the mission of Jesus and of his partners in the light of the gospel sources, thus highlighting certain features as they emerge in the Sayings source, the "miracle" or "sign" source, the Twelve source, the passion narrative tradition, and numerous other more or less hypothetical sources, we do not thereby arrive at the theological significance of the mission of the historical Jesus and his historical partners. And this does not come into view merely by interpreting an isolated simile (e.g., "disciple," "servant," [92] "fisher of men," etc.) as preserved in one tradition or another, or by simply asserting the historicity of the disciples' mission as reflected in one gospel source or another. What partnership with Jesus amounted to can be seen clearly only in the context and sequence of what Schweitzer called the "decisions of Jesus." For these led the partners to three important and new dimensions of their understanding of partnership which affected their partnership conduct in unexpected and different ways.

These three dimensions are (1) the deepened assurance of the partners' solidarity with Jesus and of Jesus' life as the sign of the Kingdom's presence; (2) the prediction of the necessary discontinuity of their partnership with him; (3) the promise of a renewed and transformed continuation of their partnership, and the assurance of ultimate reward besides uninterrupted partnership with him even in the age to come. The four "stages (Call, Choice, Mission, Consecration) in the relations of Jesus with His disciples" are important not primarily as historical sequences,[93] but as theological dimensions which, of course, presuppose "time." For in these "stages" we have an unfolding of the mission of Jesus, the growing awareness, understanding, recognition, of the mystery and yoke of the Kingdom, and thereby of the meaning of the mission of Israel, and of Jesus and his Twelve. Dibelius [94] saw in Jesus' decision to take "his followers [or "collaborators," p. 61] with him to Jerusalem, the one and only indication known to us of a development in the history of Jesus." And the interpretation of the meaning of men-fishing is affected by "the movement that Jesus set going."

What happens, then, to the Twelve, when their partner-

92. *Diakonia* is the guiding motif in T. W. Manson's study on *The Church's Ministry* (The Westminster Press, 1948).

93. A. M. Hunter, *The Work and Words of Jesus* (The Westminster Press, 1950), pp. 62 f.

94. M. Dibelius, *Jesus,* translated by C. B. Hedrick and F. C. Grant (The Westminster Press, 1949), p. 63.

ship leads them to witness the "poverty" (II Cor. 8:9), "weakness" (ch. 13:4), "obedience" (Phil. 2:8), "endurance" (Heb. 12:2), of Jesus, after witnessing and even sharing the message of salvation, of the Kingdom, to which God "bore witness by signs and wonders" (ch. 2:4), is not something unexpected. That only the Roman centurion and one of the robbers on the cross next to Jesus "had a hunch of what was going on in this death," [95] introduces an alien note when contrasting these two men with the Twelve's reaction to the cross. Not inability, let alone rejection, but unwillingness, "kicking against the goads" (Acts 26:14) as Paul did for a while, accounts for the temporary disruption of their partnership. The denial and flight of the Twelve, the "fishers of men," is a symbol of Israel's stubbornness or hardened heart in facing up to the Lord's "call" or "voice" to its mission. And as with Israel, so with the Twelve, it was not their belief that put up a barrier between them and him, but the refusal to live by "his faith" (Hab. 2:4), the refusal to live as Israel.

As the response to the call to discipleship and appointment to symbolize the Twelve was motivated not psychologically or historically, as form criticism has clearly shown, but theologically by their exposure to his preaching and other manifestations of his "special ability to effect the miraculous," [96] so also is the renewed but transformed continuation of their partnership after the temporary disruption motivated by two significant "events." One is the prayer of Jesus for the Twelve, for Peter, for Israel. The other is the Last Supper. Both are his gifts that match his demands for partnership. And the privileges and powers of that partnership cannot be had, let alone held, without accepting these gifts.

This gift and source of continuous newness and power in the word, the faith, the prayer, and the table of Jesus provides the direct link with the tradition of the exalted Lord and the commissions of the risen, exalted Jesus commencing at Easter. The men-fishing ministry as partnership in Jesus' word and deed becomes the ministry of "word and

95. E. Schweizer, *Neotestamentica*, p. 246.
96. Fuchs, *Studies of the Historical Jesus*, p. 61.

sacrament." That this ministry came to be understood and practiced in a narrow ecclesiastical and sacramental sense [97] may be due as much to the loss or lack of understanding of the parables of Jesus as to the breakdown of the Israel symbol in the ministry of Jesus and his partners. But this loss and breakdown should not be sought in, or explained by, the historical breakdown of relationships between church and synagogue. The fall of Jerusalem did at best accelerate and contribute to this, but not cause it. The same applies to the origin of gnosticism in Christianity.

In his treatment of what "the gift" was that Jesus gave to his partners at the Last Supper, J. Jeremias rightly points out two things. He calls attention to "the remarkable contrast between the universalistic emphasis" in Jesus' teaching, conduct, and also his Eucharistic words on the gift for "the many," on the one hand, and "the restricted nature of the small group to which Jesus offered this gift," on the other hand.[98] Furthermore, he points out that this contrast appears resolved when (or because) "through the appropriation of the forgiveness of sins the disciples become the redeemed community of the End time."

Helpful as this observation is, it is not altogether adequately evaluated. For the forgiveness of sins was appropriated also by all who submitted to John's baptism or who were deemed fit to become members of the new covenant community at Qumran. The difference in Jesus' way of resolving the contrast must not be seen in a different kind of gift, but in his own way of appropriating the gift and sharing the gift. It is not that one group did, and the other did not, have forgiveness, renewal, revelation, Kingdom, covenant, and the like, but Jesus had and shared a new mode of life based on this gift. Not the fact that forgiveness was appropriated, but the way in which and the purpose for which it was appropriated (as the transforming power of God's love and justice in Israel, symbol of re-

97. Bultmann, *Theology of the New Testament*, 2 vols. (Charles Scribner's Sons, 1951 and 1955), Vol. I, pp. 133 ff., 306 ff.; Vol. II, pp. 100 ff., 231 ff.

98. *The Eucharistic Words of Jesus*, pp. 236 f.

ligion and culture) makes up the uniqueness of that to which Jesus commissions and equips his disciples as partners in the men-fishing Kingdom ministry.

In Jesus' "avowal of abstinence" and invitation to "remember" him at the Last Supper, the disciples are not only assured of the end as outstanding yet near, but also called upon to test their ministry as to whether or not it is sure of its claim of doing the work of God. This test was no longer required periodically in the course and cycle of the liturgical year in the celebration of the significance of salvation history. The pilgrim's participation in the great Temple festivals brought him to confess his own and Israel's true identity. But for Jesus' partners this test was henceforth to be done "in spirit and in truth," that is, radically, rather than in the chronological sense incessantly. It was to be sought and met in the world by those "not of the world" rather than in the church. It was to be done by whatever means each one had at his disposal "in the state in which he was called" and to the degree of the measure of faith each received, rather than by any one single or particular means. That the latter does not by definition exclude institution, hierarchy, clergy, and the like, nor by Jesus' call of the Twelve include them as such, is an important point of departure.

For in Israel as the symbol of mediumship of eschatological revelation "men-fishing" retains a comprehensive connotation that in the later Gospels and epistles of the New Testament, whether originally or due to subsequent redaction, shows signs of getting broken up, fragmented, allegorized, as are other similes and parables of Jesus. The tendency grows of understanding the fishing metaphor in the domesticated, parochial sense of certain ecclesiastical, clerical activities. Patristic literature by and large confirms this tendency. The use of the fishing metaphor in early Christian art seems to be derived from sources other than Jesus' teaching; its early appearance in the catacombs suggests that it symbolized the individual's assurance of eternal life and ultimate salvation in much the same way that contemporary Jewish funerary and synagogal art interprets it.

Men-Fishing as Partnership with Jesus in the Gospel Traditions

The "Fisher of Men" Pericope. The fishing metaphor has been preserved, strictly speaking, in only one form of the gospel tradition, the special form or literary genre of "pronouncement story" dealing with Simon's and Andrew's [99] call to discipleship (Mark 1:16-18, par. Matt. 4:18-20). The immediately following pericope of the call of the sons of Zebedee, which likely in the pre-Marcan tradition already became combined with the call of the Johnson brothers, does not mention any simile besides that of "follow me." The pericope of the call of Levi (Mark 2:14; Matt. 9:9; Luke 5:27 f.) likewise has only the call to "follow." Luke 5:1-11 and John 21:1-19 are not only a different literary genre (legends), and on that ground alone must be analyzed separately, but also belong to traditions that are independent of each other as well as of Mark, and must be judged not so much in view of Mark, but on their own merit. The Marcan tradition speaks of "fishers of men," the Lucan tradition has *zōgrein,* "to catch, or bring alive," and the Johannine tradition uses only the "rock" motif in the call of Simon, and the call *poimainein,* "to feed, or tend, the sheep," in the Easter commission.

In view of only the variety of interpretations offered about Mark 1:16-20, let alone the Lucan and Johannine parallel traditions, Taylor exclaimed, "It is astonishing how widely appraisals of [this] story can differ." [100] The alternative between a purely form-critical approach [101] and one that allows for historical authenticity of vivid details as due to "Petrine reminiscences" [102] seems forced and

99. On the order "Simon and Andrew," "Andrew and Simon," and the separation of the two names in various parts of the tradition, see Dodd, *Historical Tradition,* pp. 304 f. See also P. M. Peterson, *Andrew, Brother of Simon Peter* (Leiden: Brill, 1958).

100. V. Taylor, *The Gospel According to St. Mark* (London: Macmillan & Co., Ltd., 1953), p. 168.

101. Bultmann, *The History of the Synoptic Tradition,* pp. 56 f., 62 f. See also L. Brun, "Die Berufung der ersten Jünger Jesu in der evangelischen Tradition," *Symbolae Osloenses,* Vol. 11 (1932), pp. 35–54.

102. F. C. Grant, *The Gospels, Their Origin and Their Growth* (Harper & Brothers, 1957), p. 111, *passim.* So also Taylor and many others.

fruitless to me. In the end, both approaches rest their case on the assumption that the pericope not only has something to do with the apostle, but ultimately incorporates something of an eye- or ear-witness, depending on whether one begins with the scenic details or the metaphor of the logion. In either case, the theological issue is not that of the reliability or authenticity of one over against the other. What matters is the interpretation of the intended meaning of the pericope, that is, of this form of tradition, as a whole.

The intention or tendency of this pericope does not come into focus by the eyewitness details of Peter's reminiscences nor by the fishing metaphor in the saying of Jesus whose exact and authentic form we cannot reconstruct, either. Form critics now also among modern Catholic scholars speak of the Marcan pattern of the call as having been shaped by early Christian kerygmatic and paraenetic traditions.[103] But what do these traditions contribute to the understanding of this pericope? The standard answer is that the stylized account of the call to discipleship symbolizes the meaning of radical obedience which the Lord demands from the time a person, any person, first hears his call.

But this yields nothing yet for the interpretation of the fishing metaphor. Are all called to be fishers of men? If so, the call and task of discipleship expressed here should be seen in the context of other traditions of the narrative or sayings genre which speak of discipleship as partnership.[104] But if not, what did the traditions take to be the specific meaning of this call to the task of men-fishing if it applies only to certain leaders? How does their call and special commission relate to the call to which all believers must respond? Besides the hypothetical Twelve source,[105] was there a kerygmatic, catechetical tradition on the topic of special discipleship, special calls and tasks? The reason

103. A. Schulz, *Nachfolgen und Nachahmen* (Studien zum A. u. N. T., No. 6; Munich: Kösel, 1962), pp. 109 f.

104. See below, pp. 177 ff.

105. W. L. Knox, *The Sources of the Synoptic Gospels,* 2 vols. (Cambridge: Cambridge University Press, 1953 and 1957), Vol. I, pp. 17–31.

for so widely different appraisals of this pericope lies in the fact that interpreters, both modern and ancient canonical and extracanonical, see the story in different contexts. Next to the context of the life of Jesus and of the church, that of the Old Testament, and its bearing on the interpretation of Jesus and the church, is the most significant.

The call to discipleship in the pre-Marcan tradition has four distinct features which in varying degrees determine the theological interpretation. There is first the scene itself. Part One of this study sought to clarify the economic image associated with fishing in Galilee. But here we now face the interpretation of the theological implications for the fishermen to be called by Jesus to follow him, to be eyewitnesses from the beginning, moreover to be called to "active participation in the soteriological work of the age of fulfillment." [106] In the Lucan and Johannine traditions the scenes or historical settings of the disciples' commission have been amplified by information about their previous acquaintance with Jesus in connection with their association with the Baptist (John 1:35 ff.), or by the dual emphasis in Luke that Jesus had preached in their hearing and led them to a miraculous fish catch (Luke 5:1 ff.; John 21:1 ff.) before calling and commissioning them.

Form critics speak of the fishing scenes, with or without a miraculous fish catch, as "ideal scene," that is, a production of the oral tradition which has to rest either on eyewitness or on the "fishers of men" metaphor as its authentic nucleus, or on a combination of the two. But the form critics have thereby provided us only with a nonetheless important criterion by which to judge historical narratives. They have not provided us with a criterion for the pericope's interpretation as to its historicity or as to its theological significance. Form criticism is not theology.

Secondly, there is the call itself. The call of the Lord, grace invading the world, grace becoming an event, a new salvation history or new exodus—these are some of the headlines used to describe the significance of the call.

106. T. A. Burkill, *Mysterious Revelation* (Cornell University Press, 1963), p. 32.

Here again we face several issues. One is that of the names and their sequence. We have to weigh the possibility that Andrew, who elsewhere in the early tradition was dissociated from Peter, for other but still theological reasons was here associated with Peter, who may have been originally the sole recipient of the call, or at any rate the only one to whom the metaphor "fisher of men" applied.

Then there is the element of suddenness in the call. Most commentators conclude that the story either lacks psychological motivation, characteristic of the pronouncement stories whose sole purpose is to witness to Christ, or that suddenness is a characteristic feature of accounts of the manifestation of the dynamics of revelation. Conversion is another word for the experience of what Tillich called "the divine Spirit [in] the ambiguities of life." [107] At any rate the crucial question is, What transformation, what newness of life was given and demanded when Jesus is depicted here as the medium of the eschatological revelation, or in other words when the traditional element of "the Sudden in the Scriptures" [108] is applied here to Jesus' activity?

This leads right over into another but related issue of the possible influence of Old Testament models on the literary formation and theological associations given to the "call" stories. Since patristic exegesis it has been customary to refer to Elijah's call of Elisha (I Kings 19:19-21) as a model in the minds of those who first shaped this pericope. Schulz finds the *heilsgeschichtliche Vorbilder* (salvation-history models) expressing a certain Christology and giving the whole pericope its *Sachzusammenhang* (material or theological coherence).[109] Not theological coherence or continuity, but theological critique, that is, the determination of the measure of discontinuity between the old and the new, is decisive here. The same was true when earlier we spoke of the whole mission of Jesus and his Twelve as a symbol for the recovered meaning of the mission of Israel.

107. Tillich, *Systematic Theology,* Vol. III, pp. 162 ff., esp. p. 220.
108. The title of a study by D. Daube (Leiden: Brill, 1964).
109. A. Schulz, *Nachfolgen und Nachahmen,* pp. 101, 109 f.

Thirdly, there is the issue of the task mentioned to which the call leads. The fishing metaphor has long been said to allude to Jer. 16:16 in much the same way that "Follow me" was to be a deliberate allusion to Elijah's call. In the wake of recent studies about the role of Old Testament "testimonies" as part of the earliest gospel traditions, it has been argued that the second half of Mark 1:17 and Matt. 4:19 are actual quotations or intended references to Jer. 16:16 and Ezek. 47:10.[110] This view has been challenged on linguistic grounds.[111] Other recent studies on Old Testament allusions in Mark and Matthew see no trace here at all or simply ignore this pericope.[112] What men-fishing here means cannot be determined adequately by this pericope alone. What it does say clearly about both the traditional motif of "following" and "fishing" is that the order and endowment do not come directly from God, but from Jesus as the medium of God's eschatological revelation.

The fourth feature is the early pre-Marcan combination first of Mark 1:16-18 with vs. 19 f., and then of this whole pericope with the Capernaum cycle (vs. 21-34) which Luke preserves (Luke 4:31-41) except that Luke puts the call at the end instead of at the beginning of this period. Matthew follows a totally different pattern by combining the call immediately with one of the traditional "generalizing summaries" [113] and then the Sermon on the Mount. Like Luke, the Fourth Gospel places the call of the fishermen (John 1:35-42) at the transition of Jesus' ministry from Judea to Galilee (v. 43; cf. Luke 4:44; 5:1). The call of Levi (Mark 2:14; Matt. 9:9; Luke 5:27 f.) likewise stood at the opening of another cycle in the pre-Marcan tradition which W. L. Knox called "conflict stories." [114]

110. C. H. Bird, "Some *gar* Clauses in St. Mark's Gospel," *Journal of Theological Studies,* N. S. 4 (1953), pp. 171–187, esp. pp. 174–176.

111. M. E. Thrall, *The Greek Particles in the New Testament* (New Testament Tools and Studies, No. 3; Wm. B. Eerdmans Publishing Company, 1962), pp. 42–50.

112. A. Suhl, *Die Funktion der Alttestamentlichen Zitate und Anspielungen im Markusevangelium* (Gütersloh: Mohn, 1965); Stendahl, *The School of St. Matthew.*

113. See below, pp. 196–198.

114. *Sources of the Synoptic Gospels,* Vol. I, pp. 8–16.

What Keck does for the position that the pericope of the appointment of the Twelve (Mark 3:13-19) occupies as the opening section of material combining various traditions (chs. 3:13 to 5:43, or 6:6) [115] we are indicating here about the position that the pericope of the call to discipleship (ch. 1:16-20) occupies as introduction to a larger unit (chs. 1:16 to 3:12). Even before Mark the "fisher of men" pericope became associated with two or more cycles of traditional material about activities of Jesus and his partners.

Keck speaks of two kinds of material in Mark: "one closely related to the Palestinian scene and the message of Jesus in its native setting, the other relatively unrelated to Jesus' message." [116] One shows Jesus as teacher, the other as exorcist, healer. That Jesus' partners were related to both streams of the tradition will be shown below. Whether or not the two kinds of material became combined before Mark to some kerygmatically or catechetically determined cycle is quite possible but must remain, of course, hypothetical. No less hypothetical is the thesis of Gaechter, Taylor, and others who see in these early cycles of events and sayings nothing but the original authentic order based on Petrine testimonies.

The theological significance to be derived from such pre-Marcan patterns of "disciple" pericopes as the opening section to cycles of the sayings and actions of Jesus, however, can only be that the called and commissioned disciples are immediately related to Jesus' multiform ministry. The often made inference that the disciples, called early to be his collaborators, did not at once participate actively but had first to serve a kind of apprenticeship can only be based on what the present Evangelists seem to affirm. But the pre-Marcan gospel traditions know of no such thing. When the Fourth Gospel depicts the disciples as independent partners only after Easter, and when the

115. See L. E. Keck, "Mark 3:7-12 and Mark's Christology," *Journal of Biblical Literature,* Vol. 84 (1965), pp. 341–358. Besides the "boat material" (Mark 4:35-41; 5:1-20) and the material referring to the touch of Jesus (ch. 5:21-43), we have the parable cycle (ch. 4:1 ff.) and the "generalizing summaries" (chs. 3:7-19; 4:33 f.).

116. *Ibid.,* pp. 350 f.

Synoptics depict them as getting actively engaged, disengaged, and newly engaged in different stages, we are facing, then, in both cases secondary but significant theological constructions of the subapostolic age.

The traditions employed by the later Evangelists disclose a different picture. Call to discipleship is call to partnership. The full nature of this partnership and all it entails may be unfolded in the progressive disclosure of the mystery of the Kingdom and power of God in the life of Jesus. But to speak of progression here easily misleads one into temporal or developmental psychological speculations which divert attention from the central theological issue: the experience of, and partnership in, mediating the eschatological revelation of God as salvation. The first call is substantively the same as the second call after Easter. Jesus the caller, and himself the called, together with the disciples, the called and themselves then callers, are the symbol of the New Israel, the community of the called and the calling, the fished and the fishing, who thus manifest the truth of God as power.

Underlying all four features of the "fishers of men" pericope and its traditional setting is the crucial theological question: What does following Jesus mean if it entails collaboration, cooperation, or partnership in what he is, says, or does? What does it mean that all believers must follow Jesus' call, similar to all believers' receiving the Spirit, while certain individuals are given specific tasks, similar to the Spirit's being given "more" to some than to other believers?

Two observations can now be combined: the more or less clear and deliberate Old Testament associations, indicative of the paradoxical connection between the church and Israel's salvation history, and the paradoxical contrast between all believers as called and endowed, and specially endowed leaders who are not necessarily identical with the charismatics or psychics of the community.[117] Bult-

117. See O. Linton, *Das Problem der Urkirche in der Neueren Forschung* (Uppsala: Almquist, 1932), esp. pp. 206–211. So also H. F. von Campenhausen, "Recht und Gehorsam in der ältesten Kirche," in *Aus der Frühzeit des Christentums* (Tübingen: Mohr, 1963), pp. 1–29, esp. pp. 13 f.

mann rightly saw in both these observations two different expressions of the church's understanding of itself as an eschatological community.[118]

In the sense that Mark 1:16-18 is a stylized, symbolic account of the call out of the world and into fellowship with Jesus which reaches every believer, the pericope reflects the church's self-understanding as a body of believers. This self-understanding however was to be tested and made explicit. In other words, it had to be lived. The theological issue is how the church, as the community of followers of Jesus, would manifest its life, its call, its exclusivity in the world; moreover, what, if anything, did the historical Jesus, the living and the coming Christ, have to do with all this?

If, however, Mark 1:16-18 is understood as also, and perhaps originally, giving a stylized account of how specially designated individuals came to be endowed with special gifts and authority,[119] then we face the same theological issue, this time only in terms of the church's leadership, hierarchy, or institutions. The special character of Simon's and Andrew's endowment, the task of being fishers of men, was then none other than that which also set Jesus apart from other prophets, or which set Israel apart from other religious nations: the God-given ability of witnessing to the origin and scope of this exclusivity, this eschatological character of the common "call." The "royal priesthood" of all believers does not exclude specially called "servants" or "fishers of men."

We may thus speak of the dual character of the "fisher of men" pericope. There is not an either-or about this stylized account of the call: either applicable to all believers or only to Simon and Andrew. It applies to both the church and its ministry. In Mark 1:17, as in the various accounts of Paul's call to apostleship, there may indeed be more or less clearly discernible traces of more or less consciously attempted connections between apostleship or

118. *Theology of the New Testament,* Vol. II, pp. 95 ff.

119. Stylized accounts of Paul's call are found in Acts 9:15-16; 22:15; 26:16-18, and in his own letters. For an interpretation, see Munck, *Paul and the Salvation of Mankind,* pp. 11–35.

men-fishing on the one hand and special ministries of prophet, wise man, priest, and others as known in Biblical and post-Biblical Judaism on the other hand. But the critical theological issue again is whether or not the special ministries of the old or the New Israel were properly executed. The precedent, the norm of its propriety, was for the New Israel, the Twelve, the "royal priesthood" of the new covenant, none other than Jesus. But since he himself was subject to different interpretations, identification of the true vs. the false Christ, of the true vs. the false Spirit, or of true vs. false gospel was the prerequisite task in finding criteria by which to discern between true and false ministry.

The theological legitimacy of making the fishing metaphor serve as symbol for an ecclesiastical office is not per se questionable. Questionable is, and has to be, whether the metaphor thus applied was rightly interpreted. But who is to decide that? The question is less puzzling if, instead, we ask on what grounds or by what standards one is to judge whether men-fishing was engaged in properly, regardless of whether by all believers or by the charismatic or institutional authority figure. The extracanonical gospel traditions are clear proof, besides the undercurrent of controversy within the New Testament itself,[120] that this question was answered differently by different believers and church leaders in different parts and at different times of Christianity's early expansion.

Three basic types of theological answers seem to have emerged within New Testament times, all three represented in the New Testament, while each in itself may have a bundle of divergent groups and schools. First, there is the gnostic, enthusiastic type. It may be best represented by the mysterious "wise fisherman" of the Gospel of Thomas, logion 8. Traces of this type may be seen in the tradition of the inner circle of three or five disciples among the Twelve. For only this inner circle witnesses Jesus' transfiguration, receives esoteric instruction about the end

120. See the false prophets and teachers, the wolves and Antichrists in the Gospels and Acts; the false apostles and "dogs" from the letters of Paul to those sent to the seven churches in Rev., chs. 2 and 3.

of the world, is present at certain miracles. This type may be indicated by the Zebedee-sons' request for present assurance of eschatological glory. They are those to whom Jesus' promise seems to be addressed, after he has cursed the fig tree, that they too will do what has been done to this fig tree. Some of the commissions to apostleship that speak of powers over serpents and scorpions, gifts of translations to heaven, and supernatural powers of mystical insights and allegorical exegesis of the Old Testament—these and other features, separate or combined, seem to have given rise to one kind of "fisher of men," who could claim direct descent from the historical Jesus.

The second type is perhaps best illustrated by Peter, as legislative and executive head of a church, who by laying on of hands secures or authorizes legitimacy and orthodoxy. This type is also represented by the image of Paul in Acts; [121] by Paul as transmitter of the deposit of faith through the laying on of hands in the pastoral epistles; [122] by the redactor of the Fourth Gospel by the inclusion of John, ch. 21, establishing Peter there in a position similar to that of Diotrephes as over against the "elder," the author of The Third Letter of John.[123] Problematic in all these documents is not the substance of men-fishing as ecclesiastical activity, but its theological justification.

Finally, there is the type best illustrated by the Pauline conception of the nature of apostleship, and of the Synoptic and Johannine traditions of discipleship. Of one of these traditions, the Q source, Koester said that it had "domesticated" the gnosticizing tendencies inherent in other and earlier gospel traditions. This third type became the or, rather, an "orthodox" view of the men-fishing, apostolic ministry in the church. But even in the canon of the New Testament this view of "orthodoxy" has to contend with other views which we outlined in the first two types.

By reviewing the interpretations of discipleship or partnership with Jesus in the gospel traditions other than the

121. See Käsemann, *Essays on New Testament Themes,* pp. 89 ff., 141 ff.

122. *Ibid.,* pp. 85–89.

123. E. Käsemann, "Ketzer und Zeuge," in *Exegetische Versuche und Besinnungen,* Vol. I (Göttingen: Vandenhoeck, 1960), pp. 168–187.

restricted "form" or tradition of the pronouncement story we intend to show in the following section how "orthodox" and "heterodox" interpretations of ministry could and did emerge from the common stock of gospel traditions. It is one thing to say that historically all these traditions could claim to go back to the historical Jesus and the Twelve; it is another thing to say that theologically only some but not others can claim to represent the authentic Jesus, and hence authentic, legitimate ministry.

Other pericopes dealing with discipleship that belong to the category of "pronouncement stories" or "biographical apothegms" [124] are the following: contact with prospective disciples other than the Twelve as in Luke 9:57-62, par Matt. 8:19-22. To this also belongs the tradition of Jesus' relation to his family and the saying about "true relatives" as in Mark 3:31-35 and its parallels in Matthew and Luke, but also in John 7:3 ff., and in the extracanonical traditions of Thomas, logion 99; II Clem. 9:11; and the Ebionite Gospel.[125] Then we have the pericope on Mary and Martha (Luke 10:38-42; cf. John 12:1-3), which reflects on different values of different kinds of ministry. There is also the pericope of the "strange exorcist" (Mark 9:38-40; Luke 9:49 f., with the logion quoted also in Pap. Oxyr. 1224 [126]) and the instruction to the Twelve condemning their vindictive attitude toward the inhospitable Samaritans (Luke 9:52-56). Another disciple instruction follows the incident of the rich man's refusal to follow Jesus (Mark 10:17 ff. and parallels). This pericope more so perhaps than any other was variously quoted and understood in the extracanonical tradition. Finally, one other group of pericopes belong to this category of biographical apothegms: the controversies over the disciples' conduct, such as eating with publicans and sinners (Mark 2:15-17 and parallels; cf. also Pap. Oxyr. 1224 [127]), the failure to observe the rules of fasting (Mark 2:18-22 and parallels; cf.

124. Bultmann, *The History of the Synoptic Tradition,* pp. 11–69. See also Dodd, *Historical Tradition,* pp. 302–312.

125. Hennecke, *New Testament Apocrypha,* Vol. I p. 158, Sec. 5.

126. *Ibid.,* p. 114.

127. *Ibid.,* p. 114.

Thomas, logion 75 and 104), of ritual purity (Mark 7:1-23 and parallels also among extracanonical traditions), and of the Sabbath ordinance (Mark 2:23-28 and parallels).

Discipleship in the Sayings of Jesus. Here we must distinguish form-critically between various kinds, types, or "forms" of sayings or logia. Furthermore, the narrow form-critical analysis must be expanded to include the early combination of different types of sayings of Jesus into larger units, similar to what was observed above in the narrative material. This broader form of form criticism has been called *Gattungskritik,* of which we have two recent examples in the work of M. Smith's analysis of the gospel "sermons" [128] and J. M. Robinson's study of the Q source as *Gattung,* i.e., a larger literary unit that incorporates various "forms" of logia.[129] Epistles and apocalypses are other such *Gattungen.*

1. *Similes and Other Sayings.* As wisdom teacher, Jesus is reported to have spoken of his disciples' partnership with him in the form of similes and parables. Among the similes and metaphors that apply mutually or alternately to Jesus and his disciples Jeremias lists, besides "fishers of men," those of harvest laborers, scribe's associates, shepherder's aids, and stewards.[130] In one of "the unknown sayings of Jesus" [131] the "money changer" metaphor is applied to them. Dodd comes from three different directions at the same problem. He finds in the Fourth Gospel seven parabolic sayings, similar to the Synoptic tradition, in which Jesus spoke of his (and possibly also of his disciples') role in metaphoric terms (see John 3:29; 5:19-20; 8:35; 10:1-5; 11:9 f.; 12:24; 16:21).[132]

128. *Tannaitic Parallels to the Gospels* (*Journal of Biblical Literature,* Monograph Series, Vol. VI; 1951), pp. 78–114.

129. Robinson, "*Logoi Sophōn,*" in *Zeit und Geschichte,* Bultmann *Festschrift,* pp. 77–96.

130. *The Parables of Jesus,* pp. 214 ff.

131. See Hennecke, *New Testament Apocrypha,* Vol. I, p. 88, No. 5: "Be ye competent money-changers!" If the metaphor is seen in the context of parallel metaphors cited in Plato's *Sophist* (see above, p. 13), a more comprehensive meaning than that advocated by Jeremias (*The Parables of Jesus,* p. 217) presents itself. In fact, on the metaphoric level, "money changers" and "men-fishers" appear to be synonyms.

132. *Historical Tradition,* pp. 366–387.

In his examination of the fourteen sayings common to John and the Synoptics,[133] Dodd includes sayings from different "forms" (macarisms, admonitions, etc.). But the result again shows the disciples referred to in such metaphors as servants, emissaries (John 13:16, 20), followers (chs. 1:43; 12:26; 21:22), and executives (ch. 20:23), as well as partners in prayer (chs. 14:13 f.; 16:23 f.), or generally subject to the dynamics of the new revelation expressed in the images of birth (ch. 3:3), wind (v. 8), the love and preservation of life (ch. 12:25). All of this, however, is predicated upon man's response to the medium of the divine revelation (chs. 3:18; 5:30; 6:38; 10:15; 12:47; 17:2). Hearing, seeing, believing, or knowing what God does in Jesus is to become a partner in doing the work of God.

In a critique of Bultmann's category of "I-sayings," Dodd [134] lists sayings "referring to the situation, mission or destiny of the disciples" which to him are "as much a 'you-saying' as an 'I-saying.' " Sayings in this category are characterized by what Dodd calls an "intermingling of figurative and direct expressions," which he also observes in Paul. Besides the "fishers of men," he lists the following metaphors: sheep among wolves (Luke 10:3); salt (Matt. 5:13); light (v. 14); enduring in trials (Luke 22:28); gathered harvest (v. 31) rather than harvesters! In this group he also counts the marcarism about the disciples' eyewitness (Luke 10:23). Dodd rightly dissociates these sayings from other "you-sayings" which do not refer to the disciples' historical partnership, but only to their future destinies. But whether he is justified in excluding from these "you-sayings" what he himself calls "the large body of precepts for [the disciples'] conduct" [135] seems to me as misleading and wrong here as it would be in the interpretation of the parables of Jesus.

Besides brief sayings which largely in metaphoric form refer to the disciples' involvement with Jesus as the medium of the eschatological revelation, one could list as a separate form certain parables. Thanks to Jeremias' criti-

133. *Ibid.*, pp. 335–365.
134. *Ibid.*, p. 398.
135. *Ibid.*, p. 398, n. 3.

cal study of *The Parables of Jesus*[136] we see more clearly now the role that parables and their metaphors played in the development of various theological conceptions of the church's ministry in the New Testament. But it is misleading when Jeremias excludes a number of parables from his section on "realized discipleship" in the teaching of Jesus, and at the same time includes here the parable of the great fish from logion 8 of the Gospel of Thomas. For this lends itself to confusing again the formal and material criteria for the interpretation of parable traditions.

2. *Legal Sayings and Church Rules.*[137] These sayings also contain interpretations of the nature and extent of the disciples' partnership with Jesus. To this formal category belong passages on church order (Mark 9:33 ff. and its Q-source parallels in Matt., ch. 18, and the Lucan parallels), on the disciples' mission (Mark 6:8-11 and parallels), and on the disciples' authority for disciplinary action (Matt. 16:18-19; 18:18). This form of men-fishing and its variations are all the more important as the whole question of the disciples' partnership with the historical Jesus before Easter inevitably raises the question whether Jesus founded the church, and to what degree men-fishing was an activity associated with some kind of institution or sect, however eschatologically interpreted. The Fourth Gospel incorporates these traditions of "legal sayings and church rules" only in the Easter narrative, and very sparingly and in significantly altered form in the farewell discourse.

3. *Prophetic and Apocalyptic Sayings.*[138] In these, Jesus appears more like an apocalyptic prophet than a wisdom teacher and a scribe acting as legal arbitrator or legislator. According to the tradition of post-Biblical Judaism, apocalyptic sayings may well be related to, rather than contrasted with, the sayings of priests and wise men.[139] One of

136. See especially his sections on "change of audience" (pp. 33–42), on "the hortatory use of parables" (pp. 42–48), on "the influence of the church situation," especially its missionary and organizational needs (pp. 48–66), and on the changed setting (pp. 96 ff.).

137. Bultmann, *The History of the Synoptic Tradition,* pp. 130–150.

138. *Ibid.,* pp. 108–130. On the Johannine parallels see Dodd, *Historical Tradition,* pp. 407–413.

139. See Russell, *Jewish Apocalyptic,* pp. 173–177, on apocalypticist in relation to priest and wise man respectively.

the forms of apocalyptic sayings are the macarisms or beatitudes concerning one's present or future share in salvation. Threats or curses over the loss of one's share are but the other side of the same coin. Apocalyptic sayings in the mouth of Jesus apply in almost every instance to all believers. Only in a few instances do the texts seem to refer to a special group of disciples.

These instances are not a fixed number, since they change in the process of the tradition's interpretation by the Evangelists. Mark 8:38, and the Q parallels Luke 12:8 f. and Matt. 10:32 f. (cf. II Tim. 2:12; Rev. 3:5; II Clem. 3:2) refer to either all believers or especially the appointed leaders of the church, as called to "confess" [140] and not to "deny" him. Those commissioned to serve as itinerant ministers are advised to pronounce the symbolic judgment of God on those who refuse to receive or welcome them (Mark 6:11, par. Matt. 10:14 and Luke 9:5; 10:10-12; cf. Matt. 25:34-46; [141] III John 5-10). The exclusion of the workers of iniquity (*ergatai adikias* or *anomias*) from the Kingdom can refer to all believers or, more likely, to special ministers (Matt. 7:23; Luke 13:27; cf. II Clem. 4:5; Justin Martyr, Apol. I, 16:11. See also Matt. 13:41-43; Rev. 22:11-15).

Very instructive in this connection is the series of "woes" pronounced over the scribes, especially in the Matthean version (Matt. 23:8-10) which by its composition applies these threats to some early Jewish-Christian form of scribal ministry.[142] The same change in application from Israel's ministry to that known in the church has been

140. On the different nuances of the metaphoric use of *homologein* (similar to those in the use of the fishing metaphor), see O. Michel, art. "*homologeō*," *TWNT*, Vol. V (1954), pp. 206 ff. On the important distinction between a "confession" and a credal, catechetical statement, see F. Hahn's review in the preface to his edition of A. Seeberg, *Der Katechismus der Urchristenheit* (Theol. Bücherei, Vol. 26; Munich: Kaiser, 1966), pp. xix f.

141. See J. R. Michaels, "Apostolic Hardships and Righteous Gentiles," *Journal of Biblical Literature*, Vol. 84 (1965), pp. 27–37, on other New Testament parallels to Matt. 25:31–46.

142. See E. Haenchen, "Matthäus 23," in *Gott und Mensch* (Tübingen: Mohr, 1965), pp. 29–54; G. Strecker, *Der Weg der Gerechtigkeit* (Forschungen zur Rel. und Lit. d. A. und N. T., No. 82; Göttingen: Vandenhoeck, 1962), pp. 37 f. and 216 f.

observed in the tradition of the parable interpretation. Apocalyptic symbols and metaphors, which in the parabolic teaching of Jesus may or may not have had any traditional association with certain kinds of leadership in Israel, became applied to certain roles of the church's ministry as over against all believers. The best examples are the three parables that refer to a master's or landlord's relation to his servants, to his steward, or to his householder: (1) Mark 13:34-37, par. Luke 12:35-38, the parable of the doorkeeper; (2) Matt. 24:45-51, par. Luke 12:42-46, the parable of the servant entrusted with supervision; and (3) Matt. 25:14-30, par. Luke 19:12-27, and the Nazarene Gospel,[143] about the parable of the talents. The parable of the shepherd (John 10:1-5) also belongs in this context.[144] The metaphors and symbols may have "facilitated [the] transferences," [145] but this does not interpret the theology that indulged in and promoted them.

Another form of the apocalyptic sayings, which Bultmann calls "apocalyptic predictions," contains warnings about pending persecutions and opposition which either all believers or the church's leaders will have to face (Mark 13:9 ff. and parallels). It is in this tradition that we find warnings about false teachers or prophets vigorously engaged in rival activities within the church during the period preceding "the end." [146] The tradition peculiar to Matthew preserved two such warnings (chs. 7:15; 24:11) which other traditions also reflect (Mark 13:21 f., par. Matt. 24:23 f.; cf. I John 2:18; 4:1; I Tim. 4:1; Acts 20:29 f.; Rev. 2:2, *passim;* 19:20; II Thess. 2:8-10; Didache 16:4; Justin Martyr, Dial. 35:3). The Qumran Teacher's contest with the rival fishermen in Jerusalem and the Baptist's denunciation of "the brood of vipers" provide the evidence that apocalyptic language was traditionally applied to false teachers, priests, or other leaders in Israel. On the "sifting" of the disciples, see p. 192.

143. Hennecke, *New Testament Apocrypha,* Vol. I, p. 149, No. 18.

144. Dodd, *Historical Tradition,* pp. 382–385.

145. Jeremias, *The Parables of Jesus,* p. 66.

146. On the implied differing interpretations of Spirit, see R. Scroggs, "The Exaltation of the Spirit by some Early Christians," *Journal of Biblical Literature,* Vol. 84 (1965), pp. 359 ff., esp. p. 363.

These apocalyptic sayings find their way into early Christian catechisms[147] and church orders.[148] The latter are more likely to emphasize the roles that the church's officers play in the life of the community, while catechisms by nature include all believers. But in either case the tradition has developed, each along fixed lines, certain numbers and sequences of *topoi,* i.e., subject matters presented in a fixed style and substance. Furthermore, the believer's, or the church leader's active participation in doing the work of God, and the rewards for such work, are traditionally defined along two lines: the participation and reward in the present and those in the age or world to come. To recognize the continuity and the discontinuity between the present and future age is an important task.

While we have a goodly number of critical studies on the call to and the nature of discipleship,[149] on the institution of the Twelve,[150] and on the nature of the disciples' mission,[151] we do not yet have a comprehensive study of the meaning of the symbols and metaphors used in the *topoi* on the believer's, or the leader's, active participation in

147. C. H. Dodd, "The Primitive Catechism and the Sayings of Jesus," in *New Testament Essays,* pp. 106–118. For the epistles, see Selwyn (ed.), *The First Epistle of St. Peter,* pp. 363–466. See also above, n. 140, on Seeberg.

148. As influential pattern in early Christian literature, see G. Bornkamm, *Die Vorgeschichte des sogenannten Zweiten Korintherbriefes* (Sitzungsber. d. Heid. Ak. d. Wiss., Phil.-hist. Kl., Jg. 1961; Heidelberg: Winter, 1961), pp. 24–36.

149 E. Schweizer, *Lordship and Discipleship* (Studies in Biblical Theology, No. 28; London: SCM Press, Ltd., 1960); W. Bieder, *Die Berufung im Neuen Testament* (Abh. z. Theol. d. A. u. N. T., No. 38; Zurich: Zwingli, 1961); B. Gerhardsson, *Memory and Manuscript* (Uppsala, 1961), pp. 324 ff. For a Catholic study, see Schulz, *Nachfolgen und Nachahmung.* For a general and comparative study of Greek and Biblical traditions about "following after" and "the imitation of God," see H. Kosmala's two essays in the *Annual of the Swedish Theological Institute,* Vol. II (Leiden: Brill, 1963), pp. 38–85, and Vol. III (1964), pp. 65–110.

150. For a concise review, see B. Rigaux, "Die 'Zwölf' in Geschichte und Kerygma," in *Der historische Jesus und der kerygmatische Christus,* edited by H. Ristow and K. Matthiae (Berlin: Evgl. Verlagsanstalt, 1961), pp. 468–486. See also the works of G. Klein and W. Schmithals cited above in Ch. IV, n. 56 and n. 57, and the essay by D. Flusser referred to earlier, Ch. II, n. 60. More popular studies are E. J. Goodspeed, *The Twelve* (John C. Winston Company, 1957); W. Barclay, *The Master's Men* (Abingdon Press, 1959) and *Fishers of Men* (The Westminster Press, 1966).

151. F. Hahn, *Mission in the New Testament,* esp. pp. 41–46.

and reward for partnership and cooperation with God.[152] The passive reception of the eschatological reward is one thing, similar to the passive elements that make up part of the eschatological faith and hope in every believer.[153] But active participation and partnership, both in this life and in the world to come, is another thing. Of the many metaphors applied to the partnership activities in the present, only three, listed here, are used also for the future, with two of the three explicitly stated as forms of partnership that are definitely not to be realized "before the time." The Christological basis for this argument is that Jesus in his historical ministry did not use them either.

The three terms are "judging" (*krinein*), "shepherding" (*poimainein*), and "reigning" (*basileuein*). It is clear from the context of Rev. 2:26-28 that *poimainein* is really a specification of *basileuein,* and that hence we have in fact only two basic partnership functions: *krinein* and *basileuein.* Unlike Schmithals, who finds *basileuein* unexplainable in terms of Jewish traditions and therefore postulates a Gnostic background,[154] I see both functions emerging out of the "royal priesthood" conception of the exodus tradition, which the New Testament preserves in I Peter 2:9 and Rev. 1:6; 5:10. In the latter case it is clear that the promised participation in the *basileuein* (see also Rev. 20:4, 6; 22:5; II Tim. 2:12; and Pap. Oxyr. 654, lines 5–9)[155] not only parallels that of the share in the *krinein*

152. W. Pesch, "Der Sonderlohn für die Verkündiger des Evangeliums (1 Kor. 3:8, 14 f. und Parallelen)," in *Neutestamentliche Aufsätze,* J. Schmid *Festschrift* (Regensburg, 1963), pp. 199–206; Schulz, *Nachfolgen und Nachahmen,* pp. 117–125; B. Reicke, "The New Testament Conception of Reward," in *Aux Sources de la Tradition Chrétienne, Mélanges* M. Goguel (Paris: Delachaux, 1950), pp. 195–206; J. Dupont, *L'Union avec le Christ suivant Saint Paul* (Bruges: Abbaye de Saint-André, 1952); H. Preisker, art. *"misthos,"* in *TWNT,* Vol. IV (1942), pp. 702–707 and 719–736, with bibliography on p. 699. For a biblicistic systematic study, see B. Ramm, *Them He Glorified* (Wm. B. Eerdmans Publishing Company, 1963).

153. To this category belong such phrases as "to be filled," "to be rich" (I Cor. 4:8; Rev. 3:17), "to be perfect" (Phil. 3:12), "to receive a wreath" (I Cor. 9:25) or "a prize" (Phil. 3:14; Rev. 2:10), "to rest" (Matt. 11:28 f.; Heb. 4:3 ff.); and others.

154. W. Schmithals, *Die Gnosis in Korinth* (Forschungen zur Rel. und Lit. d. A. und N. T., No. 66; Göttingen: Vandenhoeck, 1956), p. 148, n. 1.

155. Hennecke, *New Testament Apocrypha,* Vol. I, p. 100, No. 5.

function, but also is promised to all believers as members of the royal priesthood.[156]

What Paul objects to in I Cor. 4:8 with respect to *basileuein,* and warns against in v. 5 with respect to *krinein,* is in substance the same as what Jesus has to say in response to the request of the sons of Zebedee (Mark 10:35-40, par. Matt. 20:20-23): "Yes, but not now"; or rather: "Yes, but only under the condition that you also drink the cup, and be baptized with the baptism with which I am baptized." Kümmel and Cullmann have yet to come upon these verses as further exegetical evidence for alleged temporal elements in the preaching of Jesus. A statement with temporal connotations is indeed what Paul and Jesus are giving. The question, however, is whether the substance of what is said here is temporal or whether *Heilsgeschichte* is understood in chronological terms, or, as with the coming of the Kingdom and the Parousia of the Son of Man, is qualified or "fulfilled" time, which is *kairos,* not *chronos,* and yet fully historical without existentialistic confinement. This is what all the discussion seems to be about: how to account for genuine time, for the proper eschatological qualification of time.

Jesus' rebuke (*epitiman*) of the disciples' desire to exercise only the destructive side of their power in reaction to Samaritan inhospitality (Luke 9:51-56) fits in with the warning expressed after the disciples' victorious return from their mission (ch. 10:17-20). Granted they have "authority . . . over all the power of the enemy," they are told to rejoice in something even greater than that, namely, that their "names are written in heaven." The reflection on and clarification of this dialectic is constitutive for the New Testament understanding of ministry, whether of Jesus or the disciples. To state the basic unity as well as the significant variations on this subject in early Christian literature, both orthodox and heretical, requires more than mere descriptive historical or exegetical analysis.

As *basileuein* is reserved only for the end time, but can

156. G. Schrenk, art. "*hierateuma,*" in *TWNT,* Vol. III (1938), pp. 249–251. Cf. with this the two Messiahs in the Qumran tradition.

presently be exercised, though only in the form of *poimainein* (see John 21:16; Acts 20:28; I Peter 5:2; see also its perversion in Jude 12), so also is *krinein* excluded as an aspect of the disciples' present partnership with Jesus, except in the form of *elenchein* (Matt. 18:15, "to tell his fault"; I Cor. 14:24, "to convict"), *ekdikein* (II Cor. 10:6, "to punish"), or *dokimazein* (ch. 2:9, "to test") and other terms related to legal procedures. To "bind" and "to loose" (Matt. 16:19; 18:18; John 20:23) is thus also, like Jesus' own authority to forgive sins (Mark 2:1 ff.; Luke 7:47 ff.), not identical with God's own Final Judgment (Matt. 13:24 ff.; Mark 10:35 ff.). One must therefore distinguish between reigning or judging (and so with other metaphors, including fishers of men) in the full sense, which only "the end" itself will reveal, and the derived sense applicable only for the time before the end. This distinction is as crucial for the interpretation of the similes applied to the ministry in the New Testament as it is for the whole problem of eschatology.

But not only must we distinguish between one sense and another when contrasting apocalyptic sayings of Jesus with wisdom or legal sayings. There is a difference in meaning in the disciples' participation with Jesus before and after Easter, just as ministry for the Baptist disciples changed with the death of John. For the Fourth Gospel clearly indicates that with Jesus' "going to the Father" his partners will not merely continue to share in the work they have been doing all along, but that even "greater works than these" must come forth (John 14:12). The New Testament is not uniform at all on this point of what exactly the nature of these "greater works" is.[157]

Miracle Stories. The nature of the disciples' partnership with Jesus is further explained in another form of the early gospel tradition, the miracle stories.[158] The Synoptic tradition has preserved only one such account of the disciples

157. See below on the Easter commissions.

158. Bultmann, *The History of the Synoptic Tradition,* pp. 209–244; for the Fourth Gospel, see Dodd, *Historical Tradition,* pp. 174–232. Cf. also H. van der Loos, *The Miracles of Jesus, Novum Testamentum,* Supplement to Vol. IX (Leiden: Brill, 1965), pp. 216–232, on "The Miraculous Power of the Disciples."

as partners in healing and exorcism, while in the Fourth Gospel they are only witnesses of what Jesus does. It is the peculiar but not exclusive genius of the wisdom tradition that the power of God's revelation is manifest not only in history (hence, wise men as political counselors and interpreters of the signs of the times), but also in nature (hence, wise men as physicians, artists, and scientists).[159] With the Kingdom of God known and experienced to be "at hand" there merged also the "special ability to effect the miraculous" which we must attribute not only to Jesus[160] and his disciples, but also to John the Baptist and his associates.[161]

The logion tradition clearly attributes such powers to Jesus, and gives only one example of this power in the only narrative portion contained in Q (Matt. 8:5-13, par. Luke 7:2-10; John 4:46-54). But only in the Marcan tradition do we have two narratives that reflect on the disciples' share in these powers: the story of the healing of the epileptic boy (Mark 9:14-27, par. Matt. 17:14-18; Luke 9:37-43) and the story of the withered fig tree (Mark 11:20-23, par. Matt. 21:20 f.). This endowment with power is also attested in the special Lucan logion (ch. 10:19) about the disciples' authority to tread on serpents and scorpions.[162] The reasons for the disciples' temporary inability to apply these powers are listed differently in Mark 9:29, and in the Q source (Matt. 17:20), with Luke offering no explanation.[163] That people other than Jesus' disciples can also heal is recognized in the Q logion (Matt. 12:27, par. Luke 11:19); in the Marcan tradition of "the strange exorcist" (Mark 9:38-41, par. Luke 9:49 f.); and in the Acts tradi-

159. Cf. G. A. L. Sarton, *A History of Science*, Vol. II, *Hellenistic Science and Culture in the Last Three Centuries B.C.* (Harvard University Press, 1959), Ch. XXII. See also Tillich, *Systematic Theology*, Vol. III, pp. 275–282, on "the healing power of the spiritual presence and the ambiguities of life in general"; C. F. D. Moule (ed.), *Miracles* (London: A. R. Mowbray & Company, Ltd., 1965).

160. Fuchs, *Studies of the Historical Jesus*, p. 61.

161. Bultmann, *The History of the Synoptic Tradition*, p. 24, n. 1. So also Thyen, *"Baptisma Metanoias," loc. cit.*, p. 106, n. 51. Differently, E. Bammel, "John Did No Miracles: John 10:41," in Moule (ed.), *Miracles*, pp. 181–202.

162. On the use of Ps. 91 in Moses' ascension experience, see above, pp. 106 f.

163. On Jesus' inability to do miracles, see Mark 6:5.

tion of Jewish exorcists (chs. 13:6 ff.; 19:13 ff.; see also Simon Magus and his association with Philip in Acts 8:9 ff.).

But to call these examples of healing outside of Jesus and the Baptist's circle as Hellenistic and noneschatological, i.e., magical types of healing, is as misleading as the common but mistaken notion that the rabbis were non- or even anti-eschatological.[164] What this distinction intends to bring to focus is maybe better explained by first seeing the common element in priestly or Sadducean, scribal or Pharisaic, wisdom or apocalyptic theology, which Jesus once called "the power of God" as synonym for "knowing the Scriptures" (Mark 12:24). Another way of speaking of this common element is to speak of the revelation of God or what Abelson called "the immanence of God." The apocalyptic idiom of "the nearness" or imminence of God's coming is in substance no more and no less eschatological than the allegedly static view in Rabbinic, priestly, or wisdom theology. Of course, one must not go on now to the other extreme and insist that there are no differences, or "schisms," as Josephus called them. Theological diversification over eschatology is as characteristic for post-Biblical Judaism as for nascent Christianity. Even so-called gnosticism does not necessarily or by definition exclude eschatology. But as in priestly and wisdom circles, eschatology was differently interpreted in gnostic circles.

If, as Bultmann has it, the tradition of the miraculous fish catch in Luke 5:1-11 and John 21:1-14 is but the "symbolic actualization" [165] of the disciples' calling or appointment to the office of "fishers of men," then one might be equally justified in seeing in the disciples' participation in the miracle of the feeding of the multitude (Mark 6:32-44 and parallels) a symbolic actualization of their participation in the ministry of Jesus, similar to the introduction of the seventy elders as co-workers with Moses at the time of the people's craving for food (Num., ch. 11). That

164. See Rössler's study referred to in Ch. III, n. 165. Cf. L. Ginzberg, *Students, Scholars and Saints* (Meridian Books, The World Publishing Co., 1958), pp. 88–108, on "The Religion of the Pharisees."

165. *The History of the Synoptic Tradition,* p. 217.

these narratives were sooner or later in the tradition or by the Evangelists expanded to include a sacramental meaning, or, as E. C. Hobbs sees it in the case of Mark,[166] as signs of the New Exodus, is indeed evidence of the creative theological transformation of the tradition, also observable in the interpretation of the parables.

The inability of the disciples to feed the multitude (Mark 6:37 and parallels) may very well be a theological motive, similar to their inability to heal the epileptic boy, not to speak of Mark's refrain that the disciples, as partners in Jesus' work, never really understood what they were doing. To conclude from that, as Bultmann does, that therefore one cannot say anything about the disciples' participation in the ministry of the historical Jesus seems unwarranted. Just as Bultmann rightly concludes from the dogmatic judgment in John 10:41 about the Baptist that he must have indeed produced "signs," so also I conclude from the gospel traditions and their judgments on the disciples' participation that we have before us a thoroughly reinterpreted account of certain aspects of the nature of this partnership.[167]

From the fact that the sequence of events which Dodd sees preserved in the tradition of the feeding of the multitude is followed by the voyage or withdrawal, the demand for a sign, and then the disciples' or Peter's confession, Dodd plausibly concludes that the Galilean ministry of Jesus and the disciples seemed first to climax in success and popularity, but then turned into a crisis. Dodd associates this turning point with Jesus' refusal to let his mission be forced into a political channel. The same idea is part of the temptation narrative and possibly also of the disciples' reaction to Jesus' being taken captive. This change in the ministry of Jesus has often been observed. What meaning it has for the interpretation of the ministry of Jesus and of the ministry of the disciples after the Gali-

166. E. C. Hobbs (ed.), *A Stubborn Faith: Papers on Old Testament and Related Subjects Presented to Honor William Andrew Irwin* (Southern Methodist University Press, 1956), pp. 161 f.

167. See H. J. Held, "Matthew as Interpreter of the Miracle Stories," in *Tradition and Interpretation in Matthew,* pp. 270 f.

lean mission is something yet to be determined. The school of Consistent Eschatology, of which A. Schweitzer was the best-known spokesman, rightly perceived the break, but only gave it the wrong interpretation.

This change in the perspective on the nature of Jesus' own ministry, and consequently of his followers' partnership in this ministry, is a change in substance. The pattern of a successful partnership with Jesus which was followed by indications about further yet-to-be-revealed aspects of that partnership is not only common to the Synoptics (Mark 8:29-33; 10:28-31; 10:38-40; 14:29-31 and parallels) and the Fourth Gospel (John 6:68-70; 13:38; 16:31-33), but seems older than both and quite primitive in character. Therefore, historical considerations, such as when, why, and how this change in conceptions about ministry came about, or whether by chance the same change occurred as part of the climax of Jesus' Judean ministry which preceded his Galilean ministry,[168] have to be kept clearly distinct from theological interpretations.

The narrow form-critical consideration of Jesus' disciples as partners or observers in the miracle stories must be expanded to include the theological perspective to be derived from the grouping or collecting of the isolated pericopes into units and sequences. It must also be understood that these sequences mean one thing, first, in the *kērygma* of the church in which they took shape,[169] and, secondly, come to mean something else again in their use by Evangelists and apocryphal authors, but, thirdly, also yield some historical reminiscences. My own interest, however, is not in the history of what discipleship as partnership with Jesus' mission meant, but in the theology of it, specifically in the changes of the theology of the menfishing ministry.

Historical Stories and Legends.[170] These are two other

168. Dodd, *Historical Tradition,* p. 247. More cautious is Bornkamm's judgment, in *Jesus of Nazareth,* p. 155.

169. On the sequences of sayings and narratives in the precanonical tradition, see Knox, *The Sources of the Synoptic Gospels.* Cf. also Dodd, *Historical Tradition,* pp. 388–405, and L. E. Keck's essay.

170. Dodd, *Historical Tradition,* pp. 50 ff. Bultmann, *The History of the Synoptic Tradition,* pp. 244 ff.

literary "forms" that contain reflections on the nature of this discipleship. Within this form-critical unit we find three significant ideas expressed: (1) the betrayal, denial, and flight of the disciples, i.e., the emphasis on a radical discontinuity in their historical association and partnership with Jesus; (2) the preservation of a continuity between Jesus and the disciples that only he, in spite of all discontinuity, assured; and (3) the new call and commission extended in the Easter stories and their "common pattern." [171] It is important to acknowledge here also the role of the *testimonia,* that is, the citation of Old Testament passages, in the interpretation of the disciples' role before and after Easter.[172] These early "testimonies" may also have influenced the application of certain parables to the interpretation of ministry.

The Gethsemane story [173] depicts the disciples sleeping or relapsing into sleep every time Jesus is separated from them. In this, their sleepiness resembles the disciples' inability to heal during Jesus' absence from them during his transfiguration. The exhortation later appended to each story is also fairly similar (cf. Mark 14:38; 9:29). What is involved in this temporary separation of Jesus from his disciples is more than a test. What the nature of discipleship and of the disciples' participation in the ministry of Jesus is during the time he is gone "for a little while" (see *mikron* in John 16:16) is answered differently in the various sources of the gospel tradition and again in the subsequent gospel literature. The important and underlying common factor is the disciples' inability to sustain his call, whether it is the common call to enter the Kingdom or the special call of becoming partners in issuing this call.

The betrayal of Judas as one of the Twelve interests us here only in connection with the claim that the tradition's

171. Dodd, *Historical Tradition,* pp. 143 f., on Luke, ch. 24, and John, ch. 21. On Matt. 28:16-20, see G. Bornkamm, "Der Auferstandene und der Irdische," in *Zeit und Geschichte,* Bultmann *Festschrift,* pp. 171–191; H. Kosmala, "The Conclusion of Matthew," in the *Annual of the Swedish Theological Institute,* Vol. IV, pp. 132–147.

172. Dodd, *Historical Tradition,* pp. 31 ff.

173. On remnants of the Gethsemane tradition in the Fourth Gospel, see Dodd, *Historical Tradition,* pp. 65–72.

preservation of the label of Judas as one of the Twelve proves that the Twelve did indeed accompany the historical Jesus and are not the product of later theological reflection. Even if it were, as I believe it is, sure that Jesus did have a group of twelve men besides other disciples as his partners in his mission, it would yield nothing yet as to the theological meaning that the Twelve occupied first in the ministry of Jesus, with one betraying him, and then in the subsequent tradition. This says nothing yet about the validity of Meyer's hypothetical Twelve source.[174]

The disciples' inability to maintain their partnership with Jesus is further accentuated in the denial of Peter and in the reflections appended to the incident of Peter's drawing a sword "to die for his Master, rather than to die with him,"[175] at the time Jesus is taken prisoner. These accounts interpret the historical fact that the disciples, though they continued with Jesus in his trials (Luke 22:28), for a while discontinued their partnership. Why they did this, and yet "turned again," was subject to theological reflection based on Jesus' prayer (Luke 22:32; John, ch. 17), and secondly, the Last Supper in the Synoptics and the foot washing in John. Only in the Fourth Gospel does Jesus' voluntary surrender to his captors signify a third reason why the disciples are "preserved."[176] The first epoch of partnership with Jesus does indeed come to an end, and a new epoch begins. But when Conzelmann, who rightly stressed the different character of each epoch, speaks of the disciples as entering an epoch of partnership with Jesus when they are no longer protected and face only conflict,[177] he is overstating the case. For the issue is not protection versus no protection, but one kind of protection (i.e., the one which the historical Jesus and his faith provided) versus another and new kind (i.e., the Spirit, or the faith in Jesus, and the like).

174. Knox, *The Sources of the Synoptic Gospels,* Vol. I, pp. 17–31.

175. Dodd, *Historical Tradition,* p. 80, n. 1. For a critical examination of the traditions about the disciples' denial, see essays in *Zeitschr. f. Theol. u. Kirche,* Vol. 58 (1961), pp. 285–328, by G. Klein, and Vol. 63 (1966), pp. 1–32, by E. Linnemann.

176. *Historical Tradition,* pp. 57, 75 f.

177. *The Theology of St. Luke,* pp. 81, 199 f.

If Dodd is correct in his interpretation that Luke's conception of the disciples' ordeal in terms of "sifting"[178] was meant as "the sifting or purging of Israel, in preparation for the restoration of the people of God in the form of the Church,"[179] and that by contrast the pre-Lucan tradition conceived of the disciples' denial of Jesus merely as model of "the apostasy of Israel [and] similar apostasy or unfaithfulness on the part of the followers of Christ,"[180] then we see again clearly the theological reflection on three basic levels: what discontinuity in the partnership with Jesus meant (1) in the actual ministry of Jesus, (2) in the various stages and strata of the gospel tradition, and (3) in the different Gospels.

Before we turn to the "legends" about the resurrection and the new call and commission extended to the disciples as partners with Jesus, we must briefly examine the few but highly significant instances in the stories about Jesus' last days with his disciples, which consolidate Jesus' own faith, and thereby the ultimate security of the disciples' partnership in his mission. The triumphal entry into Jerusalem in the company of the Twelve is as much a parabolic or symbolic action (not only or primarily of Jesus' royal authority,[181] but of the assurance given to the Twelve that the Kingdom of God is still at hand) as was the call or appointment of the Twelve, or at least the preservation of twelve from among numerous other disciples.

The Last Supper is the second instance. In that symbolic act Jesus not only separates his destiny from that of his disciples, but also creates a new and "intimate union of will and intention" between himself and his partners.[182] But more than the example of the foot washing and the sign of surrendering himself to his captors for the sake of his disciples, the Last Supper, next to the actual death on

178. See above, Ch. II, n. 58.

179. *Historical Tradition,* p. 51, n. 1.

180. *Ibid.,* p. 57.

181. Jeremias, *The Parables of Jesus,* pp. 227 f.

182. E. J. Kilmartin, *The Eucharist in the Primitive Church* (Prentice-Hall, Inc., 1965), p. 65, presses for a sacramental view. Bornkamm, *Jesus of Nazareth,* pp. 160 f., is very reserved. Cf. J. Jeremias, *The Eucharistic Words of Jesus,* pp. 216–218 and 236.

the cross, is the last and most paradoxical claim Jesus made of the empirical reality of the Kingdom's coming.[183] That the truth of this claim rested solely on the assurance Jesus gave by nothing more than his own word, his own faith, his conduct, his obedience, and by the certainty reflected in his prayer was "the stumbling block" which he not only did not remove, but increased instead by the cross, but which believers experienced as the power of God. This was to be the new dimension of the partnership that began with Easter, but which was intimated by Jesus' conduct with his partners at the end of his life.

The Easter narratives, form-critically identified as "legends," [184] reveal an interesting pattern composed of different and separable form-critical "units of oral tradition," of which our Gospels have preserved "two types." [185] What Dodd calls "the concise type" is represented by Matt. 28:8-10, 16-20; Mark 16:14 f.; and John 20:19-21. The other, called "circumstantial type," is represented by Luke 24:13-35 (the Emmaus story) and John 21:1-14 (the fishing scene in Galilee). Luke 24:36-49 is taken as an example of the mixture of the two types.

Dodd makes plausible that the texts of the concise type are all patterned alike, beginning with the description of the disciples bereft of their leader, then of Christ's appearance, his greeting and recognition, and, for our study so important, the concluding commission to his disciples to resume their partnership ministry with him. Though the pattern in the circumstantial type is fairly similar, it is the noted "tendency to expand" the section dealing with the commission to the apostles that interests us most. Hahn made the same observation in his analysis of the two types of mission discourse preserved in the tradition, namely, that the greatest variation in the tradition was found in the opening *topos* about commission and qualification to partnership with Jesus.[186]

183. This aspect is neglected in Ladd's *Jesus and the Kingdom,* and also in John Knox's work.

184. Bultmann, *History of the Synoptic Tradition,* pp. 284–291.

185. Dodd, *Historical Tradition,* p. 143.

186. Hahn, *Mission in the New Testament,* pp. 43 f.

Dodd refers to two texts which exemplify theologically significant later expansions of the last part of the Easter narrative pattern. In John 20:19-21 the original ending ("as the Father has sent me, even so I send you" [187]; cf. ch. 17:18) was expanded by two points: (1) the gift of the Spirit, or the Johannine Pentecost, conceived of quite differently from the tradition in Acts 2:1 ff. and from the "counselor" idea in the Farewell Discourse of John; (2) the endowment with the power of "the keys," that is, authority in the church (cf. Matt. 16:19; 18:18). The other text is John 21:1 ff., where Dodd sees the whole last part of the pattern replaced by the commission to Peter to feed the sheep. Dodd takes this "in some sort" as parallel to John 20:21; Matt. 28:18-20; Mark 16:15-18; and Luke 24:44-49.

Bornkamm [188] has subjected the Matthean interpretation of the Easter legend about the disciples' commission to critical analysis, and come to some thoughtful conclusions. He believes that the order given at Easter to baptize and to use a special baptismal formula are not to Matthew's credit, but were part of an expansion of the Easter commission *topos* in one branch of the early tradition. This pre-Matthean tradition, preserved in Matt. 28:18-20, combined three elements. The tradition and then again the Evangelists worked with all three elements in establishing a proper and comprehensive understanding of ministry. The sequence of the three elements or *topoi* may be traditional. Mentioned first in Matthew is the designation of Jesus as having received "all authority," similar to the *testimonia* tradition about the exaltation of Jesus,[189] the hymnic tradition of "the name above all names" (Phil. 2:9; cf. Eph. 1:20-22; Rev. 12:10), and the Johannine tra-

187. R. Bultmann, *Das Evangelium des Johannes* (Meyer Kommentar), p. 536, n. 5, suggests that even this verse replaced an original which is better retained in Luke 24:47 (preaching repentance and forgiveness of sins to all nations in Jesus' name) and Matt. 28:19 f. (make disciples by baptizing and teaching).

188. See reference in n. 171 above.

189. See C. H. Dodd, *According to the Scriptures* (Charles Scribner's Sons, 1953), on the use of Ps. 8:4-6 (pp. 32–34), Ps. 110:1 (pp. 34–36), and possibly also Zech. 9:9 (pp. 48–49).

dition of the mission and glory of the revealer-son (John 17:18; 3:35; cf. Hermas, Sim. 5, 6:4). The second element is the commission of the disciples (Matt. 28:19 f.), followed by the third and all too often overlooked or underrated point about the assurance of continuous divine support in their apostolic work (v. 20). This should be seen in the light of the Last Supper tradition and also in the emerging adaptation of apocalytic literature to Christian use as assurance and comfort of the Lord's presence (Rev. 1:1 ff.).

Bornkamm's analysis of the pattern of these three points and of their reinterpretation by Matthew to suit his theological conviction rests on the basic premise that an original combination of Easter appearance and commission was replaced here by another but equally traditional combination of the commission of the disciples with the exaltation of Jesus. This replacement is interpreted by him as part of the general shift from Palestinian to Hellenistic Christianity. As Käsemann argues about the ministry of reconciliation in Paul as based on an earlier model that understood reconciliation in cosmic terms,[190] so also does Bornkamm pose a hypothetical "early catholicism" in the combination of the apostolic office with the redemption mystery of the exalted Lord Jesus.[191] The same conception is still preserved in the Deutero-Pauline letters (Ephesians and Colossians) and the pastoral epistles. The crucial theological issue underlying this shift in early Christian tradition is the meaning and dynamic of divine revelation. The formative stages of the gospel traditions in all their forms, and not only their Easter narratives, and the emerging theological formulations of rival factions among Christian missions, as evident in Paul, all contribute, but with different merit, to the clarification of the crucial question, Who can mediate revelation? or, How can I get a share in salvation? [192]

190. "Erwägungen zum Stichwort 'Versöhnungslehre im Neuen Testament,'" in *Zeit und Geschichte,* Bultmann *Festschrift,* pp. 47–59.

191. Cf. E. Schweizer, "Discipleship and Belief in Jesus as Lord. From Jesus to the Hellenistic Church," *New Testament Studies,* Vol. 2 (1955), pp. 87–99.

192. Bornkamm, "Der Auferstandene und der Irdische," *loc. cit.,* p. 178.

It is the merit of Bornkamm's essay, which goes beyond Dodd's helpful form-critical analysis, to have called attention to the "close connection between [belief in the exalted Lord] and a certain understanding of prophecy and charisma." [193] On this background Bornkamm views Matthew's reworking of the established pattern of narratives about the commission to disciples. Employing the sources to which Dodd also alludes, Bornkamm can show that in the pre-Matthean tradition of the Easter commission the "close connection" between exalted Lord and apostolic partnership involved exorcistic healing, glossolalia, and other "signs of apostleship" (cf. II Cor. 12:12). All those features are characteristic of a certain understanding of ministry in certain circles (e.g., Mark 16:15-18 or in the Antiochian source of Acts), in which gospel traditions were shaped and transmitted. These circles were the common source for both Paul and the "super apostles" who contested his authority; for both Matthew and the "false prophets" who, like Paul's Christian adversaries, boast of their gifts of prophecy and healing powers, but who are rejected as false fishers of men. It has been argued that the Fourth Gospel is engaged in a similar controversy fought under different symbols, which is perhaps due to its different provenance. Kragerud [194] sees this controversy in the relationship between "the beloved disciple" and Peter. Käsemann [195] sees it in the figure of Diotrephes as opposed to the author of The Third Letter of John.

The "Generalizing Summaries." These and the "itinerary fragments" are another form-critical unit in which references to apostolic partnership are preserved. In three or four of the seven instances of this tradition preserved in the Fourth Gospel,[196] the disciples are depicted as ac-

193. *Ibid.*, p. 179. See also C. F. Sleeper, "Pentecost and Resurrection," *Journal of Biblical Literature*, Vol. 84 (1965), pp. 389–399, and Scroggs' article mentioned above.

194. A. Kragerud, *Der Lieblingsjünger im Johannesevangelium* (Oslo: Universitätsverlag, 1959). H. Schlier accepts part of this thesis with qualification (see *Neutestamentliche Aufsätze*, J. Schmid *Festschrift* [1963], p. 237).

195. "Ketzer und Zeuge," in *Exegetische Versuche und Besinnungen*, Vol. I, pp. 168–187.

196. Dodd, *Historical Tradition*, pp. 233–247.

companying Jesus. In John 2:12 we also hear of the mother of Jesus and his brothers who play a significant role in the extracanonical gospel tradition, but also occasionally within the New Testament, above all in the person of James, the brother of the Lord.[197] In ch. 3:22 f. the disciples are partners in the baptism that Jesus and the Baptist administer independently. In ch. 4:1 we learn that Jesus makes (or appoints) disciples and baptizes in Judea with greater success than the Baptist, and that Jesus returns or withdraws to Galilee as "a refuge from the hostility of Judea." [198] In ch. 11:54, as in ch. 2:12, Jesus and the disciples "stay" (*menein*) in a certain place which in Galilee was Capernaum, but during their last visit in Judea they stay in the desert.

In comparing John 2:12; 3:22 f.; 4:1; and 11:54 with the "generalizing summaries" in Mark (chs. 1:14 f., 22 f., 39; 2:13; 3:7-19; 4:33 f.; 6:7, 12 f., 30) [199] we notice certain agreements with the Johannine tradition. Though they reveal a common pattern and sequence, the differences between Mark and the Fourth Gospel may suggest that here, too, we have two separate models of the same basic tradition. Mark 1:22 f. and its parallels in Matt. 4:12 f. and Luke 4:14, 31 also refer to Capernaum as does John 2:12. In Luke 4:44, which is the parallel to Mark 1:39 and Matt. 4:23, the ministry of Jesus is also depicted, including Judea.[200] The appointment of the Twelve in Mark 3:7-19, with its parallels in Matt. 10:1-4 and Luke 6:12-16 can stand comparison with John 4:1 with its passing reference to the making or appointing (*poiein*) of disciples. That there are significant changes particularly in this last instance is consonant with observations made about variations in other parts of the tradition dealing with apostolic commissions.

It is my contention that this tradition of "generalizing summaries" confirms the information from other tradi-

197. *Ibid.*, p. 324, on John 20:17 and Matt. 28:10. On James, see Schmithals, *Paul and James*.

198. Dodd, *Historical Tradition*, p. 238, n. 1.

199. C. H. Dodd, "The Framework of the Gospel Narrative," *New Testament Studies* (Charles Scribner's Sons, 1954), pp. 1–11.

200. Conzelmann, *The Theology of St. Luke*, pp. 40 f., 69 f.; p. 189, n. 3.

tions about the disciples as partners, and the special commission for this partnership in contrast to what all believers are commissioned to do, proportionate to the "measure of faith" each has in witnessing and working for the Lord. The reference in John 2:24 f. that Jesus did not trust himself to others to bear witness to him "for he . . . knew what was in man" (cf. John 12:42-43), now phrased in ways characteristic of the fourth Evangelist,[201] makes clear what the gospel traditions elsewhere reflect that the partnership of all believers and that of the appointed partners have to be clearly distinguished, but not set into opposition to each other.

Luke makes a further distinction when he has seventy or seventy-two sent out besides the Twelve, who alone are "the sharers in the 'anabasis' [or *exodos* of Jesus, see Luke 9:31] as his closest companions." [202] How the mother of Jesus and other women [203] serving him (or them, the disciples with Jesus) and the brothers of Jesus fit in here as partners of still another kind is a quite distinct problem from that of the partnership of all believers. But that all partnership with Jesus, even that of the Twelve, and even that of Mary as mediatrix, coredemptrix, or whatever else Catholic tradition has proclaimed her to be, must be distinguished from Jesus' own unique partnership in doing or mediating God's work, is emphasized in all four Gospels. This distinction is in effect the basis for the hermeneutical criterion used in "testing the spirits." In referring to Chirst as the abstract hermeneutical principle, all gospel traditions, even the so-called heretical and apocryphal ones, are united. Only in describing or analyzing Jesus as the concrete norm of this abstract principle [204] do the gospel traditions differ, even within the canonical New Testament.

Old Testament "Testimonies." This "substructure of

201. Dodd, *Historical Tradition,* pp. 234 f.

202. Conzelmann, *The Theology of St. Luke,* p. 67, n. 1.

203. M. Hengel, "Maria Magdalena und die Frauen als Zeugen," in *Abraham unser Vater,* O. Michel *Festschrift* (Leiden: Brill, 1963), pp. 243–256.

204. On the Tillichian distinction between abstract principle and concrete norm, see above, pp. 93 f.

New Testament theology" (Dodd) appears at first sight to have nothing to do with the interpretation of the men-fishing ministry. For the numerous examples of "testimonies" in New Testament literature cited by Dodd and others reflect mostly on the role of Christ in the salvation plan of God. In the passion narratives the same impression prevails.[205] But even there the quotation of two "testimonies" in connection with the disciples' predicted flight, that is, temporary dissociation in their men-fishing partnership with Jesus, merits more than passing notice. One concerns the "fall" (*skandalizesthai*) of all disciples; the other predicts that the sheep will be scattered (because) the shepherd was (temporarily) struck (Mark 14:27, par. Matt. 26:31; omitted in Luke; cf. John 16:1). In a different way, but with similar intention of indicating discontinuity and renewed continuity, Scripture is quoted in Acts 1:20. The appeal to Septuagint Ps. 108:3 with its reference to "his office (*episkopē*) let another take," meaning Judas' "share in the ministry" (*klēros tēs diakonias,* Acts 1:17, 25), is not a proof text for apostolic succession but authorization for filling the vacancy left by the apostate in order to bring the symbolic role of the Twelve back into clear focus after Easter.

The "testimonies" then imply that a proper interpretation of the activity to which the "fisher of men" metaphor refers is possible only within the context of Christianity's understanding of itself as New Israel, which does not exclude but, in some ways yet to be spelled out, always includes the old Israel. This perspective on the partnership task of the disciples is part of the following "testimonies": the Jeremiah (ch. 31:31-34) prophecy about the new covenant; the Joel (ch. 2:28-32) prophecy about the outpouring of the Spirit; the blessing of Abraham (Gen. 12:3), and the Habakkuk (ch. 2:3 f.) prophecy about the proper life of, or in, faith. Still more significant is the use made of Isa. 6:9 f., which speaks of the prophet's commission to minister to Israel even though there is seemingly no response (cf. Rom. 10:14 ff.). That this Isaiah "testimony," like some

205. Dodd, *Historical Tradition,* pp. 31–49.

others (e.g., Isa. 8:14; 28:16), came to be applied to both Jesus' historical ministry and the disciples' ministry before and after Easter is in itself an important clue for the interpretation of the meaning of partnership with Jesus. For the Twelve are not a symbol of only the New Israel but of both the old and the New Israel, and of their relationship, both to each other and to the Gentiles or the world at large.

This dimension of continued preoccupation with the role of Israel, and the substantively different interpretations that came to be offered as to the meaning of this role, have not so much been ignored as become subjected to criteria of interpretation that are alien to the problem involved. And the problem is the interpretation of the meaning of eschatological revelation as salvation. And in view of this problem it is misleading to pitch against each other Israel and Gentiles, Judaism and Hellenism, or even prophetism and apocalypticism, Temple and wisdom, scribes and magicians, normative and sectarian Judaism, not to speak of the still fashionable division between Palestinian Jewish Christianity and Hellenistic Jewish Christianity.

It is my contention that the alleged polar entities (e.g., Israel and Gentiles, Judaism and Hellenism, and the like) must not be torn apart to make up two opposing entities, nor must they be equated. The *alētheia theou,*[206] which was to be confirmed by the restricted ministries of the historical Jesus and his historical partners, symbolized by the Twelve (see Rom. 15:8), is not the same as the *alētheia theou* that was known but suppressed by the Gentiles (ch. 1:25). The two conceptions of the meaning of "truth" (*alētheia*) are not the same; yet neither are they separate or incompatible entities. What holds them together is variously designated or designatable by different symbols, such as God's plan or economy, Kingdom, mystery, or wisdom, the manifestation of God's invisible nature, or the revelation of his eternal power and deity (Rom. 1:20), new creation, spirit, life or eternal life, and many other symbols. Whether one discusses the symbols

206. Translated differently as "truthfulness" (Goodspeed, RSV), "trustworthiness" (Phillips), "fidelity" (Knox), "honor" (Schonfield).

and titles applied to Jesus or the similes and metaphors applied to the disciples, in either case the crucial task is not whether a given title or simile is Palestinian or Hellenistic, but what its theological substance is.[207] Theological diversification may indeed feed on or be fed by cultural or linguistic factors,[208] but the origin of schisms in Judaism and Christianity lies elsewhere. It lies in the very character of the indispensable role of medium or mediums of revelation, and in the understanding of revelation as salvation.

If we have learned that it is futile to speak of *the* primitive Christian community, or *the* primitive Christian *kērygma* (as futile as *the* historical covenant community in Israel), and that we can speak only of varieties of traditions, then we are led by this judgment of modern historical scholarship to face, not a historical problem, but a theological issue. And the observed syncretization or gnosticizing tendencies, whether in tenth- or eighth-century B.C. Israel or in first-century Judaism and Christianity, remain inadequately interpreted, unless or until the problem of mediumship in revelation is recognized, not as a sociological or psychological, but as a theological or hermeneutical problem.

I contend that not only must we give up all attempts at defining *the* primitive Christian community or *the* primitive covenant community in Israel, but also give up the traditional attempts at defining *the* historical Jesus or *the* historical Moses. The difference between this view and that of traditional historical skepticism—in the face of or as a result of which first the old, then the new, "quest of the historical Jesus" was launched—is that the very study of history is understood now to be the study of history's role as medium of the divine revelation. History is studied phenomenologically and hermeneutically. The men-fishing metaphor is thus properly understood as a symbol for mediumship or partnership in the revelation event. And the crucial theological task is to determine the criterion by

207. F. Hahn, *Christologische Hoheitstitel,* p. 90, calls it "inhaltliche Ausprägung."

208. On how it appears to a leading linguist, see H. A. Gleason, "Linguistics in the Service of the Church," *The Hartford Quarterly,* Vol. I (1961), pp. 17 ff.

which to judge whether or not any medium makes God truly, fully transparent. Israel does make the explicit claim that it is the medium of the *alētheia theou.* Jesus and his historical disciples make the claim that they, rather than Moses, are that medium.

Instead of stopping short of the historical Jesus and seeing "the origin and nature of diversification in the history of early Christianity" (Koester), or even in earliest pre-Pauline, pre-gospel traditional Christianity, I merely draw the last consequence from the often made observation that the very historical Jesus himself, together with his historical disciples, was a syncretistic phenomenon. By that I mean that the men-fishing ministry of the historical Jesus and that of his disciple partners contained in itself elements that were both particularistic and universalistic, anthropological and cosmological, historical and ahistorical, prophetic and magic. I am not advocating that all of these elements have become indistinguishable. But I am saying that the provenance for theological diversification is primarily to be seen in the *kērygma* before and not after Easter. It is to be seen in the historical Jesus himself, who as medium of the divine revelation, like other mediums in Israel's history, combined not only in his language, but in the very conduct of his life and ministry a diversity of aspects. This diversity was not created by the *kērygma* after Easter, but only, though often significantly, amplified or atrophied by later traditions.

The alternative about the meaning of the fishing metaphor as either Israel-directed only before Easter or universally oriented after Easter is a half-truth. For, historically, one must indeed concede that all the men-fishing Jesus and his disciples did before Easter was within the confines of Jewish territory. But from a theological point of view not even this historical judgment is adequate, as recent studies on the mission of Jesus have shown.[209] To understand the dogmatic idea of the twelve apostles one must also take into consideration the Twelve as historical disciples who symbolized the New Israel or reopened

209. For literature up to 1954, see Munck, *Paul and the Salvation of Mankind,* pp. 247–281, on "Israel and the Gentiles."

prophecy. To understand the combination of wisdom (*sophia*) theology and ecstatic phenomena in the Corinthian correspondence of Paul no less than in the Q source, one must also and first appreciate a similar syncretistic, gnosticizing combination in the historical Jesus as wisdom teacher.

Jesus and his partners do not represent only the mission to Israel but also the mission *of* Israel. This theological paradox is reflected in Munck's observation that the "apparent particularism [of the mission of Jesus and his partners] is an expression of [their] universalism—it is because his mission concerns the whole world that he comes to Israel." [210] To realize that Isa. 6:9 f. was used as a "testimony" in expressing the church's self-understanding of its mission as parallel to that of Jesus and the prophets must not mislead one to the extreme view that the ministry of Jesus, of the disciples, and of Paul's and other early Christians' apostolate was "prophetic." The more concerted, forceful, and direct the claim was made by Jesus and his disciples that through their word and deed was mediated the eschatological revelation and salvation of Israel's God, the more this claim appeared in syncretistic, gnostic form, even before Easter. This does not at all deny that with and after Easter there was continuing, accelerated, and vigorous proliferation of theological diversification.[211]

In critically assessing the interpretations of the nature and role of partnership with Jesus in doing the work of God, that is, of the nature and role of revelation mediums as reflected in Christian oral and written traditions, two points must be observed. One point concerns the degree to which men-fishing or other metaphors and similes reflecting this partnership are filled with content that derives its substance from Jesus as the perfect, final, true revelation medium, both before and after Easter. The second point concerns the relationship between Jesus and Israel, Jesus and the patriarchal promises, Jesus and the covenant, Jesus

210. *Ibid.*, p. 271.

211. Cf. A. Fridrichsen, "Jesus, St. John and St. Paul," in *The Root of the Vine*, pp. 37–62.

and the Torah, as one or as two distinct mediums of the salvation plan or mystery of God. Cullmann's concern with *Heilsgeschichte* and Munck's concern with "the salvation of mankind" are but two recent provocative attempts to keep the emphasis on the continuity between the old and the new which has also been the prevailing emphasis in patristic, in modern Roman Catholic, and in conservative Protestant exegesis. But ever since at least the rise of Consistent Eschatology and of the "history of religions" school, with its emphasis on Hellenism or syncretism, the accent has been moved to the other extreme of the radical discontinuity, not only in conceptions of the Kingdom and its coming, of Messiahship and Messianic partnership, but also in the very realization or experience of salvation.

The analysis of the fishing metaphor, first in the context of its form-critical unit, the biographical apothegm, or pronouncement story, and then also in the context of other similes and metaphors, as well as general references to discipleship as partnership with Jesus has left us with the raw material with which to reconstruct critically now the meaning attributed to the fishing (and other) metaphors in the ministry of Jesus, then in the church after Easter, and finally in the postapostolic church of the Evangelists. The sources of Acts, of the letters, of The Revelation to John, and of extracanonical material should also be included, not so much for the sake of comprehensiveness, but to make possible a theological, and not merely historical, critical analysis of the reasons and the extent that ministry came to be interpreted inadequately, and of the norm by which any ministry, and any of its claims, can be judged to be adequate or true.

Besides the literary form, or the format in which ideas of the nature and function of ministry were transmitted, we had already reason to observe that individual form or tradition units became interpreted in the subsequent gospel traditions. These are, indeed, the immediate sources of the gospel compositions. In Mark we have pre-Marcan collections of parables, of miracles, of conflict stories, the Twelve source, the "testimonies," the "generalizing summaries," the little apocalypse, the passion narrative, and others. Each of the sources common to Matthew and Luke (the Q source), and those peculiar to Matthew, to Luke, and to the Fourth Gospel, represents a stage in the church's continuous theological reflection on Jesus' ministry and man's partnership in it. The form-critical studies in the narrower, technical sense provide a bridge between *Gattungskritik* and editorial criticism on the one hand, and the quest of the historical Jesus and of the historical disciples on the other hand.

Before we return to the task of completing the analysis of what men-fishing meant in the ministry of the historical Jesus, let us briefly summarize the main elements of this raw material provided by the form-critical perspective. Strong emphasis is laid on the continuity of the historical and exalted, the past and the coming, Jesus, that is, the continuity of revelation as salvation. Continuity is emphasized in the role of the Twelve, and of their association and that of Jesus with Jerusalem. The New Israel is conscious of being the true old Israel brought to full realization of its calling as "people," "servant," "chosen" of God. The New Israel is conscious of being a medium of the eschatological revelation, but only as "followers," "disciples," "laborers," "apostles," "believers" of Christ, by whom not individuals but Israel is called to newness.

This continuity manifests itself also in the faithfulness with which sayings of Jesus, his actions and conduct of life, the general outline of his life, and the knowledge of his association with a select group of disciples was preserved in the form-critical units outlined above. It is important to remind oneself constantly of the crucial role that the historical Jesus, and with it the historical limitation of his ministry to Israel, occupies in the tradition, and this all the more as this role is often not made explicit, as in the case of the pericope of the call to the office of fishers of men.

But equally important is the emphasis the tradition places on the discontinuity of the historical Jesus and his partners, and, above all, of Easter and Pentecost, with which originate rival interpretations as to the meaning of

Jesus' ministry *to* Israel as the ministry *of* Israel. The transition in the men-fishing in Israel to men-fishing among the Gentiles was not primarily a historical process, nor was it inevitably a step from particularism to universalism, but it was a new answer given to the question that is native and essential to Israel as chosen covenant people. How, indeed, can the ministry to Israel become the means by which Israel resumes its role as "light to the Gentiles"? How, indeed, can the old covenant become truly new?

The answer to this question, and with it the insight into the mystery of Israel, the mystery of the Kingdom, the mystery of salvation history, is identified with what Jesus and his appointed partners did during their historical ministry in Israel. It is identified with his teaching, his way of life, his miracles, his visions, and his partners' participation in them. But as he went from success to seeming failure by ending up dying on the cross, so also did his partners move from success in their mission of the Kingdom's imminence and power to a seemingly ignominious end in the denial of and flight from the captured and sentenced Jesus. But the tradition has preserved isolated sayings and fashioned its own narratives which reflect, not a sense of failure, but the call to the meeting of a test, to the understanding of the mystery, to the taking up of the cross and yoke, to the drinking of the cup, and to the realization of the meaning of the baptism received (or to be received). This call is accompanied with more than promises; it is empirically verified by gifts received by those who accept the call. And the call is not merely to individuals as it is in the case of all pericopes dealing with the general call to discipleship. Rather, it is the call and subsequent appointment of the Twelve, in which the meaning of Israel is recalled and reconstituted.

No other factors are more important than the growing uncertainty and unclarity over Israel's role which contributed to the theological diversification in primitive Christianity. Syncretization, gnosticization, and Parousia delay are the result, not the cause, of the failure to realize salvation as mediated by Israel, that is, by the historical medium of Jesus and his twelve partners. As in God's fishing of Israel before, so in Jesus' commission to fish Israel and the disciples' call to be fishers of men the old Israel is renewed. Over the nature of this newness Jesus and the Baptist parted company; defining it before Easter was the meaning of Jesus' life; defining it after Easter was possible only with reference to the historical Jesus and to the historical Israel. But both did become means to opposing ends as the conflict between "orthodoxy" and "heresy" reveals by the time of Paul, and as clearly reflected in Jesus' "prophetic and apocalyptic sayings" about the false prophets, boastful teachers, and ravenous wolves.

Fishers of Men in the Theology of Mark

Mark's interpretation of the meaning of the fishing metaphor, along with that of other metaphors applied to partners of Jesus, comes into focus by an analysis of the features peculiar to Mark's account of discipleship. These features emerge clearly in the ways Mark does or does not use or modify the gospel traditions available to him. Such a critical analysis of Mark's features can be done either by examining one feature at a time or by seeing all of them as interrelated or correlated to Mark's central thesis.[212]

What Mark saw as the meaning of the commission to "become fishers of men" depends on the solution to three composite and interrelated problems: 1. How does Mark

212. For bibliographies of earlier works on the theology of Mark, see T. A. Burkill, *Mysterious Revelation* (Cornell University Press, 1963); E. Schweizer, "Anmerkungen zur Theologie des Markus," in *Neotestamentica et Patristica, Freundesgabe* O. Cullmann, *Novum Testamentum,* Supplement to Vol. VI (Leiden: Brill, 1962), pp. 35–46; É. Trocmé, *La Formation de L'Évangile selon Marc* (Études d'Hist. et de Phil. Relig., No. 57; Paris: Presses Univ. de France, 1963); J. Bowman, *The Gospel of Mark* (Studia Post-Biblica, Vol. 8; Leiden: Brill, 1965); A. Suhl, *Die Funktion der alttestamentlichen Zitate und Anspielungen im Markusevangelium* (Gütersloh: Mohn, 1965). For recent essays, see besides those of E. C. Hobbs and L. E. Keck quoted earlier, those by P. Vielhauer, "Erwägungen zur Christologie des Markusevangeliums," in *Zeit und Geschichte,* Bultmann *Festschrift,* pp. 155–169; and N. Q. Hamilton, "Resurrection Tradition and the Composition of Mark," *Journal of Biblical Literature,* Vol. 84 (1965), pp. 415–421.

view the role of "Simon and those with him," the role of "[Jesus'] disciples and Peter," the role of the Twelve as over against the other ones called—notably Levi, who for Mark is not one of the Twelve—or other followers, believers, and witnesses of Jesus who are also "taught" by Jesus but who do not get commissioned or authorized to be partners with Jesus? Why does "the content of the concept 'teaching' [which in Mark, in contrast to Matthew] is thus not fixed" [213] become "fixed" only in Jesus' relationship with those called "to be with him" (Mark 3:14)?

2. What relation exists for Mark between the disciples' consistent lack of understanding and Jesus' Messianic secret, that is, "the mystery of the kingdom of God [which is] given to [them]" (ch. 4:11)? What is Mark's understanding of the peculiar nature of the mysteriousness of the "mysterious revelation"? What reason (s) could Mark have for letting even the chosen Twelve and Peter fail to understand, fall into unbelief, and finally to "fall away," although they had received esoteric instruction and revelation about the "mystery"?

3. Why is there in Mark, unlike all other canonical Gospels, no Easter commission to Peter and the Twelve? Why is there no Marcan Pentecost from which, as in other traditions, the post-Easter church could derive its divine commission for doing the work of God in the world? Related to this is the question of what conception of the church Mark has,[214] if any at all? What does Mark see in "Galilee" by starting and ending his Gospel there? Mark lets the historical Jesus appear from a deliberately undefined somewhere and "come into Galilee" (ch. 1:14); there Jesus sees the fishermen, and in their seeing and following him they are appointed to become fishers of men. After having "gone ahead of them" to Jerusalem, despite their "rebuke" (ch. 8:32), amazement, and fear (ch. 10:32), and there to be seen no more, Mark then has Jesus

213. Bornkamm, *et al., Tradition and Interpretation in Matthew,* p. 38, n. 1.

214. E. Schweizer, *Church Order in the New Testament* (Studies in Biblical Theology, No. 32; London: SCM Press, Ltd., 1961), traces conceptions of the church in almost every book of the New Testament except Mark! For contrast, see Trocmé.

again come into Galilee, going ahead of his own disciples and Peter (chs. 14:28; 16:7) without first appearing or being seen in an Easter vision, but promising them in a message by a "young man" [215] that in Galilee "you will see him, as he told you."

Mark's Use of the Traditions. Not a single one of the forms or traditional literary units that form criticism and *Gattungskritik* can establish are missing from the Gospel of Mark. Despite his general avoidance of the Q source, Mark viewed Jesus as the wisdom teacher of sayings, as prophetic and apocalyptic discerner of truth, and as priestly and scribal discerner of right and wrong just as much as other evangelists. Despite the prominence of miracles, which are not lacking in Q, either, Mark's view of Jesus' activity is primarily that of a teacher. The exorcisms are secondary.[216] Mark's guiding principle of selecting only some and of not incorporating most of Jesus' sayings seems to be the same that is operative in his reshaping of the narrative traditions: the principle of secrecy or mystery surrounding Jesus' ministry, in which only a select few were privileged to become partners.

To give his readers, the Christians of his own day, the members of Mark's church, an intelligible clue to the interpretation of this mystery, Mark chose from Q only material suitable to his purpose. Besides using the parables of Jesus for this end,[217] Mark cites sayings of Jesus in only two sections, both of which are specially designated as esoteric instructions to the Twelve or even a specially privileged group among the Twelve: (1) the instructions following the teaching about the divine necessity of suffering and death at the hands of both Israel's rulers and the Gentiles, and (2) the esoteric revelation about "the end"

215. Cf. J. Knox, "A Note on Mark 14:51-52," in Johnson, S. E. (ed.) *The Joy of Study: Papers on New Testament and Related Subjects Presented to Honor Frederick Clifton Grant* (The Macmillan Company, 1951), pp. 27–30; H. Waetjen, "The Ending of Mark and the Gospel's Shift in Eschatology," in the *Annual of the Swedish Theological Institute,* Vol. IV (1965), pp. 114–131.

216. Rightly so emphasized by E. Schweizer, in *Neotestamentica et Patristica,* pp. 35–39, against J. M. Robinson; but also against Carrington, Manék, and others with their emphasis on baptism.

217. Burkill, *Mysterious Revelation,* pp. 96–116.

(ch. 13). Synoptic studies such as Reicke's about the four forms or *Gattungen* of early Christian preaching, and of the three kinds of preacher (Jesus, the apostles, and what Reicke calls "ordinary ministers and laymen")[218] utterly fail in the important critical task of outlining and then weighing the merits of the distinctive theology expressed by the Evangelist's modification of the traditions.

Mark's departure from the tradition is evident in two omissions that are significant for probably the same theological reason. Mark omitted all traces of a Judean ministry of Jesus with his disciples prior to his coming to Galilee. He omitted also the narratives about Easter and everything connected with it. In Jerusalem the disciples lost sight of and took leave of Jesus (ch. 14:27). But it was in Jerusalem also that both the promise of his "going before them" (v. 28) and the gift preceding his going (vs. 22-25) were given to them. The loss of sight of him, his absence, and the disciples "falling away" inevitably gets emphasized out of all proportion if one neglects to see not only Jesus' own assurance and promise of his going before them, but above all the present, ever-present gift of the new Paschal Lamb, the Eucharist.

There is another feature that easily becomes distorted in view of Mark's use of the sources. The fact that at Jerusalem the chosen disciples lose sight of Jesus and there fall away from him must be evaluated not only, as is fashionable now, on the background of Mark's use of the Roman centurion as a Gentile who alone seems to be grasping the mystery of Jesus as "King of Israel," the "mysterious revelation." There is another side to Mark's understanding of the passion, which is brought out by Joseph of Arimathea (ch. 15:42-46). This "respected member of the council" (*bouleutēs*)[219] learns, as only Mark observes, from none other than the centurion about the death of Jesus. And as the disciples of John the Baptist did at his

218. Bo Reicke, "A Synopsis of Early Christian Preaching," in Fridrichsen (ed.), *The Root of the Vine,* pp. 128–160.

219. On *buolē* as court of justice as distinct from the political Sanhedrin, see H. Mantel, *Studies in the History of the Sanhedrin* (Harvard University Press, 1961), pp. 94 f.

death, so does this man, who according to Matthew and the Fourth Gospel was a "disciple" of Jesus,[220] attend to the burial of his master. He, too, was "looking for the kingdom," for the "mysterious revelation." Jesus' prediction that the Son of Man would be delivered first to Jewish leaders and then to Gentiles (Mark 10:33) had been fulfilled. The Sanhedrin and Pilate had sentenced him to death. But for Mark there was not only a leading Gentile, but also a respected Jew under the cross, each in his own way expressing his confession and service to Jesus.

That Jesus had witnesses, disciples, followers, believers, working for him, with or without his knowledge and consent, is clearly part of the early gospel tradition preserved also in Mark. The fame or report about Jesus spreads by men other than only the appointed fishers of men, the apostles. This is clearly the case in Acts (the Hellenistic Jerusalem mission of the Seven, chs. 6 to 8; the Antiochian mission, ch. 13:1 ff.) and in Paul's letters (I Thess. 1:8 and Rom. 1:8; Paul compliments the churches for spreading the faith everywhere). The crucial theological issue is how the office of the appointed fishers of men, the apostles, is related to this "lay apostolate" of all believers.

Sandwiched between Jesus' first sight of the Galilean fishermen, and the accompanying call to follow and become fishers of men (Mark 1:16 f.), and the apostles' promise of seeing Jesus in Galilee (ch. 16:7), we have a host of witnesses for Jesus who were all eye and ear witnesses of what he had done and taught. They all had first-hand experience and knowledge of the newness and authority of Jesus' word and work. This applies to the first anonymous witness mentioned in ch. 1:28, the healed Gerasene demoniac (ch. 5:18-20) as well as the herdsmen (vs. 14-16), the strange exorcist (ch. 9:38 f.), and numerous others, and finally the Roman centurion, Joseph of Arimathea, and the witnessing women. Reicke's argument that these "ordinary ministers and laymen" had "scarcely themselves formed part of the Lord's audience" is neither

220. Lohmeyer, *Das Evangelium des Markus,* p. 350, took this as "evidence of a prolonged and repeated activity of Jesus in Jerusalem." So also Dodd, *Historical Tradition,* pp. 138 f., 246 f.

convincing to the historian, nor would it meet the challenge of the Gnostics.

It is one thing to observe with Reicke that in order to maintain "congruity between congregational preaching in the churches and the mind of Jesus" there was "the personal and literary oversight of the Apostles and their colleagues [who] clearly replaced the Lord's own oral teaching." [221] It is another thing (and here lies the crucial theological issue), how that overseeing is done, that is, the ways and means of it, and also the way it is justified theologically. The traditions underlying the Gospels, The Acts, and the letters which preserve the distinction between appointed fishers of men or apostles and those not appointed but also working for Jesus lead us to inquire what exactly the meaning of "fishers of men" is if it is not merely a simile for universal mission, let alone mission specifically to Gentiles rather than to Israel.[222]

The same issue emerges in Mark's use or, rather, introduction [223] of the concept *euangelion* in his outline of the historical ministry of Jesus and his partners. Although the gospel traditions depict many people engaged in spreading the fame (*akoē*), report (*ēchos*), or account (*logos*) of Jesus' teachings and doings, which is a *diēgēsis* (report) all its own (cf. Mark 5:16 with ch. 9:9 and Luke 1:1), according to Mark only Jesus and the appointed fishers of men preach "gospel." For Mark, only Jesus (ch. 1:10-12), and the fishers of men only in the act of preaching the "gospel" (ch. 13:11), have the Holy Spirit. The critical theological problem, however, is to assess Mark's way of making his own theological perspective explicit. Not the fact that but the way how and the reason why Mark's distinctive Christology is related to the men-fishing, gospel-preaching, and Spirit-sustained ministry is the crucial issue. The secrecy motif and the absence of Easter narra-

221. Reicke, in *The Root of the Vine,* pp. 131–132.

222. So Hahn, *Mission in the New Testament,* pp. 111 ff., esp. pp. 114–120. Similarly, and in the tradition of Lightfoot, Lohmeyer, Volkmar, and others, G. H. Boobyer and M. Kiddle in essays cited by Hahn, p. 112, n. 2. Also, H. Schlier, "Die Entscheidung für die Heidenmission in der Urchristenheit" in *Die Zeit der Kirche* (Freiburg: Herder, 1958), pp. 90–107.

223. W. Marxsen, *Der Evangelist Markus* (Göttingen: Vandenhoeck, 1959), pp. 77–92.

tives are two among other clues we have in Mark for solving this issue.

Before we outline the conceptions of discipleship in other early Christian literary traditions, a statement may be in order about the two separate issues we are facing here. First, we are facing the task of defining the meaning of men-fishing in the traditional distinction between the simile as applicable to a variety of functions exercised by preachers, teachers, healers, and the like, and the simile as applied to the chosen disciples and appointed apostles as men-fishing partners in the ministry of Jesus. Men-fishing appears here as a metaphoric expression for a variety of functions applicable to a variety of social, cultural, psychical activities.

But the metaphor stands not only for a function or variety of functions (religion as mission, education, worship, and the like). It also stands for claims exerted, for values and authority imposed by those very functions, that is, by the active (fishing) or passive (fished) participation of people in these functions. This is the theology of men-fishing in the Christian tradition. It has its basis in the historicity of Jesus' selection of a limited number of partners whose alleged historical behavior of finally "falling away" from and denying or denouncing their partnership in Jesus' men-fishing ministry raises all the more sharply the question of the meaning of their men-fishing activity as compared with that of other believers besides themselves.

Secondly, we are faced with the task of analyzing the contemporary purpose for which, and the ways and means by which, the later Evangelists and the authors of "epistles," "Acts," and "revelations" undertook to theologize about this distinction between the traditional men-fishing by any and all who are "not against us" both inside and outside the organized church as fellowship of followers (Mark 9:38), and the specific men-fishing of the appointed "fishers of men."

Some Interpretations of Men-Fishing Besides Mark's. This part can at best be only the most rudimentary outline of certain highlights in the complex historical and theological developments of primitive Christianity. Only in the gospel literature does the fishing metaphor play an important role. But the theological issue of apostolic ministry is sometimes central, sometimes not, in other canonical and extracanonical writings. A theological criterion is clearly implied by the distinction not only between appointed fishers of men and the "lay apostolate," the "royal priesthood" of all believers, but also between true and false fishers of men, between true and false prophecy, teaching, shepherding, and the like. This is clearly brought out in the prophetic or apocalyptic sayings attributed to Jesus, and in the warnings that the prophet gives when speaking in the Spirit. Besides, in early gospel and revelation traditions, this hermeneutical issue is clearly reflected in Paul's contest with those who trouble him and the churches (Gal. 1:7; 6:17), who challenge Paul's gospel and Paul's ways in Christ with another gospel, another Jesus, another spirit (II Cor. 11:4). The believers, who have the right and duty to judge by themselves and test the spirits whether they are of God or not, challenge the apostle's legitimacy, not out of some sudden theoretical scruple, but by finding themselves "bewitched" (Gal. 3:1) by rival fishers of men. Paul can speak of them in traditional fashion by comparing them with predatory animals (dogs, wolves, lions) or by using such "analogies" [224] as that of apostle, laborer, farmer, architect, guide, father, nurse, and others, and qualifying them as false, deceitful, and the like.

There are several clues to Matthew's theology of menfishing.[225] For one, there is Matthew's use of the parables of Jesus as applicable primarily to the church's leaders as subject to judgment,[226] not despite but because of their authority role in the church. Then we have Matthew's em-

224. Cf. H. M. Gale, *The Use of Analogy in the Letters of Paul* (The Westminster Press, 1964).

225. G. Strecker, *Der Weg der Gerechtigkeit,* pp. 191 ff.; Schweizer, *Church Order in the New Testament,* pp. 51–62; W. Trilling, *Das Wahre Israel,* rev. ed. (Studien zum A. u. N. T., No. 10; Munich: Kösel, 1964); G. Bornkamm, in *Tradition and Interpretation in Matthew,* pp. 15–51; R. Hummel, *Die Auseinandersetzung zwischen Kirche und Judentum im Matthäusevangelium* (Munich: Kaiser, 1963).

226. See above, p. 181.

phasis on the disciples' full knowledge of, and acquaintance with "the mysteries of the kingdom." [227] We have already reviewed Matthew's adaptation of the Easter commission.[228] Most important is Matthew's interest in Simon's role as Rock of the church (ch. 16:18 f.). Peter wields, in interaction with the church (ch. 18:18), the executive power of the keys, which could apply to both the authority in church discipline and in teaching, combining the traditional men-fishing skills of the priest, wise man, and scribe.[229] That Matthew attributes such authority not only to the church as a whole, but also to an individual apostle does not, as von Campenhausen rightly warns,[230] thereby say anything about the particular form of its use and theological justification.[231] The fact that "the basic intentions of Matthew's and Paul's theology" could be reconciled in early Christian traditions at least for a while,[232] underscores von Campenhausen's warnings.

What emerges from the study of these Matthean features is clearly one point: the New Israel, that is, the eschatological covenant community with its own order of eschatological offices, executes Christ's own authority on earth. This authority is expressed in his teachings as the new Torah; it will be valid both for the time until the end of the age, and for the Kingdom itself. Though the church and its men-fishing apostles, as well as the world at large, still await the final eschatological fishing at the judgment following the coming of the Son of Man, the criterion of the men-fishing judgment is already clearly announced in Jesus' Torah, which contains all the mysteries of the Kingdom. Where Matthew sees the new law, the teaching of Jesus as new Moses, as the link between the

227. G. Barth, "Matthew's Understanding of the Law," in *Tradition and Interpretation in Matthew*, pp. 105 ff.

228. See above, pp. 194 f.

229. W. D. Davies, *The Setting of the Sermon on the Mount* (Cambridge: Cambridge University Press, 1964), pp. 228–230, on Matthew as "closely related to [Qumran]."

230. In *Aus der Frühzeit des Christentums*, p. 28.

231. On the interpretation of Matt. 16:18 f. in early Christian literature, see now É. Massaux, *Influence de l'Évangile de Saint Matthieu sur la littérature chrétienne avant Saint Irénée* (Louvain: Publ. Univ., 1950).

232. Koester, *Harvard Theological Review*, Vol. 58 (1965), p. 289.

two conceptions of men-fishing—that which is carried on presently in the church and by its men-fishers [233] and that which the Son of Man himself will carry out at his coming—there Mark will put something else in its stead.

The features characteristic of Luke's conception of men-fishing [234] have been identified variously in the accounts of the Easter commission with the novel Lucan emphasis of a separate Pentecost [235] with which a new period begins, the age of the church, following the past age of Jesus, the time of "the gospel," [236] and preceding the age to come. How incisively the age of men-fishing with the historical Jesus differs from the men-fishing of the Lucan church and its men-fishing officers is brought out clearly and programmatically in the prologue.[237] Peculiar to Luke is "the postponement of the call" by Luke's introduction of various accounts of Jesus' activities, with even a passing remark about his Judean ministry, before the account of Peter's call and commission to catch men (*zōgrein*).[238]

That Peter "and those with him" are authorized to go men-fishing "henceforth" (*apo tou nun*) is as characteristic of Luke as is the note of the net torn because of the multitude of fish caught. The overwhelming abundance of Jesus' gift to them and of his miraculous power rather than his command after "seeing" them, as in Mark, is characteristic for Luke's view of Jesus working in the fullness of time when the disciples themselves experience unadulterated success in their men-fishing mission. Even

233. On the corresponding Matthean conception of Holy Spirit, see E. Schweizer, "Spirit of God," *Bible Key Words*, edited by G. Kittel, Vol. IX (London: Adam & Charles Black, Ltd., 1960), pp. 24–36. On Matthew's interpretation of "Gospel," see Marxsen, *Der Evangelist Markus*, pp. 92–95.

234. Besides Conzelmann's *Theology of St. Luke*, see now C. H. Talbert, *Luke and the Gnostics* (Abingdon Press, 1966), and the essays by W. C. Robinson, E. Käsemann, G. Bornkamm, and others in *Studies in Luke-Acts*, P. Schubert *Festschrift* (Abingdon Press, 1966). Cf. also E. Schweizer, *Church Order in the New Testament*, pp. 63–76; J. Jervell, "Das gespaltene Israel und die Heidenvölker," *Studia Theologica*, Vol. 19 (1965), pp. 68–96; J. Roloff, *Apostolat, Verkündigung, Kirche* (Gütersloh: Mohn, 1965), pp. 169–235.

235. Schweizer, "Spirit of God," *loc. cit.*, pp. 36–54.

236. Marxsen, *Der Evangelist Markus*, pp. 95–98.

237. See G. Klein, "Lukas 1, 1-4 als theologisches Programm," in *Zeit und Geschichte*, Bultmann *Festschrift*, pp. 193–216.

238. Conzelmann, *Theology of St. Luke*, p. 39, n. 1.

after Easter these features seem to prevail in Luke's portrait of the men-fishing activities which resemble more those of Paul's opponents in Second Corinthians and those mentioned in the commission charge of the secondary ending of Mark (ch. 16:15-18), than those in Matthew, the Fourth Gospel, or the original Mark.

Luke's choice of the verb *zōgrein* (ch. 5:10), in the double meaning of catching men and, "in so doing [bringing] them new life" [239] may be as significant as the substitute of shepherding (*poimainein*) in the Fourth Gospel appendix (John 21:15 ff.). Likewise, the torn net in Luke points to something different from that which John emphasizes by the net that did not tear with a hundred and fifty-three fish in it (John 21:11). But more important than deciding (1) whether the fruitless fishing close to shore signifies the the futile Jewish mission, and (2) whether the torn net signifies controversies between Jewish and Gentile Christians or simply the success of the church's mission to the Gentiles, and (3) whether Peter's role in Luke, ch. 5, corresponds to that in Acts, ch. 10, and (4) whether the Seventy or Seventy-two are technically also "fishers of men," the discussion over Luke's theology should focus instead on what happens to the fishers of men after Easter, when the fullness of time, the historical Jesus, and their partnership with him in this fullness is succeeded by the time of the church.

Here lies the value of Acts, and Luke's reason for writing two volumes, each of a different genre, a "gospel" and "acts." If the fishers of men before Easter were partners with Jesus in the fullness of time, which will return only at the end of time at the coming of the Son of Man, then their function after Easter must be to secure "the continuity of the Gospel (that is, of the living Jesus) within the discontinuity of the times and within the variation of the kerygma." [240] Peter and the Twelve are fishers of men from then on, primarily as "the guarantor(s) of the Gospel tradition," [241] that is, guarantors of the living and coming Jesus, guarantors of having "seen" and heard the promise

239. Hilgert, *The Ship and Related Symbols,* p. 110.
240. Käsemann, in *Essays on New Testament Themes,* p. 46.
241. *Ibid.,* pp. 89 f.

of "will see." Paul's voluntary act of visiting (*historêsai*) Peter (Gal. 1:18)[242] implies, not recognition from or by Peter, but recognition of Peter, similar to Paul's recognition of James.[243]

The emergence of a so-called "early Catholicism" in the New Testament used to be accounted for in terms of the "acute Hellenization" (Harnack), but Käsemann now sees it as due to the acute apocalyptization of Christianity, that is, "in the apocalyptic concept of the new Israel."[244] That Paul "shattered" this "apocalyptic dream of primitive Jewish Christianity"[245] appears to me to be overstating the case in the shadow still of the Tübingen school in much the same way those do who still pitch the Jerusalem Hellenists (Acts, chs. 6 to 8) against the Hebraists. There are differences, yes. But how substantive are they? How are they theologically substantiated?

Even if with Käsemann, Conzelmann, and others one sees in Luke-Acts a theology of history replace the primitive apocalypticism, the issue for us here is whether or not, and if so, how substantively, this change did affect the conception of fishers of men. Von Campenhausen wants us to see that what changes there were in the conception of the nature of the church, of the ministry, and the like did not seriously affect the church's life till the controversies of the second half of the second century.[246] But does not Bauer's view of orthodoxy and heresy in primitive Christianity[247] lead us to think otherwise? Can, indeed, must we not look at the acute apocalyptization of Christianity as only one and parallel movement to the acute gnosticization or syncretization which, as in post-Biblical Judaism, though

242. See W. D. Davies, *The Setting of the Sermon on the Mount,* pp. 453–455.

243. On the role of James, see Thomas, logion 12; see below on the Gospel of Thomas. Cf. W. Schmithals, *Paul and James.*

244. Käsemann, in *Essays on New Testament Themes,* pp. 91 f. See also his essay on "Early Catholicism in Paul" in *Zeitschr. f. Theol. u. Kirche,* Vol. 60 (1963), pp. 75–89. Cf. Koester, *Harvard Theological Revue,* Vol. 58 (1965), p. 315, n. 106.

245. Käsemann, in *Essays on New Testament Themes,* p. 92.

246. In *Aus der Frühzeit des Christentums,* pp. 28 f.

247. Cf. Strecker's report on his own new edition of Bauer in *Journal of Bible and Religion,* Vol. 31 (1965), pp. 53–56.

distinct movements, may be like two sides of the same coin? And the coin stands for the interpretation of the mysterious, that is, eschatological, revelation of God which, in all its finality remaining mediated *in* history, predicates that history as ended, fulfilled.

The gnostic or gnosticizing view of the men-fishing office is perhaps best, and historically first, illustrated by the Gospel of Thomas.[248] If the Thomas tradition is a source independent of the Synoptic traditions, similar to what Dodd contends about the *Historical Tradition in the Fourth Gospel,* then we have here a theology of men-fishing in a different key. Should these various traditions have their origin in some activity of the apostolic fishers of men in a given area, then Thomas' view may be representative of how apostleship came to be understood in eastern Syria around Edessa, just as Paul's letters are representative of views current in parts of Asia Minor and Greece,[249] and as Peter represents views held in Palestine and parts of western Syria.[250] Each apostle was the authority for his church; each responsible for a version of Christianity that is indigenous not so much to an area as to an individual apostle.

If Thomas is, as Koester makes plausible, the twin brother of James, hence, a relative of Jesus, then it is quite possible that the "polemical note" which Conzelmann detects in the composition of Luke 4:16 to 5:11, "reflecting the rivalry of two groups, one evidently gathered round Peter, and another round the relatives of the Lord," [251] could allude to this early overlapping of western and eastern Syrian apostolic men-fishing activities. Likewise, Pauline, Petrine, and Apolline missions did intersect at least for a time or limited area only. The picture in Acts where Peter is succeeded by James is similar to the picture in the Gospel of Thomas where James is superceded by Thomas. To speak of succession may be quite in order, provided it

248. For a comprehensive review of research on Thomas and a bibliography about each of three basic approaches to Thomas, see Koester, *Harvard Theological Review,* Vol. 58 (1965), pp. 291–306.

249. *Ibid.,* pp. 306 ff.

250. *Ibid.,* pp. 284–290.

251. *The Theology of St. Luke,* p. 43.

is not misunderstood in the later sense of succession as per se and by the rite of the laying on of hands thereby legitimating the apostle's, or his successor's authority, as intimated by the pastoral epistles and Luke's own view set forth in Acts.

Like Matthew's basically Petrine, western Syrian view of apostleship, Thomas develops his own view also from the Sayings of Jesus or from Jesus as teacher, prophet, wise man. Thomas does it only more exclusively so, and yet in a version that is as different again from the Q source as each of them is different from the Johannine Sayings source. What Koester says about Q, namely, that it has "domesticated the Logoi through a particular apocalypticism,"[252] is equally applicable to the Thomas and the Johannine Sayings *Gattung*. For Thomas to choose the *Gattung* of Sayings for his interpretation of the meaning of the men-fishing task is as significant as Luke's choice of the gospel *Gattung* for one period and of the *praxeis* or "acts" *Gattung* for the following period.

Though absent from his disciples, Jesus is still with them. In Mark he *is* with them as the one who is "going ahead" of them. In Acts it is the Spirit or as Spirit that Jesus is with them. In Thomas, Jesus, "the living one," manifests himself as such in the continuity of his wisdom teaching as the continuity of revelation in the discontinuity of time, as the *kērygma* in history. Apocalypticism in Acts was replaced by history; in Thomas it is replaced by wisdom. Whether this wisdom is gnostically understood and interpreted in Thomas can be decided with certainty only by putting Thomas on the same level as the developed gnostic systems of the second century.

The same applies to Acts. To see intimations in Acts of a legalistic "Catholic" interpretation of the apostolic office is possible only from the vantage point of the late second century as von Campenhausen rightly claims. This, however, does not deny that changes did take place. What I do call into question is that such changes in the emergence of indigenous types of apostolic Christianity, as

252. Koester, *Harvard Theological Review,* Vol. 58 (1965), p. 301.

there assuredly were, must not be looked at as at once displaying the full later dogmatic content and juridical format. What the relationship of this primitive canonical and extracanonical material is to the later tradition (the Scripture vs. tradition problem) is one thing. It is another thing, for which I contended earlier in this study, that the ministry of the historical Jesus, rather than the indigenousness of individual apostles, let alone of different areas or cultures, is the primary exhibit for a case of syncretism and apocalypticism in its first Christian form.

Thomas, the fisher of men, the apostle of the living Jesus, executes his call by exposing men to the mystery of the Kingdom through teaching which, like that of the historical Jesus, was largely, almost exclusively, in parables, similes, or symbols. In that sense Thomas views his men-fishing ministry as does Mark, who links it with the "mysterious revelation" in which the fishers of men, and only they, become partners. What separates Thomas from Mark is the lack, not so much of the passion narrative and apocalyptic material, but of making these motifs explicit.

The conceptions of apostleship, and other "analogies" or similes applied to this ecclesiastical office as distinct from mere function, should be analyzed also as to their use in other documents of the New Testament. But that must be reserved for another occasion. There are at least two more distinct developments noticeable in the New Testament: One is that associated with Paul, as evident in his letters, and in the pseudepigraphical traditions of the pastoral epistles, and the letters to the Ephesians and Hebrews. The other is associated with the name of the apostle John, in the Fourth Gospel, in the letters attributed to him, and the Apocalypse. By documenting the variety of traditions before and besides Mark, it is hoped that thereby Mark's theology will more clearly come into view. Within and among the existing theological diversification Mark chose his own particular stance. Returning to the theology of Mark in conclusion is not for the purpose of setting it up as a normative model, but only to highlight its individual characteristics which later became modified by Mark's association first with Paul, then with

Peter,[253] each of whom recognized the however temporary or otherwise limited significance of Mark.

Fishers of Men in Mark. The Evangelist Mark uses two basic keys to unlock the problem of the meaning of men-fishing: one is the (since Wrede) famous motif of the Messianic secret; the other is the motif of seeing and being seen by Jesus. The choice of the "sight" idiom predisposes Mark for concentrating on the narrative material that makes Jesus "visible," but the "secrecy" motif demands the language idiom—hence, Jesus as teacher of parables. E. Schweizer's view of Jesus as for Mark preeminently the teacher of the mystery of the Kingdom deserves full emphasis. But when he explains Jesus' choice of the parables as "accommodation to their [i.e., the disciples'] limited ability to understand (*Anpassung an Verstandesfähigkeit*)," and then takes their consistent lack of understanding as evidence of the impenetrable and alien character of God's eschatological revelation,[254] Schweizer confuses the issue. Burkill's view of the nature of "mysterious revelation" in Mark is similar to Schweizer's when he claims that the failure to comprehend Jesus was "neither a freak of chance nor even an outcome of human volition, but a provision of God's sovereign purpose."[255]

Neither mysteriousness per se nor inscrutability of God's purpose is the nature of Mark's conception of the "mysterious revelation." To be sure, the inability of the disciples, though specially trained and secretly taught by Jesus, is not mere unwillingness. Here lies the shortcoming of a one-sided existentialistic interpretation and the decisionism it advocates. For Mark, the mystery becomes intelligible, and Jesus' call obeyable, not at one but at two points; and it is the second point that necessitates the omission of Easter narratives. The first point is Johannine in character: the mystery of the Kingdom is revealed in the cross. Jesus as the symbol of Israel, the medium and interpreter of God's plan, of salvation history, of the power of God, becomes intelligible only at the point

253. Cf. *ibid.*, p. 314, n. 100.

254. In *Neotestamentica et Patristica*, pp. 39 f.

255. *Mysterious Revelation*, p. 116.

where/when in his faithfulness and obedience until death he confirms his mediumship, his role as savior.

The other point, comparable to the second focus in an ellipse, concerns the apocalyptic element which Marxsen to a degree rightly identified but misleadingly associated with the localized Parousia expectation of the Marcan church in Galilee. The resurrection of Jesus is only one historical stage among others in the Marcan conception of "gospel" whose "beginning" (ch. 1:1) lies with the Baptist's announcement of the imminence of the Kingdom, but whose "end" comes only with "seeing" the Son of Man. This is the essential bipolarity of Mark's theology to which Burkill refers.[256] But when he says that for Mark "the earthly ministry is not the sphere of divine revelation, but the appointed antecedent of such revelation," [257] or again that "the earthly ministry of the Messiah can hardly be in an unqualified sense the locus of revelation," [258] then too much is made of a good thing.

Historical revelation, whether as Israel or Jesus, by definition excludes even looking for a locus of revelation in an unqualified sense. Mark is not interested in "overcoming the bipolarity," [259] but in qualifying, that is, in interpreting it. That also applies to Jewish apocalypticists as much as to Cabalists or to Christian prophets and Gnostics. The apocalyptic categories in the legend tradition about Easter, transfiguration, and Pentecost are not eliminated by Mark; "seeing" Jesus or "having" the Spirit is for Mark not a static past historical or future mythological entity; it can be had only in "being" with Jesus, who for Mark is always "going ahead." As in Heb. 6:20 (forerunner); 12:2 (pioneer); 13:12 (suffering outside the gate), with believers being exhorted to follow or go forth, so in Mark, Jesus can be "seen," and Spirit can be "had" only in being where Jesus is gone or going, or in going into the direction from which he is coming. According to Mark, only appointed "fishers of men" know or have experienced the scope of that "being with Jesus," not in spite of but because they temporarily but thoroughly "fell

256. *Ibid.*, p. 177.
257. *Ibid.*, p. 173.
258. *Ibid.*, p. 179.
259. *Ibid.*

away," denounced and "denied" Jesus. Only the appointed fishers of men, the apostles, are directed to go forth to Galilee and there to "see" him "as he told you."

Mark is not what Dibelius called a passion story with a long prologue; that would recognize only one of the two poles pointed out earlier. No, Mark is, similar to The Revelation to John, an account of the apocalypse of Jesus for which both past and present are but prologue. Partnership with Jesus' full authority and power is fully realized only in the act of overcoming fear (Mark 16:8) or sleep (ch. 14:37, 40), or overcoming one's disposition for the things of men (*phronein ta tōn anthrōpōn,* ch. 8:33). It is possible only in what Paul called overcoming the offense of the cross. The conclusion of Mark's Gospel is deliberate: the apostles are scattered; the shepherd is absent. Instead of imagining them on their way home to Galilee, they may well be imagined as sitting in closed rooms around the Lord's Table, hesitantly but faithfully celebrating the covenant and promises Jesus had come to confirm (Rom. 15:8 f.). But Mark gives no indication whether the fishers of men were again "with Jesus," were again on the road and following him into Galilee.

Leaving it open-ended as he does, Mark underscores the promise that only those who do become "obedient to the heavenly vision" will indeed "see him." They will indeed be rewarded but only as those who continue to accept the gift Jesus increased with every day of his life: the gift of the power and certainty of God which came to them in the "newness" of Jesus' teaching. The future tense in Mark 1:17: "I will make you become fishers of men" has the same significance as that in ch. 14:62: "You will see the Son of Man sitting at the right hand of Power," or as in ch. 16:7: "There you will see him," or as in ch. 13:11 with its promised Marcan Pentecost. They have "become," and then "are," fishers of men only and as long as they are partners, participants in what Burkill called "the whole career of Jesus [as in Mark's eyes the] fulfillment of the purpose of God." [260] But when Cullmann likewise says that the apostolic, men-fishing commission received its

260. *Ibid.,* p. 172.

content from "the fulfillment of the Messianic function that Jesus himself exercised," [261] then clarification is demanded. For by omitting the Easter commission, Mark qualifies this tradition by saying that the career of Jesus has only just begun, or, to modify Cullmann's phrase, Jesus' Messianic function is still being exercised.

For Mark to place the call of the disciples to become fishers of men at the very beginning of the Gospel can therefore not mean what it does in Luke: authenticity of men-fishing based on the historical reliability of their witness.[262] "Primarily concerned" as Mark is with the pre-Easter period [263] because of his "effort to establish the connection forward with the life of the church," [264] the Easter commission in Mark can therefore not simply have been dropped as "falling outside the scope of his work." For, as Burkill himself observes, the "required connection forward is not really established," which may give us the clue as to why it was dropped.

By omitting the Easter commission Mark does not deny, ignore, or otherwise downplay the presence of Christ in the world or in the church, as implied in G. Barth's essay,[265] but rather gives it a different interpretation. In this he is closer to the author of The Revelation to John and his view of the presence of Christ (Rev., chs. 2 to 3) and its relation to his coming than to Paul, Matthew, or the Fourth Gospel. The "prolepsis of the power (*dynamis*) of the Son of Man" which Tödt sees expressed in the manifestations of "authority" or "newness" in Jesus' historical ministry came variously expressed in the various combinations of gospel traditions.[266] What Tödt does for Christol-

261. *Peter: Disciple, Apostle, Martyr,* 2d rev. ed. (The Westminster Press, 1962), p. 220. On Marcan soteriology, see now E. Best, *The Temptation and the Passion* (Society for New Testament Studies, Monograph Series 2; Cambridge: Cambridge University Press, 1965).

262. Burkill, *Mysterious Revelation,* pp. 31 f.

263. *Ibid.,* p. 250.

264. *Ibid.,* p. 251. Cf. also Trocmé, *La Formation de l'Évangile selon Marc,* p. 68, on Mark's "Exposé des véritables intentions ecclésiologiques de Jésus."

265. In *Tradition and Interpretation in Matthew,* p. 111.

266. H. E. Tödt, *The Son of Man in the Synoptic Tradition* (The Westminster Press, 1965), pp. 294 ff.

ogy and Fuchs for the interpretation of Christian existence in general based on "the christological coherence of [Mark]," [267] I want to do for the interpretation of Mark's view of the apostolic, men-fishing office.

The authority, newness, and proleptic power that Jesus manifests, and which he promises also to his called and appointed partners, is for Mark not juridically conceived as executive, judiciary commission. But a specific commission it is none the less. The apocalyptic orientation of Mark's theology does not exclude the conception of delegated authority as such, nor that of divine law [268] or wisdom teaching. The prominent role that the special, almost esoteric, quality of the partnership with Jesus has in Mark's account of "the Gospel of Jesus Christ, Son of God," and of its "beginning," suggests that Mark wants to be just as explicit about the role of Peter and the Twelve, as is Matthew or the other Evangelists. Mark does not ignore the issue expressed in the traditional Easter commissions or in Matt. 16:18 f.; he only has his own way of interpreting the substance and scope of this men-fishing commission to Peter and the Twelve; he has his own way of explicating the criterion by which to judge whether or not this commission is being carried out adequately.

And the criterion for Mark is "to see Jesus." For in seeing him, following him as the forerunner, the new exodus, and only thereby to come to see him, the secret of the Kingdom is revealed: only to them, only through him. The first thing the appointed fishers of men "see" in Mark is Jesus' "coming into Galilee, preaching the gospel of God" (ch. 1:14). The last thing they "see" is the supper and his voluntary surrender to his captors. The next time they "see" him—if at all—is when again he comes into Galilee.

What Mark has taken over from the tradition are the following elements: The divine commission to be fishers of men, which makes them proleptically exercise divine

267. *Studies of the Historical Jesus,* p. 118, n. 1.

268. Cf. E. Käsemann, "Sätze heiligen Rechtes im Neuen Testament," in *Exegetische Versuche und Besinnungen,* Vol. II (Göttingen: Vandenhoeck, 1964), pp. 69–82.

power as authority, does not come from God directly, but through a medium, a new medium; not Torah or Moses, but Jesus. Without constant contact with Jesus (his "presence" or the followers' "faith," prayer, and the like), this commission is ineffective, powerless. Temporal disruption of this contact (the "absence" of Jesus or the "flight" of the disciples), which renders them ineffective, is one thing. Substantive disruption ("denying" Jesus, "blaspheming against the Holy Spirit"), which renders them illegitimate, is another thing.

The fallen-away disciples, and Peter who denied Jesus, not the believers in general, are called again to follow Jesus as he goes ahead into Galilee. This suggests that Peter's denial did not automatically and forever lead him to forfeit his commission. The once made call is binding for those who heard and accepted the call. In this sense also is Israel's call irrevocable, as Paul shows. Loose talk about Israel's forfeiting its inheritance because of its rejection of Christ is as misleading and harmful as post-Reformation talk has been about episcopacy and papacy having forfeited their rights. Whether Rome's argument of a *de iure* authority or Rabbinical arguments about Israel's *de iure* "advantage," as Paul called it (Rom. 3:1), are adequate enough to reflect the full scope of the "spiritual blessings" (*ta pneumatika,* Rom. 15:27), is another question.

That the called fishers of men fell short and fell away finally is not Mark's emphasis. That the fishers of men had authority to heal and perform miracles also is not peculiar to Mark. What sets the future leaders of the church apart from the rest of the believers are two points, according to Mark: It is they who are first called when Jesus comes into Galilee (chs. 1:14 and 14:28; 16:7). It is they who are taught by Jesus directly, privately, about the "secret of the kingdom"; the Messianic secret is fully disclosed to them at the Last Supper. Other believers or disciples of Jesus may "see" Jesus on the cross. But only the appointed fishers of men "see" the Eucharistic Supper; only to them has been given the secret of the Kingdom, just as Israel's divinely commissioned fishers of men have "the keys of knowledge" (Luke 11:52).

But unlike Matthew, and unlike the Rabbinic fishers of men, the teaching of which Mark speaks does not concern the words or law of Jesus; it solely concerns the substance of what can be "seen" in Jesus. This is for Mark as empirical as the signs in the Fourth Gospel. As the medium of the eschatological revelation, Jesus empirically manifests forgiveness and healing and resurrection as present signs of, but not as the presence of, the Kingdom of God. It is in this substance of what can be seen in Jesus that the fishers of men actively share and collaborate. But like Jesus' own Kingdom ministry that becomes for Mark fully legitimated by what Jesus does, so also the ministry of Jesus' partners manifests its divine legitimacy by what they do. That the gospel must be preached to all nations (chs. 13:10; 14:9) is for Mark something which, like the call to self-denial and cross-bearing, every believer should do.[269]

Wherein, then, does men-fishing differ from evangelizing? Is there for Mark any difference between fishers of men or apostles and the preaching of the gospel? As a function, acting as men-fishers is, like Paul's conception of apostleship, merely one function among others, such as serving, shepherding, witnessing, interpreting tongues, wielding executive or administrative powers, prophesying, healing, baptizing, teaching, and other activities. Our study of the use and understanding of fishing metaphors in non-Christian traditions has shown that the metaphor could apply to any number of activities. It is thus as neutral a metaphor as apostle-*shaliaḥ* is. Its substantive meaning can therefore not be defined functionally, but only theologically. This means for Mark that the men-fishing function attains its peculiar Christian characteristics by the act of "seeing" Jesus.

And Jesus is for Mark also more than the sum total of his functions as teacher, prophet, healer, visionary, or whatever else could have historically been seen in the syncretistic phenomenon that was Jesus. Jesus called Israel-

269. Cf. E. Schweizer, "The Church as the Missionary Body of the Body of Christ," in *Neotestamentica*, pp. 317–329.

Jerusalem, the eschatological community, the people of the covenant and of the promises, to make it come to itself, its mission and destiny. Jesus' sole purpose in "coming out" (Mark 1:38) is also the substance of the men-fishing commission: not only to preach, heal, and the like, but also to interpret, to theologize, if you will. The fishers of men are not only functionaries; they are also and foremost representatives; not just partners, but representative partners; not just belonging to Christ (Mark 9:41), but "bearing the marks of Jesus." How representational Mark felt about this commission is indicated by his emphasis on the fishers of men working "two by two," which was characteristic of some non-Christian men-fishing as well.

That their legitimation is open and subject to critical examination is indicated by Mark in two ways. Lacking the Easter commission leaves them with no other authority than that which comes from "seeing" Jesus, "the same yesterday and today and for ever" (Heb. 13:8). Whether they have indeed "seen" Jesus is something which those who get "fished" by them can—indeed, must—themselves judge (cf., e.g., I Cor. 11:13), for they, too, have "seen" Jesus "publicly portrayed" (Gal. 3:1). The historical, crucified Jesus is one way, Jesus the coming Son of Man is the other way, by which Mark sees fishers and fished alike assess or judge each other, with both sides subject to being "fished" by him when they come to "see" him as he "sees" them.

Men-fishing for Mark is not mission as function but as office. For a while Peter, for instance, operates in Jerusalem, functioning as one of "the eschatological regents."[270] Later he functions as itinerant men-fishing apostle (e.g., I Cor. 9:5). But these different functions are secondary compared with the scope and theological justification of his office as the Jesus-appointed fisher of men or as "Rock" in the case of Peter. Like other fishers of men specified by name, Peter has been entrusted with a privilege others do not have, the use or abuse of which others, however, are competent to judge. For "the truth of the Gospel" is not clerical, ecclesiastical; neither is it democratic or subject to majority vote. The office of the fishers of men, the privi-

270. Bultmann, *Theology of the New Testament,* Vol. I, p. 37.

lege and duty entrusted to it, is none other than a delegated, active share in the ministry of Jesus to Israel and a reflection of the ministry that is Israel's—the ministry of the chosen, of the nation called holy among the nations, of the kingdom of priests among the kingdoms of the earth. It is the ministry both of and for the royal priesthood of the called. It is the appointed office, analogous to other appointed "offices" such as that of parents over children or that of every kind of political, juridical institution (*ktisis*) ordained for men (I Peter 2:13), which is dedicated and committed to watching discerningly over the growing realization of "God's truthfulness" (*alētheia theou,* Rom. 15:8) within the church, and through the church in the world. It is an office not appointed by the church but for the church.

What critical, judgmental aspects there are to the execution of the men-fishing task is best indicated by what is said to be the veiling character of Jesus' own parabolic men-fishing activity or of Paul's apostolic ministry (cf. II Cor. 4:2-6; 10:1-6). While fishing as function is not yet sifting, as harvesting is not yet sorting, and as shepherding is not yet separating, the fisher's "open statement of the truth" (*phanerōsis tēs alētheias,* II Cor. 4:2) aims at the conscience of every man. The tools of fishing, or as Paul says, the weapons of apostolic warfare, "are not worldly, but have divine power," by which every man's thought can be "taken captive," or fished and caught, "to obey Christ" (II Cor. 10:3-6). Mindful of what manner of spirit they are of (Luke 9:55), fishers of men must use the authority which the Lord, not the church, has given them, "for building up and not for tearing down" (II Cor. 13:10).

Where Paul employs more gnosticizing language,[271] probably due to his opponents' predilection for "wisdom," and "mystery," Mark uses prophetic idiom. Refusing to hear and receive the prophet is to refuse that which the prophet is preaching.[272] As partners of the historical Jesus,

271. See D. Lührmann, *Das Offenbarungsverständnis bei Paulus und in Paulinischen Gemeinden* (Wissenschaftl. Monogr. z. A. und N. T., No. 16; Neukirchener Verlag, 1965).

272. Cf. J. Gnilka, *Die Verstockung Israels* (Studien zum A. u. N. T., No. 3; Munich: Kösel, 1961).

the fishers of men are called to give "testimony" also to unbelievers by such prophetic, symbolic acts as shaking off the dust that is on their feet (Mark 6:11). Mark does not, however, speak of the power of the keys given to them. But he does speak of mountain-moving faith and the power of prayer which they are expected to display (Mark 9:29; 11:22-25). The display of divine power in these and not in other forms of authority is as function the prerogative of all followers of Jesus, but as office and charge it is the calling only of the fishers of men. They, however, although possessing this charge, can use this authority as power only if and when they "see" Jesus, as he "sees" them (Mark 16:7; 1:16 f.), which for Mark is "by faith" only, not yet "by sight."

APPENDIX I

Philological Observations

Halieus is used in its literal meaning in Isa. 19:9; Ezek. 47:10; Mark 1:16, par. Matt. 4:18, and Luke 5:2. It is used metaphorically in Jer. 16:16 and Mark 1:17, par. Matt. 4:19. Other designations for fisherman that appear in Patristic Greek,[1] but not in the Septuagint, New Testament, or apostolic fathers, are *ichthybolos, ichthyolkos, ichthyothēras, ichthyothēreutēs.* The angler, the only fisher symbol in early Christian art for the first three centuries, is not mentioned in Old or New Testament; *ankistrothēreutēs* is found only in Patristic Greek; *aspalieutēs* only in non-Christian literature. The same with the terms *diktubolos, diktueus, diktuthēras, sagēneus, sagēneutēr, sagēnobolos,* and others. *Amphiboleus* appears once in the Old Testament (Isa. 19:8), and occasionally again in Patristic Greek.

Designations for fishing spears vary as do those for nets and angles, each suited for a particular species of fish. Of the spear we know the *schoinos* (a reed as arrow or short javelin), *belos* and *bolis* (harpoon or arrow), *akōn* (javelin or dart), and the large *enchos* or *lonchē* (lance or spear). Only *belos* and *bolis* appear in Biblical literature. In the Septuagint both terms are used literally as well as metaphorically; in Eph. 6:16 and Patristic Greek only metaphorically.

The three kinds of casting nets all go under the general

1. G. W. H. Lampe (ed.), *A Patristic Greek Lexicon* (Oxford: Clarendon Press, 1961).

designation *amphiblēstron*. According to Clement of Alexandria, who probably gleaned the information from the widely circulated *heurēmata* literature, we learn that casting nets were invented by the Sicilians (see *Stromateis* I. 16). *Amphiblēstron* in the literal sense occurs only once, in Matt. 4:18. All three references in the Old Testament are metaphorical: Ps. 141:10; Eccl. 9:12; Hab. 1:15-17; the same in I QH 2:29; 3:26; 5:8, but not in Christian literature. The verb *amphiballein* also occurs only once in the New Testament and then only in the literal sense, in Mark 1:16; but Patristic Greek uses it also metaphorically. A. W. Mair in his introduction to Oppian's *Halieutica,* p. xli, said that "the primary meaning of casting net seems pretty well established, but it could easily be extended to any sort of net."

The *sagēnē* appears in its literal sense in Isa. 19:8; Ezek. 47:10; and Matt. 13:47. Metaphorically, it occurs six times in the Old Testament, but never so in Christian literature. Different kinds of dragnets are used in fishing, fowling, and hunting. The same is true of *diktuon,* the most general designation for net. The term is used in the New Testament only in the traditions about Jesus' call of Galilean fishermen to discipleship (Mark 1:18 f., par. Matt. 4:20 f.; and the related passages in Luke 5:2 ff.; John 21:6 ff.). In the Old Testament, *diktuon* is used at least nine times metaphorically, only once literally in connection with hunting (Symmachus' reading of Gen. 22:13). In Patristic Greek it is used only metaphorically. *Linon* occurs only in Patristic Greek and only metaphorically. On a variety of other nets, see Oppian, *Halieutica.*

The *ankistron* is used in the literal sense in Job 41:1 f.; Isa. 19:8; Matt. 17:27; in the metaphoric sense in Hab. 1:15; Ezek. 32:3; II Kings 19:28, but not in the New Testament. The earliest patristic reference to "hook" in the metaphoric sense is Ignatius, Magn. 11:1. An analysis of the meaning of ropes dangling from fishes' mouths in synagogal art is given on pp. 123 f. The term for "wicker basket" (Hebrew, *ākōn;* Greek, *onkion*) is not found in either Biblical or patristic literature. Only in a medieval German woodcut does the wicker basket appear as symbol of the papal tiara on the head of Peter, the fisher of men (see H. Roeder, *Saints and Their Attributes,* p. 23; Henry Regnery Company, 1956).

Among the tools used in hunting or fowling are the net or snare, and the trap. *Pagis* is not used in the literal sense in either Testaments and Patristic Greek. Metaphorically, it is used widely in the Septuagint, the Dead Sea Scrolls, the New Testament and patristic literature. See J. Schneider, art. *"pagis,"* in *TWNT*, G. Friedrich (ed.), Vol. V (1954), pp. 593–596. *Skandalon* also appears in the same literature, but used exclusively in the metaphoric sense. See G. Stählin, art. *"skandalon,"* in *TWNT,* G. Friedrich (ed.), Vol. VII (1964), pp. 338–358. Less frequently referred to are the following tools: the noose or loop (*brochos*), used metaphorically in Prov. 6:5; 7:21; 22:25, and once in the New Testament in I Cor. 7:35. The verb *brochizein,* and the noun *brochisma* appear in Patristic Greek. Then there is the basket used in fowling: Hebrew, *kelub;* see Jer. 5:27 where the Septuagint substitutes *pagis.*

The metaphoric use of some other hunting tools is quite interesting. Hunters or fowlers use ropes or cords (Hebrew, *ḥebel;* Greek, *schoinia*). In the literal sense, but not related to hunting, ropes are used in CD 11:17; John 2:15; Acts 27:32; in the metaphoric sense, in Ps. 140:5; 119:61; Job 18:10. In Prov. 5:22 *seira* is used; metaphoric but unrelated to hunting in Ignatius, Eph. 9:1. The Hebrew tradition that spoke of "the cords of death" (or Sheol), as in II Sam. 22:6; Ps. 18:5 f.; 116:3; I QH 3:8 ff.; 5:30; 9:6, was translated as "pangs (*ōdin*) of death" in the Septuagint, in the New Testament (Acts 2:24), and Patristic Greek. On *speira* as the cord passing through the top meshes of a net (dragnet or casting net), see R. Eisler, *Orpheus,* p. 277.

Fetters (*pedē* or *peza*) appear related to hunting in the metaphoric sense only in Aquila's version of Ezek. 19:4. It is mostly used when speaking of prisoners of war. The pointed stick (Hebrew, *sotet;* Greek, *hēlos*) is used metaphorically as a "scourge" in Israel's side which intermarriage with foreigners is rated to be (Josh. 23:13). It is used metaphorically, but also in other senses, in Patristic Greek. Another thorny implement used in hunting is the *tribolos,* which appears in the metaphoric sense only in Prov. 22:5. Of pits and trenches used in hunting, we have the following terms: *bothros* or *bothunos,* which occurs metaphorically in Ps. 7:15; 57:6; Prov. 22:14; 26:27; Eccl. 10:8; Isa. 24:17 f. = 47:11 = Jer. 48:43 f.; possibly also in Ps. 94:13 and Barnabas 11:2. The noun as well as the two verbs *bothrizein* and *bothreuein* are used in their metaphoric sense in Patristic Greek. Another word for a hunting trench or pit is *seiros,* metaphorically once in Prov. 5:22. Identical with Sheol or Hades, *seiros* is used in Ezek. 26:20; 31:14; 32:18, *et passim;* also, II Peter 2:4. Related to *seiros* is *phrear* (cf. Rev. 9:1 f.). Still another term is *koilasma,* metaphorically used only once in Isa. 8:14, but never in Christian literature.

Fowlers make their catches with sticks (*rhabdos*) covered with birdlime (see C. Schneider, art. *"rhabdos,"* in *TWNT,* Vol. VI [1959], p. 967:22 f.). In the battue style of hunting, hunting marks, that is, "rags or feathers hung on cords along the enclosed hunting-ground," [2] were used in the chase of animals toward the prepared traps, nets, or pits. Assisting in the chase at times were hunting dogs or specially hired beaters. Hunting dogs are referred to in the metaphoric sense in Ps. 22:16-20 where Aquila and Symmachus prefer "hunters" to "dogs." Another reference is in Ps. 59:7 f., 15. In Phil. 3:2 and Ignatius, Eph. 7:1, "dogs" refer to heretics chasing their prey. See also Eisler, *Orpheus,* p. 51, n. 3a, and pp. 59 f. Strategically placed and timed, the hired beaters sound off terrifying (*phobos*) noises to bring the animals to the hunters in wait or into the traps. The "sound of terror" is used metaphorically in Isa. 24:17 f.; I QH 8:33. See also Gerleman, *Old Testament Terminology,* pp. 8 f., and Oppian, *Cynegetica* IV:120 ff.

The hunt concludes with the animals being killed (*sphazein*). O. Michel, art. *"sphazein,"* in *TWNT,* Vol. VII (1964), p. 932:10 f. comments on its metaphorical use. Of interest is also the bow (*toxon*), used literally by Ishmael and Esau (Gen. 21:20; 27:3), metaphorically in Job 20:24; 29:20. Its use in warfare has been commented

2. Gerleman, *Old Testament Terminology,* p. 6; for examples from Greek tradition, see Eisler, *Orpheus,* pp. 166 f.

on by R. de Vaux, *Ancient Israel,* pp. 243 f. Of theological interest is the use of the bow in metaphoric battles, such as in I Sam. 2:4; Ps. 11:2; 37:14 f.; 64:3, but especially when used of God's actions in history, such as in Ps. 7:12; Hab. 3:9; Lam. 2:4; 3:12, *passim.* To speak of idolatry as a "treacherous bow" (Ps. 78:57; Hos. 7:16) is synonymous with "net" or "snare." Another hunting tool that doubles, both literally (e.g., I Sam. 17:40; Zech. 9:15) and metaphorically (e.g., I Sam. 25:29) as weapon in warfare, is the stone in a sling (*sphendonē*), not mentioned, however, in the New Testament and apostolic fathers.

The act of fishing is variously referred to. *Halieuein* is used only metaphorically in Jer. 16:16; I QH 5:8; John 21:3; and in Patristic Greek. *Amphiballein* is used in the literal sense only in Mark 1:16; metaphorically in Hab. 1:17, and in Patristic Greek. The verb *sagēneuein* is not found in Biblical literature or the apostolic fathers. However, H. G. Liddell and R. Scott, *A Greek-English Lexicon* (rev. ed. by H. S. Jones, R. McKenzie, *et al.;* Oxford: At the Clarendon Press, 9th ed., 1953), *sub voce* document from Herodotus and Strabo the metaphoric use of the phrase *sagēneuein anthrōpous,* which adds further weight to the thesis that the gospel use of the "fisher of men" metaphor has its long-established antecedents. Another verb is *helkein,* used metaphorically in Ps. 10:9; Hab. 1:15, and so probably also in John 21:6, 11; Hermas, Visions, III, 2:6; and 5:2. It continues to be used so in Patristic Greek.

To catch something with a dragnet can be called *syllambanein,* of fish in Luke 5:9; of men in I Clem. 12:2; *Martyrium Polycarpi* 5:2, *passim.* On its metaphoric use (e.g., Ezek. 12:13; 19:4, 8; Ps. 10:2), see G. Delling, art. *"syllambanō,"* in *TWNT,* Vol. VII (1964), pp. 759–762. Related in meaning is *epilambanein* (Luke 20:20), and *synechein* (see H. Koester, art. in *TWNT,* Vol. VII (1964), pp. 876 f., in Septuagint, and pp. 881 f., in New Testament). The verb *ballein* is used either with the words for line and hook (Matt. 17:27) or casting net (ch. 4:18). It can be used metaphorically in Patristic Greek.

Applicable to fishing as well as fowling or hunting are

the verbs *thēreuein* and *pagideuein;* the latter is used only metaphorically in I Sam. 28:9; Eccl. 9:12; and Matt. 22:15. See, on this, J. Schneider, in *TWNT,* Vol. V (1954), pp. 595 f. The verb *thēreuein* is used in its literal sense in Gen. 27:3, 5, 33; Lev. 17:13; Job 38:39. Metaphorically, it is used (1) of God's mighty acts in history, Jer. 5:6; 16:15; (2) of man's fateful existence in general, Eccl. 9:12; (3) of man-made misfortunes of the believer, Job. 18:9; Ps. 59:3; 94:21; 124:7; Lam. 3:52; 4:18; (4) of magicians hunting souls, Ezek. 13:18, 20. It is used in Patristic Greek, but in the New Testament only once, Luke 11:54.

Another verb of interest is *haliskein,* used mostly metaphorically of the power of money (Sirach 31:3), lust (Prov. 11:6; Sirach 9:4), words (Prov. 6:2; Sirach 23:7), as well as of God's mighty acts in history (Isa. 8:15; 13:15) or at the end of history (ch. 24:18). The noun *halōsis* is used in the literal sense in Jer. 50:46 (cf. Isa. 33:1; Jer. 50:2, 24; 51:41), but metaphorically in II Peter 2:12, and in Patristic Greek. The verb *agreuein* is used in the Septuagint mostly metaphorically; so also in I QH 2:29; 8:34, once in the New Testament, Mark 12:13, and documented also in Patristic Greek. The noun *agra* is found only in Luke 5:4, 9, but never in Septuagint or Patristic Greek. It also served as a title of Artemis in Athens.

It is to Gerleman's credit to have renewed the knowledge that the Hebrew verb *ṣrr* or *ṣrh;* Greek, *synkleiein,* literally, "to hem in," has something to do with hunting (see his *Old Testament Terminology,* pp. 10–12). The verb is used in its literal sense in Luke 5:6; metaphorically, in Ps. 30:9; 78:50; also in I QpH 5:6; I QH 3:9; cf. O. Michel, art. *"synkleiō,"* in *TWNT,* Vol. VII (1964), pp. 744–747. Terms taken from warfare, which in their metaphoric meaning overlap with hunting or fishing metaphors, and therefore are relevant for our discussion, can be seen, e.g., in Plato's *Sophist,* 222 C or throughout the Old Testament. Representative samples are *harpazein,* "to seize" or "snatch"; *piazein,* "to oppress"; *aichmalōtizein* (or *-teuein*), *kratein, sylagōgein, lambanein,* "to capture"; and others.

Of special interest is the verb *zōgrein,* literally, "to catch alive." Its literal meaning may best be seen on the background of ancient Near Eastern traditions of war (see, e.g., R. de Vaux, *Ancient Israel,* pp. 247–257, and Y. Yadin, *The Art of Warfare in Biblical Lands,* 2 vols.; McGraw-Hill Book Company, Inc., 1963), and Israel's Holy War tradition (see De Vaux, *Ancient Israel,* pp. 258–267). The verb is used in the metaphoric sense only once in the Old Testament, in Jer. 5:27; only twice in the New Testament, Luke 5:10; II Tim. 2:26. L. H. Brun, "2 Tim. II, 23-26," *The Expository Times,* Vol. 41 (1930), pp. 235–237, reads "preservation of life" as the meaning of *zōgrein.* In Lampe's *Patristic Greek Lexicon* the verb is credited with the dual meaning of "catching alive" and "restoring to life." In the Corpus Hellenisticum we have an important corroborating testimony in Lucian for interpreting the fishing metaphor as synonymous with "reviving" (*anabioun*). It is the contention of E. Hilgert, *The Ship and Related Symbols,* p. 110, that Luke, in changing the Marcan metaphoric use of *halieis,* deliberately used *zōgrein* in the dual meaning. *Zōgrein anthrōpous* is then quite different from the above mentioned metaphoric use of *sagēneuein anthrōpous.*

APPENDIX II

Fishers of Men in Early Christian Iconography and Patristic Literature

Iconography. The examples shown or cited in studies of ancient art with fishing scenes are often taken not only as evidence of the purely decorative use of the fishing metaphor (as in the late first-century A.D. hypogeum of the Flavian House), but also as proof that the literary and iconographic use of the metaphor was widely spread and commonly understood in antiquity.[1] This, of course, applies to Christian as well as Jewish iconography and the use each made of fishing scenes.[2] Whether more than purely decorative values are expressed depends on how the scene is placed, whether in church and synagogue or catacombs, whether alone or in a composition with other scenes and symbols. But the conclusions to be drawn from the context within which a fishing scene is found must remain as tentative as those drawn from literary references to the fishing metaphor which happen to be contemporary with the work of art.

The earliest and most important iconographic evidence that we have to date of the fishing metaphor in Christian

1. See J. Wilpert, *Die Malereien der Katakomben Roms* (Freiburg: Herder, 1903), p. 263.

2. See above, pp. 123–126, on synagogal iconography. See also G. Kretschmar, "Ein Beitrag zur Frage nach dem Verhältnis zwischen Jüdischer und Christlicher Kunst in der Antike," in *Abraham unser Vater,* O. Michel *Festschrift* (Leiden: Brill, 1963), pp. 295–319, and H. Strauss, "Jüdische Quellen frühchristlicher Kunst: optische oder literarische Anregung" (Zeitschr. f. d. Neutest. Wiss., No. 57; 1966), pp. 114–136.

art is from the early third-century Chambers of the Sacrament in the catacomb of Calixtus.[3] In one of the chambers the panel shows a single fish hooked at the end of a line held by a standing fisherman. The panel is flanked on the left by a panel showing Moses striking water from the rock, while on the right follows a panel with the baptism of Jesus. Water is the element common to all three panels. The fish appears to be pulled from the very waters Moses provided miraculously.[4] Whether that makes the fisherman a symbol of baptism, as Wilpert suggested,[5] and as contemporary Alexandrian theologians understood the literary fishing metaphor,[6] can be considered as only a possibility at best.

In what is known as Room A 2 of the Chambers of the Sacrament the fishing scene is flanked by different panels, one depicting a eucharistic (?) table with seven disciples (allusion to John, ch. 21?) gathered (by fish and wine?), and another depicting the raising of Lazarus. That such a composition of panels reflects a specific theology which the artist does not invent for the occasion but only reproduces from what he has consciously learned or unconsciously absorbed from the contemporary teaching has been claimed by Wilpert (pp. 155 f.) for this piece of catacomb art, as Goodenough, Kraeling, and others have claimed about the Dura-Europos synagogue panels. This applies also to the composition on an early sarcophagus where an orans figure is flanked by a fisherman on one side and a shepherd figure on the other.[7]

The interpretation of the meaning of these fishermen figures is controversial. Does it refer to baptism or does it

3. Besides Wilpert, see also H. Leclercq, *Dictionnaire d'Archéologie Chrétienne et de Liturgie,* Vol. III:1 (1913), cols. 157 f.; for a non-Christian parallel, see Vol. XIII:2 (1938), col. 2879.

4. On the drinking of water from the rock, see I Cor. 10:4. Cf. E. Becker, *Das Quellenwunder des Moses in der altchristlichen Kunst* (Zur Kunstgeschichte des Auslandes, Vol. 72; Strasbourg, 1909); Goodenough, *Jewish Symbols,* Vol. VI, pp. 191 ff.

5. *Die Malereien,* pp. 153 f., 263 f. See also above, pp. 139 f. on Carrington and Mánek.

6. E.g., Clement of Alexandria, *Paedagogus,* III.10.52:2.

7. See Leclercq, *Dictionnaire d'Archéologie Chrétienne et de Liturgie,* Vol. XIII:2, col. 2879, Fig. 10021.

not? Does the figure represent Christ, or Peter,[8] or some other apostolic fisher of men? We commented earlier on divergent interpretations of the angling fisher on the late third- or early fourth-century funerary jar from Grottaferrata.[9] That the fisherman is depicted almost exclusively as angler throughout early Christian art should make one hesitate to accept Eisler's verdict that "the angler-glyph of early Christian art is due to the influence of the same prophetic passages in the Old Testament which gave birth to the allegories about the net-fishing in [the New Testament]." [10]

The juxtaposition of fishers who are spreading nets with the Jonah story on Christian sarcophagi [11] or frescoes [12] admits all sorts of interpretations. Clearly related to Christ is the fisherman figure in the engraving on an old silver ring with the inscription *Salvator* in mixed Greek and Latin letters. Eisler [13] also refers to "an old Christian goldglass" which shows Christ as fisher.[14] It is Eisler's contention that all bishops used to wear a fisher ring as "ensign of episcopal dignity" before finally, but not until the thirteenth century, only the pope was privileged to wear the famous "fisher ring." [15] A different connotation is given to the fishing metaphor by the floor mosaic at the entrance to the *katēchumeneion* (the Christian education building) at Aquileia which depicts net fishers hauling in a big catch. Eisler takes this as "symbolic representation of the fishing for men by means of the missionary preaching of the kingdom of God." [16]

8. On Peter's replacing Moses as teacher and miracle worker, see G. Stuhlfauth, *Die Apokryphen Petrusgeschichten in der Altchristlichen Kunst* (Berlin-Leipzig, 1925), and E. Dinkler, "Die ersten Petrusdarstellungen," *Marburger Jahrbuch f. Kunstwissenschaft* 11/12 (1938–1939).

9. See above, Ch. I, n. 56; and pp. 83 and 124.

10. *Orpheus*, p. 79.

11. *Ibid.*, p. 161.

12. *Vorträge der Bibliothek Warburg*, II, pp. 204–206.

13. Leclercq, *Dictionnaire d'Archéologie Chrétienne et de Liturgie*, Vol. XIII:2, col. 2882, Fig. 10028.

14. *Orpheus*, p. 66, n. 2; cf. Leclercq, *Dictionnaire d'Archéologie Chrétienne et de Liturgie*, col. 2881, where he refers to two glass medallions of "le Christ pêcheur."

15. *Orpheus*, p. 60, n. 2; and plate XXXVIII.

16. *Vorträge der Bibliothek Warburg*, II, p. 303.

More sacramental or mystical significance is attached to the fishing symbol when it appears in juxtaposition with the sacred vine as in mosaics at Orléansville and Sertei. As artistic compositions they are surprisingly similar to the Bacchic scenes in the men-fishing tradition of the Dionysian cult.[17] The same mystical significance is seen by Eisler in the juxtaposition of fisher or fish with lamb and milk pail or with fish-meal scenes. A recent interpretation of the fishing symbolism in early Christian art allows for *bildliche Motiveinflüsse* from popular bucolica, i.e., traditional Greek pastoral poetry, and from funerary meal rites, besides sacramental associations.[18] Not to be overlooked or underrated, as it is here, should be the influence of the *halieutica* tradition.[19]

Patristic Literature. The symbolism of fisher and fish occupied and intrigued the early fathers quite extensively. This fact was recognized early by Cardinal J. B. Pitra who provided a still useful survey of the patristic material.[20] We now have F. J. Dölger's extensive writings [21] in which the symbolism of fish and fishing is analyzed in its syncretistic context. The philological observations presented in Appendix I gave a first indication of the widespread use of fishing and hunting metaphors in patristic literature. The fact that among the metaphors used are some which do not go back to either Old or New Testament proves what the iconographic material also does independently—that the patristic interpretation relies on, or is motivated by, other than strictly Biblical traditions. In Part One of this study it was shown how this very digression led to a distorted identification of the economic milieu of the Galilean fishermen. There is likewise a diversity of theological interpretations of the fishing metaphor emerging here in patristic literature which cannot claim Biblical

17. *Orpheus,* pp. 283 f.; see also above, pp. 67 f.

18. C. Andresen, art. *"Fisch,"* in *Die Religion in Geschichte und Gegenwart,* 3d ed., Vol. II (1958), p. 968.

19. See above, pp. 16–20.

20. *De Pisce Symbolico* (Paris, 1855). See also Eisler, *Orpheus,* pp. 71–74.

21. Besides five volumes on the ΙΧΘΥΣ symbols, there are many articles by Dölger on the same subject scattered in numerous periodicals.

authenticity, no matter how hard it tries by means of allegorical exegesis.

What follows is a mere sampling of the variety of theological ideas that came to be associated with or expressed by the fishing metaphor. No attempt is made to assess these observations critically, either historically or theologically. One of the late patristic or rather medieval examples cited by Eisler [22] refers to God's fishing of Leviathan by means of a fishing rod which is the genealogical tree of Jesus, and a hook depicted as the cross of Jesus. Only with reference to evil is the fishing metaphor apparently applied to God.[23] Not so with Jesus. He can be called fisher of men in two basic senses: one applied to his catch of men as his apostles, the appointed fishers of men; the other applied to Jesus' men-fishing of all men. The fact that the symbol of the fisher came to be applied to Jesus less and less is explained by Wilpert as due to the growing preference for the fish symbol which seems to have replaced the fisher symbol by the third century.[24]

Eisler cites two examples of Jesus as fisher of men. One is found in the hymn appended to the *Protreptikos* by Clement of Alexandria in which Jesus is invoked as shepherd of lambs and fisher of men. The other example Eisler cites is from Gregory of Nazianzus who is reported to have said that "Jesus, who is called the fisherman, fishes himself with the drag net; he bears every hardship, in order to recover from the deep the fish, which is man." [25] In a category by itself is the fishing Jesus does when appointing apostles. Marcion said that Jesus "took and seized Paul," [26] but Chrysostom later speaks of Paul's being fished (*halieuein*) by Jesus after his resurrection (in Hom. 30 of his homilies on Matthew). By Jesus' call, Peter becomes the ecumenical fisherman (*ho tēs oikoumenēs halieus*), as he is called in Chrysostom (in his homily on Matt. 18:23);

22. *Orpheus,* p. 28, citing the *Hortulus Deliciarum* of Herrad of Landsberg.

23. On God's "hunting" through designated agents, see references to Theodoretus Cyrrhensis, in Lampe, *Patristic Greek Lexicon,* s.v. *agreuein.*

24. *Die Malereien,* p. 264.

25. *Orpheus,* p. 66, n. 2.

26. See Grant (ed.), *Gnosticism,* p. 104.

Cyril of Alexandria calls Peter a "hunter" (*thēreutēs*).

Only some of the fragments have been gathered in H. Smith's edition of the *Ante-Nicene Exegesis of the Gospels* [27] about the various interpretations of the gospel pericopes dealing with the call to become fishers of men. In post-Nicene exegesis, the variety of interpretation increases. But one thing remains constant: the notion that certain people were appointed to engage in this men-fishing activity which Origen once identified as "the gift of the word." That the successors of the apostles for quite some time were looked upon as fishers of men is evident in a letter of Paulinus of Nola to Bishop Delphinus referring to the bishop as the fisher who "let down the hooks towards me, to draw me out of the deep and bitter flood of the world, so that I should be soon a prey of salvation. . . . I am thy fish." [28] Note, however, the distinction here made between "getting hooked" and "falling prey to salvation." We will return to this point immediately.

Another distinction appears to be made between different apostolic methods of fishing. This distinction is all the more important as by contrast the adjectives *halieutikos, zōgreutikos,* and the adverb *halieutikōs* become in Patristic Greek synonymous with "apostolic" or "episcopal" in general. Eisler has a quotation from St. Bruno Signiensis which refers to the apostles as fishers of men who brought the fish to "swim about in the stream of baptism, caught with the hook of faith [or creed] and in the nets of holy preaching." [29] Clement of Alexandria (Paedagogus III.10.52:2) explicitly states that Jesus commissioned Peter to fish men "through water." Whether Carrington's recourse to the lectionaries of the early church, which include the "fishers of men" pericope within the same reading as the ministry of John the Baptist and the baptism of Jesus,[30] can serve as proof that the men-fishers were primarily working as baptizers is a precarious inference at best.

27. Translations of Christian Literature, Series VI (London, 1925), Vol. II.

28. Eisler, *Orpheus,* p. 72.

29. *Ibid.,* p. 51.

30. P. Carrington, *According to Mark,* pp. 44 ff.

The most important fishing tool or method is preaching. But here an interesting distinction is made, based on whether the fishing activity is seen directed at mankind in general (conversion) or at the church in particular (regeneration). We had observed earlier (see p. 47) that early Christian apologists had interpreted the rapid spread of Christianity as due to the God-given rhetorical skill of the otherwise uneducated, uncouth Galilean fishermen. In his homily on Jer., ch. 16, Origen claims that Jesus, after educating (*paideuein*) the disciples, gave them "the gift of the word" (*charin logou*), and that as "fishers of Jesus" (*halieis Iēsou*) they set out to "gather up" men by casting their nets, the Word of God, in the form of God-given, "inspired" new rhetoric.

What the substance or content of their preaching was is variously defined. In a commentary on the feeding of the five thousand (Matt. 14:13-21), Cyril of Alexandria interprets the report that the disciples used five loaves and two fish as referring to the five parts of the Mosaic Pentateuch and to the fishermen's apostolic and evangelistic activity.[31] In his commentary on Matt. 13:49-50, Cyril speaks of the fishing power of (1) the *kērygma,* and (2) the holy creeds (*mathēmata*) which contain "marvelous and complex teaching." This apostolic fishing is seen and developed in three different contexts: the men-fishing of heretical teachers; the non-Christian pagan teachings that rely on *eloquentia Platonica* and not on the *simplicitas apostolica* (Jerome); and the universal men-fishing carried on by evil spirits.

Apostolic men-fishing was conceived in two independent ways. First of all, it applied to getting men started on the road to salvation, that is, converting or "hooking" them. To be rescued from the "seas of troubles" (Clement), the "life of disorders" (Cyril), from being "irrational" (*apsychoi, alogoi;* cf. Origen, and Barnabas, ch. 10), are some of the phrases used to describe what the fishes are to be fished from. The Gnostics, of course, have their own detailed descriptions of the nature of things from or out of

31. See J. Reuss (ed.), *Matthäus-Kommentare aus der griechischen Kirche* (Texte und Untersuchungen, Vol. 61; Berlin, 1957), fragment 174.

which men are to be fished (see above p. 82). Using the whole arsenal of fishing tools, men are said to be caught and dragged out of one sea and transferred to swim and live in another sea. The sea from which they are pulled is identified by Origen with the Pauline passages on dying to the world and to sin. But by a complete transformation, that is, the result of letting oneself be fished, the result of turning from error to truth, the fish are brought to life by the same fishers who, by the Word of God, offer them "another life" (Origen).

In Apollinaris of Laodicea, however, the fish of Matt. 17:27 becomes a *typos* of the church. Held down in the brine of unbelief and superstition, and submerged (again) by (the same old) disorder and distress of pleasures, it is the church that must be brought up, fished, and rescued by the apostolic men-fishing.[32] Thus is preserved here an element of the meaning of men-fishing which early threatened to become almost completely replaced by equating it with foreign mission, conversion, catechetical instruction preceding baptism, and the like. But "in the beginning it was not so."

32. *Ibid.*, fragment 88.

Subject Index

(Citations are by pages. However, figures following the Roman numerals refer to footnote numbers of the respective chapters.)

Index of Modern Authors

(Roman numerals refer to chapters; figures after the colon refer to footnotes. Page references are marked by "p.")

Scripture Index